W0232474

FACULTY EXPERIENCES IN ACTIVE LEARNING

FACULTY EXPERIENCES IN ACTIVE LEARNING

A Collection of Strategies for Implementing
Active Learning Across Disciplines

Edited by J. A. Keith-Le and M. P. Morgan

J. Murrey Atkins Library
at University of North Carolina Charlotte

Copyright © 2020 J. Murrey Atkins Library at UNC Charlotte

Suggested citation: Keith-Le, J. A., and M. P. Morgan, eds.
*Faculty Experiences in Active Learning: A Collection of Strategies
for Implementing Active Learning Across Disciplines.*
doi: https://doi.org/10.5149/9781469660042_Keith-Le

This work is licensed under a Creative Commons CC BY-NC 4.0
license. To view a copy of the license, visit http://creativecommons
.org/licenses.

ISBN 978-1-4696-6003-5 (paperback: alk. paper)
ISBN 978-1-4696-6004-2 (open access ebook)

Published by J. Murrey Atkins Library at UNC Charlotte

Distributed by the University of North Carolina Press
www.uncpress.org

CONTENTS

ACKNOWLEDGMENTS

This book is dedicated to the students and instructor in the spring 2019 LBST 2213 Anthropology and Philosophy of Science class who were present in one of our large active learning classrooms during the most tragic event our campus has ever faced. The dedication recognizes the survivors of that horrific day, April 30, 2019, and honors the memory of two students, Ellis Reed Parlier and Riley Howell, who lost their lives.

#ninerstrong #weareallniners

Special thanks goes out to the spring 2019 ENGL 4183/5183 Editing with Digital Technologies English students for their help copyediting this book.

Additional recognition is extended to A. E. Auten, D. M. Sacco, and D. N. Spoor who served as APA ninjas at the eleventh hour. Thank you.

J. Garvey Pyke, EdD, UNC Charlotte, Center for Teaching and Learning

Active learning improves student learning. After seven decades of research and practice proving its efficacy, it is now at the forefront of instructional innovation throughout higher education. Clearly, the faculty and academic leaders at UNC Charlotte agree, as seen through the evidence all around us on campus. New classrooms are being built with active learning as the primary design consideration. Old classrooms are being retrofitted to allow for greater flexibility in setup and usage. And faculty are designing student experiences centered around interaction and engagement—both in class and out of class.

Many years ago, I learned that one of the essential components of a successful teaching center is to "highlight the good works of our faculty." At UNC Charlotte, that is very easy to do. We have many dedicated professionals who put student learning first and are ready to share their wisdom and experience with others. Scholarly teaching is not confined only to the colleges of education but is found in every discipline, just as you will find in this book. I congratulate the authors for their hard work and their good works, and I am grateful to be their colleague. Together, through reflective professional practice and knowledge dissemination, we are all helping each other in keeping student success a top priority.

Leveraging People, Space, and Systems to Ignite Active Learning

JULES A. KEITH-LE, HEATHER MCCULLOUGH, RICH PREVILLE, AND KURT RICHTER

Sparking Change

In 2014, the University of North Carolina at Charlotte (UNC Charlotte) sparked change with a commitment from leadership to stop building new theater-style lecture halls and, with a partnership between the Center for Teaching and Learning and Classroom Support, to build two state-of-the-art, evidence-based, active learning classrooms. At the same time, a faculty community of practice (the Active Learning Academy) focusing on active learning methodology in course design and in the classroom was formed. The academy's mission is to create a community of practice among instructors who are interested in promoting active learning. It additionally provides a space for faculty to become familiar with best practices and new technologies, while receiving support from active learning experts and instructional designers on challenges. The Active Learning Academy has grown steadily in size each year with members representing all colleges and departments on campus. Through additional partnerships with the Provost, Registrar's Office, Facilities Operations, Disability Services, and Environmental Health and Safety, UNC Charlotte continues to build flexible and needs-based active learning spaces across campus. Long-term strategic plans are moving the campus from a departmentally controlled classroom scheduling model to a central scheduling model that prioritizes placing Active Learning Academy members in active learning teaching spaces.

From Then Until Now: History

Active learning is rooted in American educational literature as early as 1924 when John Dewey described it as "an active, personally conducted affair" and "something an individual does when he studies" (Dewey, 1924). In their seminal work, Bonwell and Eison (1991) define active learning as students "doing things and thinking about the things they are doing." Yet definitions of active learning only begin to scratch the surface of a large practice of pedagogical methods. It is often clearer in practice than in definition. When one sees active learning in practice, it is often a dynamic educational experience. Active learning practice at UNC Charlotte has had a large and diverse following in the ranks of our instructors over the years. Our efforts to support them with community, professional development, resources, and tools are evidenced in the chapters of this book.

The design of teaching spaces, particularly in higher education, has not always supported activities like those observed in active learning classrooms. From their acoustics and lighting to their aisle widths and seating density, most traditional learning spaces are designed for information to flow one way—from the front of the room and toward the audience. Active learning classrooms are different. Active learning classrooms, or ALCs as we call them, are designed to support movement and sound to and from all directions and among different groups, from conversations within the same group to conversations among different groups to an instructor giving instructions one-to-one or one-to-many. The pedagogy, technology, and room furniture all serve one purpose in an ALC: to facilitate collaborative learning.

UNC Charlotte began its journey to provide more coordinated pedagogical and technological support for active learning methodology in 2014. With strong support from Academic Affairs, two classrooms in Kennedy,[1] the oldest building on campus, were renovated to support an active learning environment. Plans for these classrooms included hosting larger classes, setting the stage for faculty to employ student-centered teaching that was collaborative and hands-on, and offered technology-assisted interactive options. The Center for Teaching and Learning (CTL) and Classroom Support (CS) partnered in developing and providing technical and pedagogical support to instructors who used the renovated classrooms.

The SCALE-UP Model

Ideas around redesigning the university teaching spaces began in the 1990s, and J. M. Wilson (1994) termed this new model the *studio classroom.* The studio classroom was one space that was meant to serve as lecture hall, discussion forum, and lab (Baepler, Walker, Brooks, Saichaie, & Petersen, 2016). Dr. Robert Beichner, our colleague at North Carolina State University, has been working on the student-centered active learning environment with upside-down pedagogies (SCALE-UP) project since the 1990s. Beichner formed a group of more than two dozen schools to collaborate on designing classrooms that could merge the concept of lab and lecture in a way that would provide a new alternative to the traditional method of teaching (Beichner et al., 2007). The pedagogical framework supporting the SCALE-UP model creates environments that lead to cooperative learning, which encourages students to be engaged in the learning process, reduces lecture time, and teaches students how to solve their own problems and find the answers to the questions themselves (Beichner et al., 2007). The continued collaboration among Beichner's "adopters" can be followed on a website hosted by North Carolina State University and supported, in part, by the U.S. Department of Education's Fund for the Improvement of Post-Secondary Education (FIPSE), the National Science Foundation, and Hewlett-Packard (North Carolina State University, 2019).

UNC Charlotte reached out to Beichner, consulting with him on the design and the construction of two new active learning classrooms. We followed the design of the SCALE-UP model as we worked to renovate the Kennedy building to house not one but two of these

---

1. As a result of the tragic events of April 30, 2019, the Kennedy Active Learning Classrooms have been permanently closed and will be repurposed to include a contemplative space documenting the history and honoring the victims.

classrooms. One large ALC can seat up to 126 students, and a smaller ALC seats 36. These classrooms were needed to support instruction, discussion, group work, and entire class interaction. Flexible seating consists of round table-pods that support team interaction among students. Each pod seats nine students and provides three university-supported laptops, an instructor microphone for speaking to the class as a whole, speakers that engage with the room's integrated sound system, and a digital display that can be controlled using a touch-panel switch by any of the computers at the pod. The instructor's lectern also features a digital display allowing for control of all digital monitors in the room, multiple drop-down projection screens, handheld and lavalier microphones, and the ability to push out multiple forms of media at the touch of a button. The wireless capability and layout of the room unchain the instructor from the lectern and promote instructor–student engagement moving around the room. Instructors have the power to share materials with all the tables' digital displays or to share each table's work with the entire classroom.

The CTL has always believed that our mission is to guide instructors to become reflective teachers, critically reviewing and refining their own learning practices, and to engage in professional development in place through this work. The new ALCs provided an opportunity for transforming instruction. However, that opportunity needed careful cultivation and support to be realized.

The new classroom spaces attracted considerable attention from faculty across campus. The demand to teach in the space was high. However, the CTL and CS recognized that instructors would need guidance and support to transform their teaching in a way that maximizes the potential of the learning space. As a result, any instructor who taught in one of the new ALCs was required to participate in the faculty community of practice, the Active Learning Academy (ALA) that included both technical and pedagogical training. The program also included regular interactions with instructional technologists and designers. Faculty acknowledged that the deliberate effort required to modify lessons and instructional approach was often significant. The instructional designers recognized that faculty skills developed over time and through regular and deliberate participation in the ALA. Campus interest in active learning grew, and after several years, the ALA expanded to welcome faculty who taught in any style classroom.

The Active Learning Academy

The CTL chose an academy model of training because of the strong history of peer-led training to engage faculty in professional development and to have lasting impact. In the 1960s and 1970s, education training focused on methodologies that included experiential learning (Bonwell & Eison, 1991). This training encompassed programs that included new math, learning by doing, and activities that fell generally under the heading of active learning (Bonwell & Eison, 1991). In the 1980s, this kind of learning expanded through programs that taught reading through the writing process and saw the beginning of the science, technology, engineering, and mathematics (STEM) movement (Bonwell & Eison, 1991). The active learning methodology seeks to pair instructors who are open to this kind of learning with the high-tech support of our active learning classrooms. UNC Charlotte's ALA sought to do just this, while also providing a community for them to collaborate on pedagogies, activities, and using the new classrooms in their instruction.

The first ALA piloted from fall 2014 through spring 2016 with the participation of 109 academics from all across the campus. At the end of the first cohort, UNC Charlotte hosted its first Active Learning Conference. Dr. Robert Beichner spoke about the active learning space there, where he addressed questions of why active learning is such an effective means of instructional practice, how to promote active learning at the university level, and the value of learning for all students in such an environment. Members of the UNC Charlotte ALA participated in an interactive poster session demonstrating their unique approaches to instruction and sharing their successes in the classroom. This inaugural event has morphed into an annual Spring Active Learning Expo hosted at UNC Charlotte, where ALA faculty showcase the work they are doing around active learning and share resources.

The Richter Active Learning Continuum

Former CTL Senior Instructional Technologist Dr. Kurt Richter's vision and depth of experience contributed to the development and continued success of the ALA. Richter was the instructional technologist who designed and led the first cohorts of the ALA. When identifying the learning objectives and goals supporting the academy, he created the Richter Active Learning Continuum, a framework for the transformational process faculty would experience as they embraced moving away from the traditional "sage on the stage" and toward the active methodology supporting a new role of "guide on the side." Richter included key elements that would be transformed, including: grouping, seating, work products, teaching style, assessment, and dialogue (see Figure i.1). This model is still one we follow today. As each year's ALA cohort forms, teams of engaged faculty work to move their courses and teaching from traditional lecture to full implementation of active learning practices.

The Active Learning Academy Today

After the pilot, the ALA transitioned to an annual cohort that followed the academic calendar, beginning in the fall and culminating in the spring with a large event promoting the research and service in active teaching and learning of its members. The model for the academy depends on faculty leaders in active learning who serve as facilitators of smaller teams of cohort participants. Team facilitators are supported by a university-funded stipend and coordinate monthly meetings among their team members where they examine course designs and teaching methods, and experiment with ways to transform their courses using best practices in active learning methodology. The CTL provides cohort support by scheduling special active learning events and scholarly speakers, and sharing the latest in research and tools with academy members. At the end of each cohort, UNC Charlotte hosts the Spring Active Learning Academy Expo, where teams showcase, demonstrate, and actively share what they have worked on over the past year with the campus at-large. Faculty who participate in the ALA have been given priority scheduling for active learning classrooms.

In 2018, strategic organizational improvements were made to the academy. These improve-

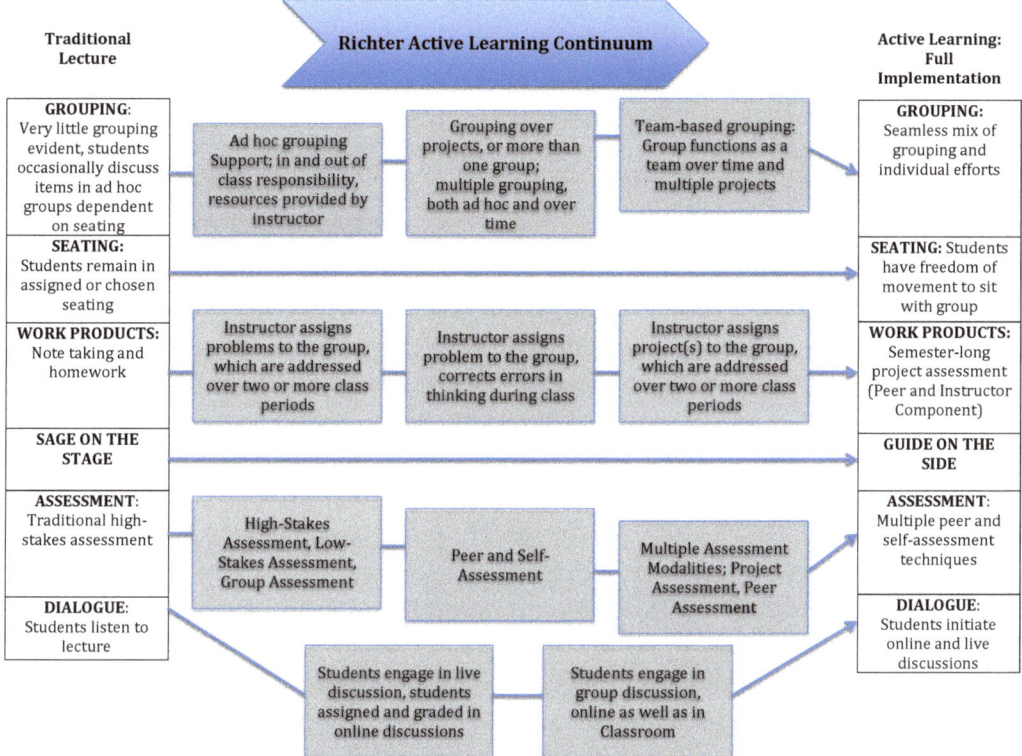

Figure i.1. Richter Active Learning Continuum.

ments included recruiting veteran academy members to work on writing and publishing this book and building a framework into the academy that allowed for members to grow to become facilitators. Additionally, awards for "Excellence in Active Learning Leadership" and "Emerging Active Learning Leader" are given out annually at the end of semester event.

More Active Learning Classrooms

In 2014, there was a great deal of discussion between CS and CTL about supporting the flipped classroom model. The number of faculty adopting the practice had outgrown the two original ALCs, and other spaces on campus were not ideally arranged to support active learning. With the support of Academic Affairs, CS changed their mission statement to include support for learning environments that improve student and faculty experiences in the classroom and, importantly, support for the creation of instructional media.

As of 2019, there are 20 ALCs in use or under construction on the UNC Charlotte main campus. Seating capacity ranges from 36 to 128. The newer rooms have all been designed to meet departmental needs for flexibility, both in budget and space. They have movable tables and chairs, multiple digital displays and projectors, smart board technology, a facilitator podium with a master control panel, sound integrated throughout using microphones and speakers, and various types of whiteboard surfaces to write on. UNC Charlotte recently received a $67,000 grant from Steelcase Education's Active Learning Center program to add a new active learning classroom and conduct assessments and research on the impact of the newly designed space. Future plans focus on larger active learning spaces to continue replacing traditional theater-style lecture halls.

Impact on Faculty and Student Success

As an institution of higher education, student success is at the forefront of every decision UNC Charlotte makes involving the scholarship of teaching and learning and campus space allocation. The Freeman et al. (2014) meta-analysis of student performance in active learning versus traditional learning in STEM classes found that active learning increases student performance. The average exam scores increased by 6% in the active learning classes. Another major finding from the Freeman et al. (2014) study is that students in the traditional lecture classes were 1.5 times more likely to fail than those who were in active learning classes.

This research led UNC Charlotte to examine the preliminary impact of active learning on our campus. In a survey of faculty members who were participants in the ALA, 47% of faculty surveyed reported that they needed more preparation time for an ALC course when compared to a traditional course, but 83% were extremely likely to request an ALC again.

In a survey of students conducted on the impact of ALC use at UNC Charlotte, students reported an overall trend of positive reactions and improved student success. Of the students surveyed, 65% responded that they "somewhat" or "strongly" agreed that they were more engaged with the subject matter in an ALC than in a traditional classroom. Survey results also showed that 64% of students responded that they "somewhat" or "strongly" agreed that they were more supported by their peers in an ALC than in a traditional classroom.

Of the ALA faculty who participated in the survey, 50% reported better student performance in an ALC when compared to a traditional classroom, with 33% reporting equal performance. The initial measure of DFW ("D", "F"/fail, and withdraw) rates for nonwhite versus white students in active learning classrooms was 9% versus 14%. This finding suggests further study is needed surrounding the impact of the ALC on DFW rates. The survey found no significant difference in student achievement by gender or race in ALCs, suggesting the environment of the ALC may act to mitigate gender and race differences found in traditional classroom settings.

The Active Learning Academy's Book

This book is the direct result of the work at UNC Charlotte leveraging people, spaces, and systems to ignite a campus-wide culture of active learning methodology. The authors of the following chapters are faculty who have been ongoing participants in the ALA over multiple cohorts and many years. Each chapter tells a story about their journey to move away from traditional lecture and toward full implementation of active learning. The authors of this book hope the reader will find useful resources or ideas within these pages that can spark change across all institutions of higher education.

References

Baepler, P., Walker, J. D., Brooks, D. C., Saichaie, K., & Petersen, C. I. (2016). *A guide to teaching in the active learning classroom: History, research, and practice.* Sterling, VA: Stylus Publishing.

Beichner, R. J., Saul, J. M., Abbott, D. S., Morse, J. J., Deardorff, R. J., Bonham, S. W., . . . Risley, J. S. (2007). The student-centered activities for large enrollment undergraduate programs (SCALE-UP) project. In E. F. Redish & P. J. Cooney (Eds.), *Research-based reform of university physics.* College Park, MD: American Association of Physics Teachers. Retrieved from https://projects.ncsu.edu/per/Articles/Chapter.pdf

Bonwell, C. C., & Eison, J. A. (1991). *Active learning: Creating excitement in the classroom* (ASHE-ERIC Higher Education Report No. 1). Washington, DC: The George Washington University, School of Education and Human Development.

Dewey, J. (1924). *Democracy and education.* New York, NY: Macmillan.

Freeman, S., Eddy, S. L., McDonough, M., Smith, M. K., Okoroafor, N., Jordt, H., & Wenderoth, M. P. (2014). Active learning increases student performance in science, engineering, and mathematics. *Proceedings of the National Academy of Sciences of the United States of America (PNAS), 111*(23), 8410–8415. doi:10.1073/pnas.1319030111

North Carolina State University. (2019). SCALE-UP: Student-centered active learning environment with upside-down pedagogies. Retrieved from http://scaleup.ncsu.edu

Wilson, J. M. (1994). The CUPLE physics studio. *Physica Teracher, 32*(9), 518-523. doi:10.1119/1.2344100

CHAPTER 1

Logistics of Active Learning

NICOLE SPOOR, TONYA BATES, PILAR ZUBER, AND STEPHANIE STEWART

Introduction

Active learning has been shown to be an effective way to teach in most disciplines, but the logistics of developing a course using active learning principles or moving a course from standard teaching methods to active learning strategies can seem overwhelming. To help you smoothly implement active learning strategies, this chapter focuses on the logistics of active learning at all stages of a course, from course development to postsemester reflection, and also addresses content coverage, classroom setting, class time, syllabi, and establishing groups. The chapter concludes with advice about implementing small changes during the semester and finding resources on campus to help with moving toward active learning.

Content Coverage

Course Development

One of the most frequent concerns for those who have not previously used active learning strategies is the amount of class time these strategies consume. Face-to-face class time is a precious commodity; for many reasons, such as accreditation or licensure requirements, some content absolutely must be taught during the semester. However, adding active learning strategies does not mean decreasing content coverage. It does mean thinking about how to cover content in a different way. Strategically looking at what content must be taught during class and what students can be trusted to learn on their own is a starting point for including more active learning in the classroom.

During Class

Adopting a flipped classroom model will help you meet content coverage requirements. In a flipped classroom, students are exposed to content prior to attending class and then use their knowledge during in-class active learning activities. Not only does this increase engagement during class, but it also increases content retention because students see the content more than once and use the content in multiple ways. Having students using the content in multiple ways makes the flipped classroom model a good strategy for reaching diverse learners.

You can use various methods to move a course to a flipped classroom model. Lectures can be a good place to start, especially if they take up the bulk of your face-to-face classroom time. In place of a lecture, assign a reading that addresses the same content. You can also have your students watch voice-over slideshows or prerecorded lectures through the course management software. However, as with all out-of-class coursework, you may be concerned that students will not view the readings or lectures prior to class; this concern can be addressed in several ways.

Hold students accountable for the content during in-class active learning assignments by emphasizing how the material will be used during class. This will increase the likelihood that students will complete the readings and watch the lectures. The in-class active learning activities become assessments for content covered prior to class time. You should establish the importance of completing readings and watching lectures early in the course, so students understand their importance as well as how not completing or watching them will hurt their grades. You can assign reading or lecture quizzes within the course management system. Automatically graded quizzes will help you hold students accountable without creating more work for yourself. For in-class quizzes, using a polling software, like Poll Everywhere, will allow you to review answers in real time and automatically collect grades. iclicker

Implementing active learning strategies for content is not always just moving in-class lectures to recorded lectures or voice-over slideshows. Active learning activities that have students become the "expert," such as think-pair-share and jigsaws, both discussed in more detail later in this chapter, force students to engage actively with the content and their peers.

After Class/Postsemester

Reflecting on the effectiveness of each activity used during a class session or throughout the semester can help you determine changes that need to be made for both upcoming classes and future iterations of the course. Analyzing student feedback about specific active learning strategies will help you gauge student perceptions of the activities. However, be careful about jumping to conclusions about the activities themselves: Activities that fail to go as planned or that are not met with student enthusiasm may simply be improperly aligned with the course content.

Classroom Setting

Many classrooms are not set up for active learning activities, but that does not mean that there is not a way to adapt a classroom to facilitate active learning; some classroom setups will require more out-of-the-box thinking than others. Classroom size, seating arrangements, and available technology are all space issues that must be addressed when designing active learning activities.

Course Development and Preclass

It may be difficult to think about the space you will be using during the development of your course because you do not know where you will be teaching, and the location of your class can change every semester. What you can do is be prepared for any setting that you might be faced with and think about how your activity could be adapted to various possibilities.

Classroom size is one variable that should be considered during the course development phase. If your classroom is large, how will you manage the activity? If you have a small classroom, how can an activity be adapted to minimize the need to move around the room? Minimizing space requirements is especially important when you are instructing many students in a relatively small classroom. Another important consideration is seating arrangements. Although a classroom with movable furniture is the best scenario for many active learning activities, most activities can be adapted to any type of classroom. If the class has stadium seating with fixed seats, students might have to move into groups along the walls or at the front of the classroom. If desks cannot be moved, then chairs can be. You might also choose to incorporate activities that do not have any special seating requirements.

Technology availability in the classroom is something you should consider during course development. Some active learning strategies require each student to have access to a computer; others only require low-tech tools, such as whiteboards, sticky notes, and markers. If you plan to use high-tech tools for your active learning activities, the course development phase is a good time to determine which tools you hope to have. You may be able to request classrooms with that type of technology or to use one of the active learning classrooms on campus.

You will definitely want to view your classroom once you have been assigned a location. You probably will not be able to change anything about the classroom to which you are assigned, so you must adapt your course to the space you are given. If you assess the classroom early in the course development process, you will have time to make any necessary adjustments to your active learning strategies. When you visit the classroom, you should visualize your activities and their space requirements to address issues that may arise. Keep in mind class size, seating arrangements, and available technology.

During Class/Postsemester

Once your class begins, you may find that even more adjustments are necessary. Remember that implementing active learning in your course is an iterative process. You may find that the setup of the classroom does not work well for one type of activity, and adjust your assignments to use one that better fits the class setup.

Reflecting on the seating arrangements should not only occur after each class but also when reflecting upon your active learning strategies. What type of activities worked best for the space you had to work with? What activities might be better suited for another space? What activities need to be adjusted to accommodate the space you had?

Time

As you design an active learning course, you will need to account for time constraints imposed by the university's class schedule. Accounting for these constraints will help you as you develop the course, manage in-class activities, and plan future iterations of the course.

Course Development

Class meeting times at UNC Charlotte are generally scheduled for 50, 75, or 165 minutes. Each meeting schedule has its benefits and challenges. Early in the planning of your course, consider which one of those class lengths might work best for your course and your active learning goals. To help determine this, consider the following questions.

What are your course objectives? In a heavily content-based course, breaking the information down into smaller chunks might be more beneficial to students. In a course that is more skill-based, a longer class meeting time would better lend itself to multistep, problem-based learning activities.

How large is your class? Consider how the number of students affects how much actual "learning time" you have available. When assessing possible activities, think about the amount of time it takes to get the class settled and ready as well as the time required to get the activity going. In general, larger sections will require more time for both.

At what level of student is your course aimed? This is similar to the first question but takes into account the expected experience of students likely to be enrolled in the course and how they might respond to activity-based learning. This is also related to attention span. Shorter bursts of active learning activities work better when students tend to have shorter attention spans, as opposed to the longer, multi-step, independent learning activities.

What time of day does your class meet? The temperament of your students may be related to the time of day that your class meets as well as the class length. While a 165-minute evening course is often most convenient for students who work full-time while completing their degrees, they are likely to be tired. Consider the timing of the activities during class time and how that impacts their engagement in class.

Some of the above questions may appear to assume that you have control over your course schedule, and we acknowledge that is not always the case. A course that is ideally scheduled for 75-minute meetings twice per week may need to be scheduled for a 165-minute meeting on a Tuesday night due to departmental needs or classroom availability. Despite these challenges, focusing on active learning activities to enhance the class time you find yourself in can go a long way in overcoming these challenges.

Preclass

While you have likely considered and selected your activities in the course development phase, you may need to reassess and adjust activities after you have had an opportunity to gauge your class's personality. When beginning to implement activities, you might find that your students take longer than you originally intended. Please note that this does not necessarily mean that your activity did not work; your class may just take more time to start or may have become deeply engaged in the activity. Other changes to consider are how you introduce the activity and the time it takes students to respond.

During Class

Be flexible. While you do not want your class to dictate how things go, you do want to allow for and encourage positive responses. If students are engaged in an activity, allow the activity to continue past the time allotted for it and eliminate or shorten another activity to accommodate the class schedule. Conversely, if the activity is not taking as long as you thought it would, try to gauge whether or not you can add to the activity to enhance the learning and engagement.

After Class/Postsemester

Assessment of timing after class does not need to be formal. You may find it beneficial to keep some written notes for longer-term planning, but much of your assessment and adjustment will be during the semester between class meeting times. One thing to note is that the success of activities is often based on instructor confidence and the personality of the class. Not every activity will work every semester for every class. If you teach multiple sections, you may find that the activities working in one section do not work in others. Consider how the class meeting time may have affected how well the activity worked for particular sections. You may find yourself making adjustments in timing based on the individual section personalities.

For long-term planning, keeping track of the impact of timing on your active learning strategies and your course success can help to make a case for changing the timing of your class meeting. You may find that a course taught for years in the 165-minute, once-per-week format actually works much better in a 75-minute, twice-per-week format.

Syllabus

A course syllabus serves a variety of purposes. It is often thought of as a technical document that lists and briefly describes academic policies and provides a schedule of topics that will be covered during the semester. The syllabus is provided to students at the beginning of the semester, generally as a Word or PDF file posted to the learning management system (LMS). Students are told that they are expected to read and be familiar with the content of the syllabus, but after that, the syllabus tends to fade into the background. As such, it is easy to see how the syllabus has come to epitomize passive learning. However, because the syllabus sets the tone at the beginning of the course, it is a key component of active learning strategies.

Course Development

The majority of the course syllabus is put together during the planning stages of the course. There are a few things to consider when getting started. First, be familiar with requirements for syllabus content. Colleges and academic units generally have minimum requirements for syllabi. These requirements usually dictate which university policies and resources must be included on the syllabus, along with recommendations for others to include. Colleges and other academic units may also have specific requirements for college-level policies or other information that must be included in all syllabi. Legal Affairs has developed a resource that includes suggested language for policies and notices that can be accessed from the legal affairs website. While the language is not required, it may be helpful to students to see similar language across syllabi.

After the policy/resource requirements are addressed, consider the course-related content that either needs to be included or may be helpful to include. Most commonly, this includes an outline of course topics, descriptions of course assignments, course- or instructor-specific policies, and a class schedule. Additional course components to consider include plain language descriptions of course goals, objectives, and hints for doing well in the course.

By the time you have included all required components, the syllabus will have become a long, burdensome document that few people want to read. As such, the challenge becomes how to make it into an active learning experience for your students. Here are some suggestions. These suggestions can be taken individually or in conjunction with each other, depending on your comfort level with integrating active learning.

Consider the overall structure and order of your syllabus. While colleges and academic units have requirements for syllabi, they generally do not require the content be presented in a particular order. Students are more likely to be engaged with the syllabus if it focuses on the course-specific content toward the front.

Use a syllabus quiz. A syllabus quiz can be as simple as a handful of multiple-choice questions that cover the main points of the syllabus. But the effect that it has is much more powerful; a syllabus quiz requires students to read the syllabus. Integrating a syllabus quiz into the LMS requires students to log in to and interact with the LMS early on in the semester and gives students an opportunity to "practice." Giving a syllabus quiz in class can help students understand your expectations for out-of-class readings and assignments. An in-class quiz can be done individually or in groups and can be provided through technology, like Poll Everywhere or Kahoot!, that decreases your grading workload. In terms of keeping students engaged with the syllabus throughout the semester, questions from the syllabus quiz can reappear at multiple points of the semester, such as at the midterm exam.

Embed the syllabus into Canvas or another LMS. Using an electronic version of the syllabus can turn it into an interactive introduction and guide to the course. Leveraging a system such as Canvas allows you to set up pages with hyperlinks, images, and audio and video files. In Canvas, the syllabus can be set up as a module that must be completed prior to other course material, such as the syllabus quiz, being accessed. Something to consider with embedding the syllabus into Canvas is that Canvas does not have an option to print, so no file version exists. This may have implications if you are required to keep a shareable file version of the syllabus. After setting up the syllabus in Canvas, it is possible to copy and paste the pages into a Word document as a backup or alternate file version. It is tedious to do the first time, but relatively easy to update as you go along.

Preclass/During Class

After the syllabus has been developed, you will need to think about how you want to approach introducing the syllabus to your students. The first day of class is often considered to be "Syllabus Day" in which the instructor spends the class period going through the syllabus. Though reviewing the major points of the syllabus during class time is always good practice, the first day of class may not always be the best day, particularly if your course tends to have a great deal of initial turnover. You may find that the second week of class is a better time to review the syllabus or that consistent references to the syllabus throughout the first few weeks of the semester work just as well. Questions related to the syllabus may also be used as bonus questions on exams or other tests.

After Class/Postsemester

The syllabus is not going to be a course component that you will be reviewing after each class meeting. More likely, the syllabus might be adjusted when major changes, such as schedule adjustments, are made. Be sure to notify students of any changes made and, if helpful, why the changes were made.

Most syllabus changes will be made after the semester while you prepare for the next iteration of the course. Between semesters, you might consider what was effective and what was not. Feedback can be derived from the syllabus quiz scores as well as the types of questions that students asked throughout the semester.

Establishing Groups

Group work has long been a cornerstone of active learning. We know it is an integral part of student development and can see its value in our courses, but integrating group work into course design can be difficult, especially if you have taught the course without it before. Below are some options for using groups.

Course Development

As you consider how to integrate groups into your course, one of the first things to consider is how you want to use the groups. Groups in active learning can be used as part of a graded group project (or series of projects), or to enhance class meeting time, or a combination of both. Part of this planning includes determining the relationship between grading and group work. If you choose to use groups just for class meetings, you may choose not to have any part of the grade based on these activities or perhaps just a small part. If the groups are part of a formal project, then consider a proportion of the course grade that adequately corresponds to the amount of the course workload represented by the group project. You may also take into consideration whether each group member gets the same grade or if the contribution each group member made affects their assignment grade.

Once you have decided the role of groups in your course, you must decide how you will form them. The two basic options for structuring groups are formal groups and informal groups. Formal groups are those in which the groups are established early on in the semester and students stay in those groups throughout the semester, generally culminating in a project or other outcome. Students can be assigned to groups by the instructor or can be permitted to choose their own.

By assigning students to groups, you will get to determine the makeup of the groups and create diversity. Diversity among groups can be based on traditional demographic characteristics as well as skills or other personality traits. The downside to assigning groups is that students do not always respond well to being told whom to work with, which can increase the workload for the instructor as you will have to help students navigate the group process. Allot time for these issues, but know that it is not always possible to anticipate every possible issue.

While allowing students to choose their own groups may reduce the potential for conflict, conflict-free groups may not always be in students' best interests because they do not reflect the workplaces your students may be entering into. The disadvantage of students choosing their own groups becomes apparent in courses where students within the same major take several courses together. They know each other well and tend to choose to work together in groups as they are familiar with each other's strengths and weaknesses. Though it is important that the students learn to recognize skills within themselves and in others, conflict-free groups limit the opportunity for students to be challenged and develop new interpersonal skills and conflict-management skills

Informal groups are those formed ad hoc during class time to complete activities. These groups help increase in-class student interaction. Likewise, having the students complete tasks in groups and report back to the class automatically decreases class time spent on passive learning.

Preclass

Once you have established how you intend to use groups in your course, both in terms of class activity and group formation, you must consider how you will implement the groups in your course.

Group size depends on the task or assignment. Consider the roles necessary to complete the assignment and how many students may be required to fill those roles. Determine if the workload can be distributed equally to ensure that you can provide each student with enough work and a beneficial learning experience. Depending on the assignment, you may define the roles for students or they can choose the roles they prefer.

Assign groups using a variety of methods. Groups can be assigned randomly using Canvas or other methods. If you choose to assign groups purposefully, you will need to collect data about the students in your course to ensure your assignment goals are met. Common ways are described below. They can be used alone or in combination.

Have each student complete a survey of your design. Create your own survey instrument in which you collect data on the characteristics you wish to know. This can be a paper survey, or a survey created and administered in the LMS. Use an established system such as CATME (https://info.catme.org/). CATME can be used throughout the group project, not just to put together the groups. You might also use personality surveys such as the Myers–Briggs Type Indicator to assess personality types and create groups based on personality types. These are helpful for establishing groups in which students play to their strengths or groups in which students are challenged to develop a new skill. Use course-related data such as academic performance to that point. While this may create some unevenness within a group (e.g. a group member not carrying their own weight), it may help prevent creating entire groups of "superstars" and those of less motivated students.

Group purpose will determine group composition. Prior to utilizing informal groups, evaluate what the task is, how much time it will require, and how groups will report back. Options for putting students into groups during class can be systematic (e.g. counting off and grouping by number), by interest (e.g., ask a poll question and group students based on answer), or based on proximity/convenience (e.g. the people around them). Applying a combination of these options will vary the makeup of the groups and allow students to work with an assortment of class members throughout the semester.

During Class

Both formal and informal groups can be used during class time. The formal project-based groups can be afforded class time to work on projects in an environment where the instructor is there to provide immediate feedback. Maintaining the same groups throughout the semester both for projects and in-class meetings establishes the importance of group development as part of the active learning process. Students become accustomed to sitting together and getting into groups earlier, which can cut down on time spent in class. This is quite useful in large courses that meet for the shorter 50- or 75-minute sessions, where taking 10 minutes to get into groups severely impacts time set aside for learning activities.

However, too much repetition can lead to stagnation in the group experience. Groups may become like-minded or somewhat predictable, which may result in a less than active learning experience as students are less likely to be challenged. Task-based learning becomes less about the process involved in reaching the outcome and more about how quickly they reach a conclusion—the "We are done discussing" syndrome. Providing opportunities for students to interact with different class members often leads to increased engagement with the course and course goals.

Though it may be somewhat time consuming to alternate how informal groups are formed in class time, ensuring that the method for putting together the groups is in line with the group activity often leads to better outcomes. Placing group formation instructions on a PowerPoint slide so students can read them as well as hear you give the instructions will both cut down time requirements and lessen student confusion. Using groups consistently throughout the semester and setting early expectations for group work are crucial. This is particularly helpful in a standard auditorium/lecture hall classroom style where it is not always obvious to students that they can work in groups in this type of physical setting.

Another important consideration for group work during class time is keeping students accountable for their work (i.e. keeping them on task). Students must be expected to report back in some way. Active learning spaces often, at a minimum, have whiteboards on which groups can write their response or other outcome. In a standard classroom space, you may choose to use other means, such as poster-sized Post-It notes, to present responses, worksheets, or other note pages that students submit at the end of the class period. You may also decide to use electronic response systems like Poll Everywhere or Kahoot!. These means have the added benefit of allowing you to grade group participation.

After Class/Postsemester

Depending on how you choose to implement groups in your course, the after-class assessment will come either in the form of a quick assessment or a grade for the activity. A quick assessment of how well the activity worked in the classroom setting might simply involve notes to yourself about any changes you wish to make for the future. The future could be the next class meeting, later on in the semester, or the next semester.

If the grading scheme for the course involves giving grades for group work, then there is work to be done in between classes. Low-stakes, informal group activities during class time can generally be graded quickly, particularly if electronic feedback is used. High-stakes group work will take longer to grade, but this time requirement is likely something you have already considered in developing the assignment. Group assignments have the advantage of fewer actual assignments to grade; rubrics specifically set up for group assignments can set expectations for students and ease some of the grading burden.

An aspect of after-class/postsemester assessment is feedback regarding the individual student contribution to the group (e.g. the accountability factor). Accountability can be established by having students submit a separate assessment of individual contributions using a simple form, either paper or electronic, in which each group member rates and describes the contributions of all group members. Using a system like CATME can help to track and provide feedback. The assessment can come at multiple points: during the project, after the project, and at the end of the semester. The feedback can be integrated into the course/project grade or used for future planning.

Making Small Changes

Active learning is not an all-or-nothing model. Sometimes the best way to implement active learning strategies is to make small changes. Small changes may even be the most effective way to present information content. Small changes can also be a useful way for the instructor to become more comfortable with active learning.

Course Development

Moving an entire course to an active learning model may seem overwhelming. It also may not be feasible to always engage students in active learning activities. Active learning does not mean having to include group-based learning projects that last for multiple sessions or the entire semester. Active learning also does not mean that you have to keep your students active the entire session. Implementing one or more quick active learning strategies can be effective in increasing student engagement with the course material. If you are moving an older course to an active learning model, choose a few small strategies or activities appropriate for the subject matter and try them out. Sometimes small changes are more effective than a complete overhaul.

During Class

Although there is almost an endless number of small changes that could be made to increase active learning, this section will outline some of the most popular. Use of technology that involves students in the classroom may be one of the easiest ways to engage students. For example, UNC Charlotte provides access to the polling software, Poll Everywhere. Students can use their computers, tablets, or cell phones to record attendance, answer questions, and share ideas. Many applications make it easy for instructors to "gamify" course content. Having students interact with course content in the form of a game is an easy way to increase active learning. Rather than just asking questions and getting responses from a few students, usually those who would be engaged with the content in any format, gamifying your questions encourages everyone to be involved. Kahoot! is one very popular and easy-to-use application to use for gamifying content.

Many K–12 active learning strategies are quick and easy to implement to support content that students read before or during class. In a think-pair-share activity, students think about what they have read and then share their thoughts with a partner. The partners then share their thoughts with the entire class. This activity can be scaffolded by providing students prompts or questions that they should reflect on and discuss with their partner. The same content may be assigned to everyone, or each pair might address a particular section of the reading. A think-pair-share activity not only gives students the chance to reflect and discuss, but it also provides experience in speaking to an audience.

Jigsaws can be particularly good active learning strategies for deep or heavy content. Groups are assigned a particular section of the reading and then work together to determine how to best summarize and share the information in their section with others. One student from each group joins with members from other groups to form a new group in which they each "teach" the rest of the group their section of the content. Another approach would be to have each group prepare a minilesson on their assigned content and share it with the entire class.

There are also small changes that can be made to get students moving in the classroom. Movement increases focus along with engagement and should not take a lot of time. Simply taking frequent breaks during a lecture to have students move across the class and discuss the content with a student they do not usually work with is an effective way to include active learning in your classroom. Having students brainstorm by moving to a whiteboard to write down their ideas or using notecards that students place in categories scattered throughout the classrooms are other ways to provide a stimulating active learning experience.

After Class/Postsemester

Regardless of the strategies, always remember that active learning exists on a continuum. Although some instructors are excited to dive into the deep end of active learning, even just being willing to dip your toes in can help your students. Reflecting upon the strategies you choose to implement can help you to figure out what works in your courses and perhaps move you toward implementing more extensive active learning strategies in the future.

Ask for Help!

Course Development and Preclass

Remember that you are not alone. This book has been compiled by UNC Charlotte faculty from the Active Learning Academy. The academy can help connect you with instructors who have tried these student-centered strategies. Observe your peers doing active learning though the Center for Teaching and Learning's Teachers Observing Peers Program. The course you observe does not have to be in your discipline for you to get ideas about what you can do in your course. You might get an idea for your large enrollment course, nonmajors' course, etc.

If you think you are not that creative, do a quick online search for the active learning idea you have. You might be surprised to find how many ideas are already out there and ready for you to implement. A few tweaks may be all that are necessary so you can have an activity ready to go for your next class.

The textbook publisher's website is another place to look for resources. Scroll through your course textbook to the critical thinking questions at the end of the chapter and transform them into an in-class think-pair-share activity or case study. You can use adaptive learning from your textbook to generate an activity for the material that your class needs to review.

Joining a community of practice like the Active Learning Academy at UNC Charlotte can be beneficial. Attending a professional development conference can help you discover strategies for teaching in your discipline. If you cannot attend a conference, join a professional listserv that will help you connect with other instructors through email.

During Class and After Class

Having help when implementing a new teaching tool is always a good idea. The first time you try something, ask an expert to be present. Having someone there who could answer technical questions allowed me to focus on the specific content. Using teaching assistants, undergraduate preceptors, colleagues, etc. is also recommended.

If you have a summer course or smaller section, you can practice the activity. After the activity, you should collect feedback or a reflection from the participants. Some ideas for prompts are: Thinking about the big picture, what is the most important thing you learned about (insert your topic here) today? What did you get out of the class activities that you would not have gotten out of a lecture?

After class, review the feedback and student reflections. You might get ideas about how to improve the second or third iteration of your activity.

Conclusion

A move to active learning can improve student engagement and learning, but implementing active learning may feel overwhelming. This chapter includes many considerations and ideas to help make the transition easier. The move does not have to be extreme and could include just adding small active learning activities. Any changes are well supported on campus.

CHAPTER 2

Strategies to Incorporate Active Learning Practice in Introductory Courses

MOHSEN DORODCHI, LAUREL POWELL, NASRIN DEHBOZORGI, AND AILEEN BENEDICT

Introduction

Science, technology, engineering, and mathematics (STEM) discipline courses, and especially their introductory courses, are reported to have high failure rates. The long lecture-based format of teaching in introductory courses has shown very unsuccessful results. For example, historically, the drop"D", "F"/fail, and withdraw (DFW) rates have been reported to average 30% for introductory programming courses (Watson & Li, 2014). Students also complain about the time required and the fact that the introductory programming course demands more time than they have (Kinnunen & Malmi, 2006). Our interpretation of this issue is that students do not have enough time to digest the materials conceptually and relate their programming skills to analysis and algorithm development. When integrating active learning into such courses, significant improvements were reported over traditional lecturing. A thorough study by Freeman et al. (2014) showed that active learning leads to increases in examination performance (average increase of half a letter grade), while decreasing the failure rates. Furthermore, the study proved that while active learning achievements hold across all of the STEM disciplines and occur in all class sizes, course types, and course levels, it is particularly beneficial in small classes and in increasing performance on concept inventories.

This chapter is focused on introductory courses. The distinguishing factors that make introductory courses unique include: (a) they are offered in multiple sections with large class sizes, (b) they provide students with gateway courses into their major, and (c) freshmen experience college-level gateway courses for the first time as the foundation of their majors. Considering these features, along with the large size of such courses, special attention needs to be paid when teaching them. Beyond the content, faculty should focus on study skills, team skills, and skills for cooperative learning because they are essential to student learning.

The organization of this chapter is as follows:

- An overview of practiced active learning in introductory courses in different disciplines.
- An overview of cooperative learning versus collaborative/social learning.

- A presentation of the course model that we have been practicing for the past few years.
- The integration of our model along with innovative practices designed by us and other educators for teaching introductory courses in active learning. We present our class model that relies on student preparation and reflections on their learning.
- A discussion on how to use students' self-assessment and reflection on the teamwork and course materials to adjust and enhance the activities. In this section, we first discuss the data acquired from students' self-assessments and reflections to identify factors such as positivity, grit, and their impacts on their learning. Next, we discuss the design and adjustment of the course activities in a direction that helps students learn and perform more effectively. At the end of this section, we discussed the effectiveness of integrating self-assessment and reflection into introductory courses.
- A summary of the chapter and future directions for our findings.

Overview of Practiced Active Learning in Introductory Courses

In their work, Bonwell and Eison (1991) discussed opinions on the methods for active learning and the obstacles to its adoption. Some of these obstacles include instructor fears of being unable to teach sufficient content, the amount of preparation work required, and large class sizes. These hurdles, however, have not proven insurmountable. Active learning has demonstrated its effectiveness across disciplines and has demonstrated that it can improve both the performance and satisfaction of students.

According to Prince's (2004) survey, support can be found for multiple variations on active learning in engineering classrooms. Prince began by addressing the challenge of quantifying student classroom experiences to compare different techniques. He discussed active learning, cooperative learning, collaborative learning, and problem-based learning in engineering classrooms. After examining studies, he concluded that evidence supports the effectiveness of all these methods. Collaboration and cooperation promote positive outcomes and should be encouraged in the classroom.

Student satisfaction can be dramatically improved by incorporating active learning methods into a classroom. In Armbruster, Patel, Johnson, and Weiss (2009), students were dissatisfied with the traditional lecture-based course model in an introductory biology class. Because of this, instructors chose to reorganize the course according to active learning principles. They added problem-based activities to their lectures that students were asked to solve in small groups that would remain together for the semester. Another method to encourage students to participate more actively was the addition of "clicker questions" to each lecture that counted toward a student's participation grade. The classes were also given weekly quizzes, administered using "clickers," that were worth a small portion of the final grade. To measure the effectiveness of these methods, student evaluations and class performance were compared across three years, with the earliest year being taught in a traditional lecture style and the latter two years using active learning methods. Student performance improved, as did student satisfaction. Interestingly, while some students gave negative comments about the use of the weekly quizzes, other students listed the quizzes as highly helpful. The writers believe that this, combined with student comments, showed evidence that the quizzes made the students more aware of their own learning.

Active learning can be used effectively in large classes. Deslauriers, Schelew, and Wieman (2011) conducted a study on a first-year physics course. Eight hundred fifty students were divided among three sections in large, theater-style lecture halls. This course had been taught in a traditional lecture format using PowerPoints, instructor demonstrations, and "clicker" quizzes, which were not paired with discussion, to evaluate overall student understanding. During the 12th week of the course the authors conducted an experiment. In order to have a direct comparison of the two participating sections, one author taught the 12th week material as usual, while in the other section the material was taught by two of the authors. They integrated multiple active learning strategies, including assigning reading before class, which for consistency was also assigned to the control section, giving quizzes on that reading, and soliciting feedback in class. Additionally, they added a discussion component to the clicker quizzes and had students work in small groups to prepare written answers to questions. A test was prepared and administered to both classes when the experiment concluded. Students in the experimental section performed better on the test and, according to evaluations, were more satisfied with the material.

Instructors in a course on renal pharmacology experimented with a flipped classroom model combined with a more active teaching style (Pierce & Fox, 2012). They assigned students to view recordings of lectures before coming to class for activities. The in-class activities used a Process Oriented Guided Inquiry Learning (POGIL) design and were oriented around applying what they had learned from the videos to perform patient care. The instructors also required students to answer questions and perform calculations during the activity. Student evaluations were favorable, and student scores on the final exam improved under the new methods. The POGIL method encouraged students to consider applications of their studies, and it better prepared them for the final examination.

In contrast to the science and engineering classes discussed in this overview, McCarthy and Anderson (2000) used active learning in a history class and a political science class. Instead of a traditional lecture and discussion, the researchers used a role-playing exercise in a history class and an activity completed in pairs in a political science class. Students in more traditional classes were compared to the experimental classes, and the experimental classes performed better.

The positive impact of active learning across introductory courses is difficult to quantify, but it is equally difficult to deny. It has been used in classes across STEM disciplines and in humanities classes. While the exact methods do and must vary, the importance of focusing the student on the learning is well supported.

Cooperative Learning versus Collaborative/Social Learning

Active learning is generally defined as any pedagogical practice that engages students in the learning process. Active learning helps both student cognition and metacognition by engaging students to do meaningful learning activities and to think about what they do (Bonwell & Eison, 1991).

In research, active learning is often referred to by other names such as cooperative learning or collaborative learning. It is a challenge to provide a universally accepted term for active learning because there are multiple active learning techniques, and educators adopt different names based on their methods. However, it is possible to provide some generally accepted definitions and to highlight distinctions in how common terms are used (Prince, 2004).

In particular STEM fields, student engagement in active learning is mainly in the form of teamwork. Teamwork plays two important roles in active learning; one is peer learning that helps students learn from each other, and the other is about improving social skills. Teamwork in active learning has been introduced using different terms such as cooperative learning or collaborative learning, depending on the point of the teamwork.

Collaborative learning refers to any pedagogical technique that requires students to work together in small groups to accomplish a common goal (Prince, 2004). Therefore, collaborative learning can include all group-based instructional methods, including cooperative learning (Millis & Cottell, 1997; Smith & MacGregor, 1992).

However, some researchers believe there are distinctions between collaborative and cooperative learning and that they have different philosophical roots (Bruffee, 1995; Panitz, 1999). In either definition, the core of collaborative learning is the emphasis on student interactions rather than on learning activity.

Cooperative learning is defined as a structured teamwork where students pursue common goals while being assessed individually (Millis & Cottell, 1998). This type of teamwork has five specific aspects: individual accountability, mutual interdependence, face-to-face promotive interaction, appropriate practice of interpersonal skills, and regular self-assessment of team functioning.

While different cooperative learning models exist (Stahl, 1994; Slavin, 1983), the common element across them is a focus on cooperative incentives rather than competition to promote learning.

Based on given definitions, we believe collaborative learning can be more applicable in introductory-level courses in which students need to interact with each other and learn more social skills while learning from each other in a socially supported environment. This social aspect is important because it improves students' communication skills and prepares them for upper-level classes and the professional environment. It also makes learning a fun experience while motivating students to be actively involved due to social pressure in teams. This type of teamwork best suits less challenging and sophisticated concepts where students get a chance to learn from peers and fill the gaps between team members' backgrounds.

On the other hand, we believe cooperative learning on a larger scale can be applied in higher-level classes and capstone courses where a project is defined as a common goal and all team members apply their knowledge to accomplish the goal and develop a final product. In this form of teamwork, less emphasis is on learning and more on applying what they learned. Cooperative learning is more structured, and usually team members have assigned tasks and roles. It is more suitable for advanced and challenging topics where tasks are distributed among the team members.

An Active Learning Introductory Course Model

The teaching paradigm has been shifting from traditional lecture-based teaching methods to designing learning experiences, processes, and environments for students (Duderstadt, 2008). An integrated course design starts with analyzing the "situational factors," followed by formulating the "learning goals" as well as designing the "feedback and assessment procedures." The design and selection of the teaching/learning activities fulfills this process (Fink, 2003). Activity-based active learning seems to be one of the desirable delivery methods for such teaching and learning activities, providing both excitement and fun while emphasizing learning (Bonwell & Eison, 1991; Dorodchi & Dehbozorgi, 2017; Sanders, Boustedt, Eckerdal, McCartney, & Zander, 2017; Xinogalos, 2016). Considering the above factors, a coherent course would have a complete alignment among the activities, the assessment, and the learning goals and outcomes (Dorodchi et al., 2018). In addition, the need for an educational measurement of student knowledge aligned with activities and learning goals that goes beyond traditional tests and the methods to make inferences about student learning are instructionally essential in this model of course design (Pellegrino, Chudowsky, & Glaser, 2001).

One major issue in implementing active learning and a flipped classroom is making sure students come to class prepared. For the introductory courses, our experience showed that the preparation materials should be well structured and in line with the class activities. Therefore, in our course model, we have adapted Kolb's experiential learning cycle as shown in Figure 2.1 to make sure that the course materials and activities are developed with proper relevancy and consistency. The model visualizes Kolb's traditional four-stage model including preparation before the class, the class activity, and the postclass activities followed by the reflective observation. By replicating the reflection stage multiple times throughout the cycle, as shown in Figure 2.2, students are directed to properly conceptualize a particular course objective at different levels.

In other words, instead of having reflection only once as the last stage of Kolb's model, our model has three distinct stages with reflection integrated throughout. Students plan for the upcoming week with prep work assignments, have active learning experiences in class, and then extend their learning on assignments at home. By integrating reflection throughout all these steps, our model becomes a three-stage process with reflection: prep work that helps students prepare for upcoming classes, in-class activities to further learn and experiment on the material, and postclass assignments that extend concepts from the course so students reflect on each of these aspects multiple times throughout their learning.

Such a model also provides opportunities to design the activities in such a way to both challenge students step-by-step while encouraging them to enjoy the group and social aspects of team activities (Dorodchi et al., 2017). When designing activities for each phase and creating tests for assessing students' learning, Bloom's taxonomy was also applied. An example of one week's iteration is shown in Figure 2.3.

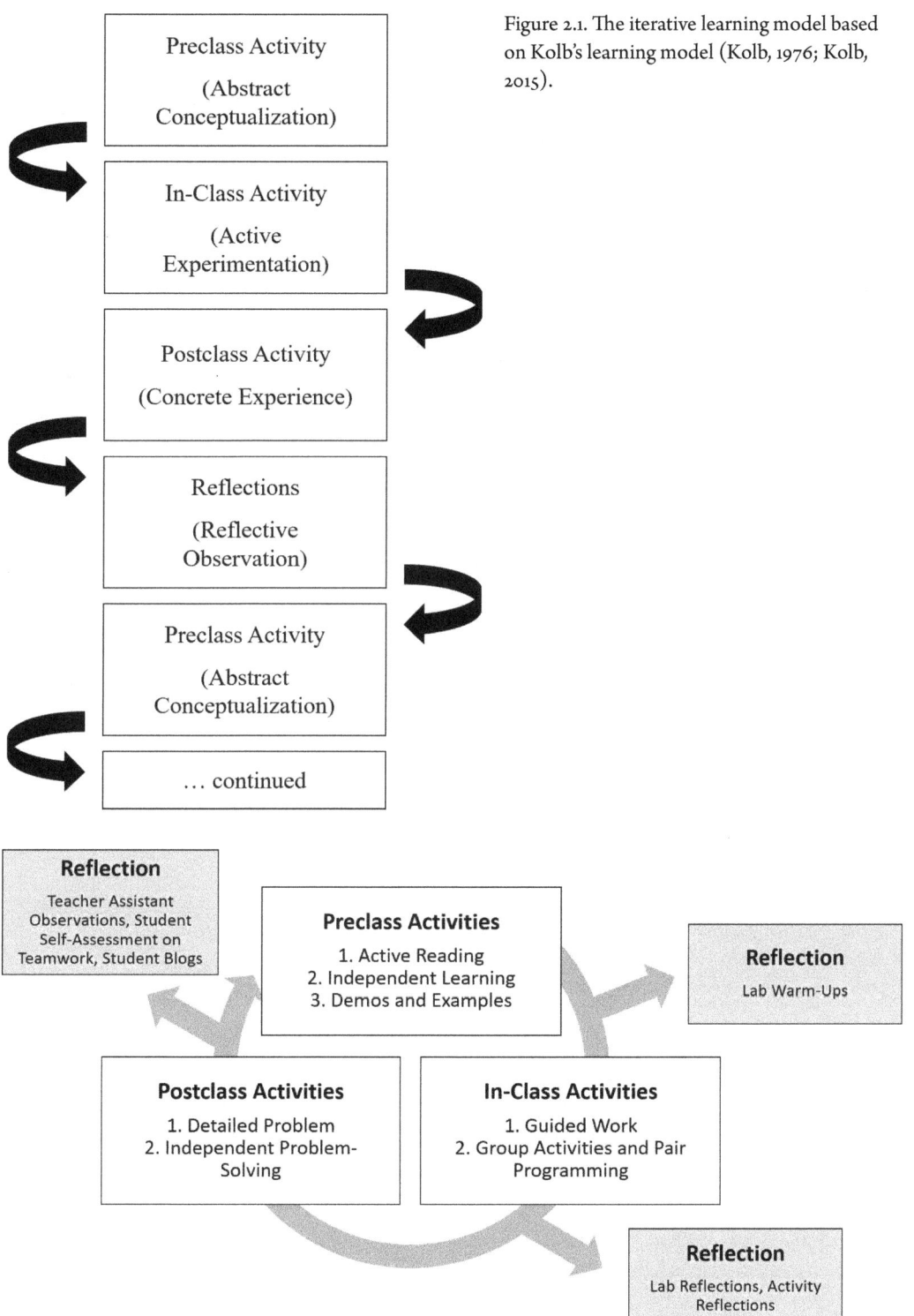

Figure 2.1. The iterative learning model based on Kolb's learning model (Kolb, 1976; Kolb, 2015).

Figure 2.2. Our course model with integrated reflections.

How to Comment

You will also need to know how to properly comment for next Lab.

 The icon to the left will be used a lot in Lab 2 as a reminder to comment. Follow the steps below to learn more about commenting.

...

1. About how long did this work take you (pre- and postlab) *(Enter time)*

2. List two things you have learned from pair programming. Describe them briefly. *(Short Answer)*

3. How do you declare an integer as a primitive data type? *(Multiple choice)*

4. Proper commenting is just to make things look nicer, but it's not required. *(True/False)*

5. What must be imported to use the Scanner? *(Multiple choice)*

...

Activity 1: Declaring Variables to help Children learn Geometry

You are asked to write a program for elementary school children to play with and learn about geometry. The program will teach them about shapes, areas and perimeters. As the start, we want you to just write a program about rectangles.

1. Start with your **block comment**!

...

1. Which activities did you finish on/before the checkpoints? *(Select all)*

2. After Lab 2, how confident are you in your mastery of variables, math operations, and user input? *(Likert Scale)*

3. How was your experience with pair programming? *(Select all: 😄 Excellent, 🙂 Moderate, 😐 Bad, ...)*

4. Why is using math operations and variables important in programming? *(Short answer)*

...

Program 1: Convert Pounds into Kilograms

Write a program that converts pounds into kilograms. The program prompts the user to enter a number in pounds, converts it to kilograms, and then displays the result. One pound is *0.454* kilograms.

...

Figure 2.3. Illustrating the flow of one week's lab cycle, taking sample instructions and questions from a preclass activity, reflection, in-class activity, reflection, and postclass activity.

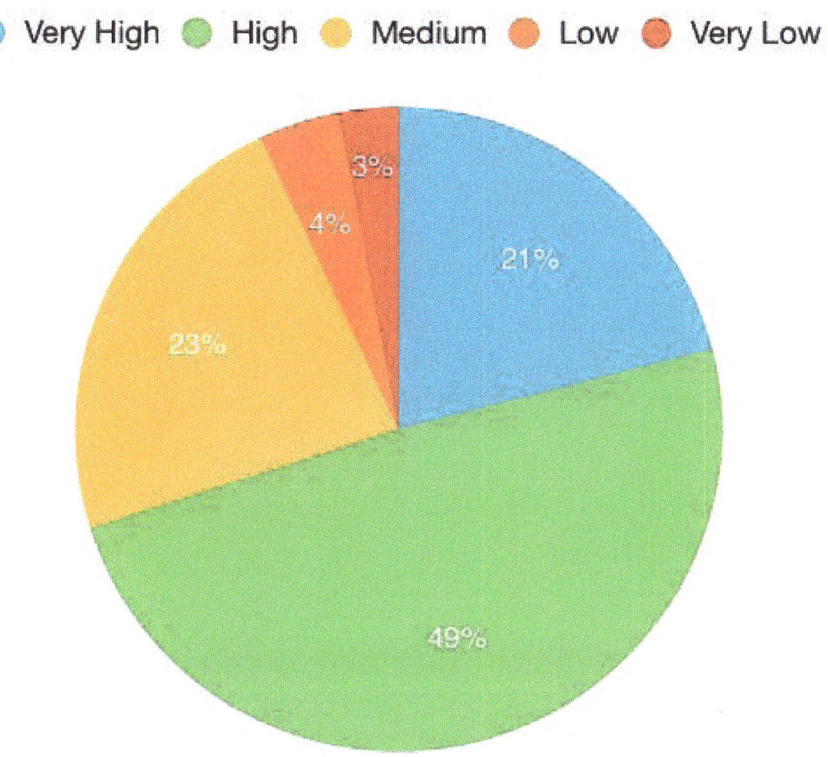

Figure 2.4. Students' perceptions about how much they learned about Java programming.

First, the students complete the prelab homework (a type of preclass activity, as shown in the cycle in Figure 2.2) meant to prepare them before coming to the lab as shown in Figure 2.3. Then, at the beginning of the lab, a "lab warm-up" is completed (a type of reflection) that asks questions relating to their preparation work. The lab itself is a type of in-class activity where students complete programming activities to strengthen their knowledge of what was learned that week. After lab, students complete the lab reflection (another type of reflection), responding to questions about the lab itself and their own learning experiences. Finally, students complete a postlab assignment (a type of postclass activity) independently for homework to further review what they have learned. Many of our own reflective prompts were aimed at having students think about their own learning experiences, hence metacognitive attributes can be included in our data. Figure 2.4 shows an example of a question from one of the reflections that asks the students near the end of the course "How much do you think you learned about Java programming?" As shown in this case, very small percentages claim they did not learn anything. Most feel they learned something or learned very well.

The reflection provides opportunities for students to talk about their learning at different levels. We think it also encourages students to think about their progress and level of understanding throughout the course. Some of our reflective prompts were designed in this way. However, we did not only include reflections just a few times throughout the semester. Instead, it was an iterative process that occurred much more frequently, such as at the end of many in-class activities. Furthermore, we did not limit our prompts to students' attitudes toward their learning experiences but asked a mixture of questions regarding many different aspects of their learning experiences.

Designing the Activities for Activity-Based Active Learning

In this model of the introductory course, we have a combination of lectures and labs. Each class or lab session includes several activities done in small groups with a duration of about 15 to 45 minutes per activity. In this section, we discuss how we designed the activities. We intended that students would do multiple activities focusing on one aspect of the course objective in a class period or lab from fundamentals to more challenging levels. We also provided opportunities to design different forms of activities to keep students interested. We call this model of activities "staged diversified activities" as explained below.

Staged Diversified Activities

As mentioned before, our course follows an activity-based active learning structure emphasizing collaborative learning that includes a spectrum of activities. Primarily, we start with warm-up activities closely related to the preparation activity before the class. We gradually transition the activities to more challenging ones using diverse methods, such as clicker-style quizzes, LMS (learning management system) individual and group work, pair programming, scratch-off quizzes, etc. We have observed that students learn better by diversifying the activities. We ask students to think and discuss the major concepts of the course while doing the activities. The goal is to facilitate the learning through transitioning from simple to more challenging concepts as well as using staged diversified activities. By scaffolding the activities, we can provide a smooth flow of concepts and make sure that students work together efficiently, implementing peer instruction and learning. Furthermore, switching between types of activities is helpful to sustain student interest. Diversifying activities prevents the effect of "getting used to it." Our observation showed that students face a plateau in their learning after a few weeks into the semester without a well-prepared, diverse set of activities. Finally, we split the activities into two major parts, leaving time in between for a Kahoot! quiz to discuss the major points of activities while assessing their learning.

In addition, we propose infusing different activity checkpoints into the activity-based active learning (ABAL) class to maintain the pace and keep all groups of students synchronized. Activity checkpoints are good times for discussions in the class. For introductory courses, activity checkpoints are essential to keeping all students engaged and on the same pace as explained here.

Activity Checkpoints

Given the time limit of each class and the need to complete many different activities per session, we use activity checkpoints. Checkpoints are spread throughout activities mostly to provide demonstrations or feedback from the instructor and to make sure all the students in large classes are learning at the same pace.

One guideline for scaffolding activities is to break tasks into smaller, more manageable pieces with feedback at the checkpoints (Silver, 2012). Both the switching of activities and the use of checkpoints allow us to enforce timely completion of the different types of activities while keeping students engaged.

Estimating realistic time limits for activities is another challenge in ABAL classes. We have evolved a scheme over time based on trial and error while testing and timing the activities ourselves, observing the students in class, and evaluating their feedback. The following brief summary of two case studies shows how we implement the discussed activity scaffolding.

Case Study 1: Checkpoint in Search-and-Sort Activity on LMS

In this class activity, students worked in pairs to complete a guided activity inside the LMS on one of the advanced and major concepts of the course. By this point, around the end of the course, the major constructs of programming, including looping, methods, and arrays, have been covered in detail with good repetitions, and students are ready to learn the search-and-sort algorithms. Many computer science algorithms require students to know the search-and-sort algorithms in depth. The activity is split into several sections, labeled "Section 1: Searching" and "Section 2: Sorting" and separated by checkpoints with proper timing per section. At the time of the checkpoint, the instructor provides overall class discussions to review some of the essential concepts with students as a short, on-demand lecture and/or a Kahoot! quiz. This gives the opportunity to adapt to the students' current needs and fill in any gaps in their learning. Breaking up the activities also helps the students deal with manageable portions of the content. In addition, the instructor has a chance to assess student learning before moving on to the next activity.

Case Study 2: Class Discussion Through Clicker-Style Quizzes (e.g., Poll Everywhere, Kahoot!)

Clicker-style short quizzes are offered between activities and sometimes during the activity checkpoints. These are used to assess student understandings of the completed class activities, provide low-stakes practice problems, and measure the effectiveness of our activity and checkpoint breakups. In hopes of reducing the performance gap between the practical and theoretical components of our course, we have designed a series of Kahoot! quizzes to provide students with constant and consistent feedback and practice. With more consistent assessment of the learners' knowledge and experiences, we are better able to determine and meet the students' learning needs.

Throughout iterations and with constant formative feedback from the quizzes, we were able to tweak the relevant in-class activity content and design questions to follow a smooth scale of easy questions building up toward more challenging ones following the algorithm (Dorodchi et al.,, 2017). Below, we showcase an example sequence of questions used in a clicker-style quiz:

- Question 1: What is scope?
- Question 2: What does the snippet below display?

```
for (int i=0; i < 5; i++) {
    System.out.println(i);
}
System.out.println(i);
```

Figure 2.5.

- Question 3: What does the snippet below display?

```
int i = 0;
for (i = 4; i < 5; i++) {
    System.out.print(i + " ");
}
System.out.println(i);
```

Figure 2.6.

- Question 4: What does the snippet below display?

```
for (int i = 0; i < 5; i++); {
    System.out.print(i + " ");
}
```

Figure 2.7.

Before completing the above quiz, students would have completed the relevant activities. Question 1 is a simple and conceptual problem that reviews the students' ability to recall and understand the definition of scope. Question 2 scales up in difficulty and applies scope into a loop problem related to the most recent in-class activity completed. Students are expected to synthesize their understanding of scope and their practice in the recent in-class activity to answer this question. Students are expected to notice that the variable i is used out of scope. Question 3 showcases an example where the variable i is properly used to avoid the scope issue. By asking various questions relating to the same concept—scope—we can further reinforce the learning of students, including those who have gotten the previous question wrong. It is important to note that the instructor can see the progress of the class (including percentages of correct and incorrect responses) and thus provide additional explanations in between questions. Question 4 gets even more complex by quizzing students on for-loop exceptions with semicolons; students must first notice the misplaced semicolon and then also understand the complications caused by this misplacement. Question 4 combines the concepts from all three previous questions (for-loops and scope of the iterative variable).

In this section, we have covered our scaffolding strategy for our Kahoot! quizzes. These quizzes assist in identifying the learning gaps between our class activities and our lecture test concepts. Furthermore, it provides opportunities for more consistent assessment and feedback loops. The findings gained by witnessing the students' overall knowledge and where they may be struggling provide us the insight to tweak in-class activities and better scaffold Kahoot! quizzes. We can then build a bridge between the concepts learned in class and the concepts students are tested on in the lecture tests.

Student Reflections

Reflection is generally described as the process of giving meaning to experiences. It is a deliberate process in which people "capture their experience, think about it, and evaluate it" (Boud, Keogh, & Walker, 1985). As explained before in the learning model for the course, students need to reflect on their learning to conceptualize the major course contents.

In addition, reflection can also be used to discover the factors that make the most impact in teaching as well as hidden issues. The instructor needs to be aware of student learning experiences to support evidence-based teaching. In teaching, sometimes the instructor may go by "intuition" rather than evidence, and such intuition may not always be relevant (Guzdial, 2015). The evidence-based model in education is defined as "the integration of professional wisdom with the best available empirical evidence in making decisions about how to deliver instruction" (U.S. Department of Education, 2002). Therefore, to improve overall performance in introductory courses using active learning, we need to first discover the factors that affect student success and failure. Based on such discoveries, we may start to make improvements in our pedagogy.

We particularly investigated reflective writing as a way to have students reflect on their learnings, course content, and group work. In reflective writing, students think and write about their learning experiences to glean insight from them. Reflection is beneficial for students as it helps them to think more critically about their experiences and to challenge their own assumptions (Mezirow, 1990).

Many examples exist in engineering and computer science (CS) education literature about integrating reflective practices into courses and learning environments. Turns, Sattler, Yasuhara, Borgford-Parnell, and Atman (2014) provide a variety of examples from engineering and have created a framework for thinking about elements of reflection. Others have created pedagogies that include student reflective practices for engineering (Adams, Turns, & Atman, 2003; Shekar, 2007) and CS courses (Dorodchi et al., 2018). All these works indicate that the reflective practice not only benefits the student but also can also benefit instructors and administrators by improving at-risk classification and time to predict at-risk students (Dorodchi et al., 2018).

Statistical Analysis of Reflections

In this segment, we show descriptive statistics of the collected reflections to demonstrate results of some of the reflections as well as how the analysis can help with the scaffolding process. Analyzing reflections to gain insights into the student learning experiences can help us adapt

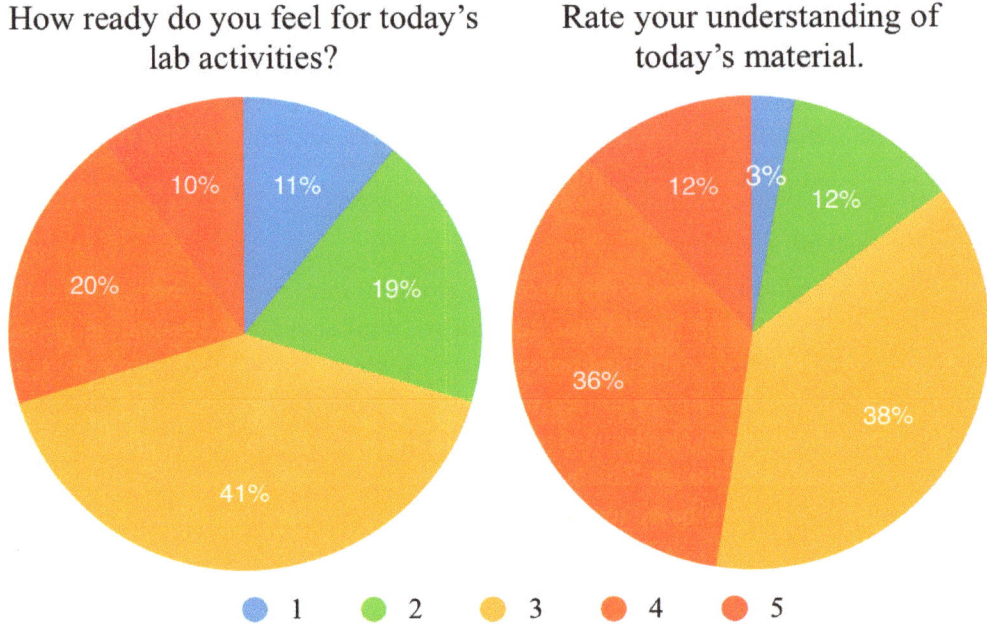

Figure 2.8. Comparison of students' perceptions before and after the lab activities.

class activities and discussions to the students' needs. Figure 2.8 is an example of a pretest/posttest practice that compares the students' perspectives about their level of readiness before the start of the lab session to their assessment of their own understanding at the end of the lab. The combined data of fall 2017 and spring 2018 semesters indicate that only 15% of students felt less competent at the end of the lab while that number at the beginning of the lab was about 30%. Such data provide useful feedback to instructors as far as the effectiveness of lab or class activities.

In Figure 2.9, students' level of interest toward programming at the beginning of the course is compared to their level of interest toward the entire computer science discipline at the end of the course. These pre/post questions were designed because it has been reported that some students quit the computer science discipline due to the difficulty of programming courses. As shown, the high level of interest changed from 40% to 54%.

The level of student confidence in performing programming tasks is also an important point of concern for faculty who teach programming courses. In Figure 2.10, using two posttests, we measure the change in the level of students' confidence from their own perspectives on two highly reported (as indicated by unigrams) challenging topics (i.e., methods and arrays) after the corresponding lab activities. This data can help evaluate the implemented scaffolding and provide information for possible additional activities to balance out the students' levels of confidence, if necessary.

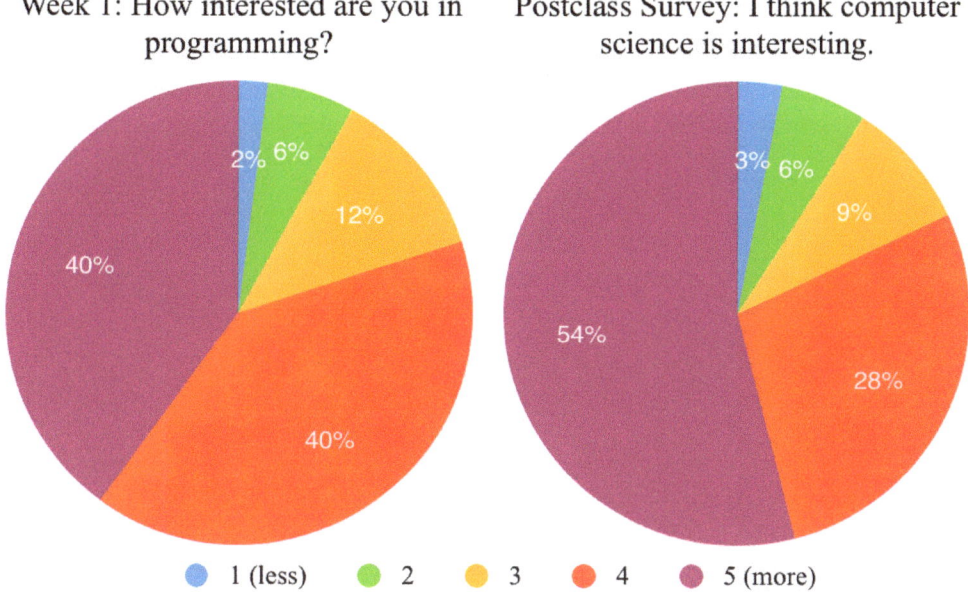

Figure 2.9. Comparison between student interest in programming and computer science at the beginning and the end of the course.

Reflection provides substantial information about students' learning; however, immediate analysis of this information is quite challenging. More elaborate analysis of the reflections is discussed in another chapter in the book called "A learning analytics approach to assessing student risk in active learning."

Reflection on Teaching Using This Active Learning Model

We have been practicing using active learning for a while and have been through different levels and a number of iterations.

Working in groups, while often advantageous, is not always easy for students. One of the advantages of this model of active learning is its flexibility in handling different student needs for group interaction. As all students are responsible for turning in their own work and can complete the majority of it on their own, students who do not want to work with their group members or who have group members who are behaving poorly are not unfairly penalized. This creates an environment that encourages collaboration without making students resent forced grouping or tying the grade of active students to their nonparticipating peers.

The feedback from the clicker-style quizzes such as Kahoot! or Poll Everywhere quizzes is another important aspect of this model. After or during an activity, students are often reluctant to ask conceptual questions. This makes judging difficult if more clarification or a minilecture

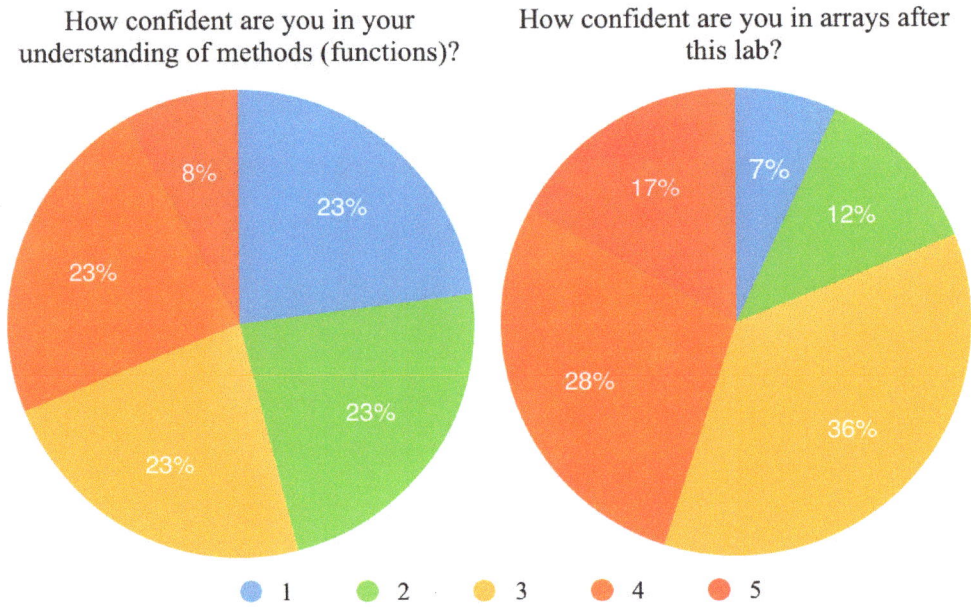

Figure 2.10. Students' perceptions about two challenging areas in computer science after the first exposure in the labs, rated from least (1) to most (5) confident.

is needed. Seeing the results makes it easy to supplement the explanation if students are struggling and helps students understand where they need help without the pressure of an exam.

Conclusions and Recommendations

Active learning in introductory courses presents unique challenges, such as unbalanced background related to the course content and team-based activities in addition to the level of motivation. A lack of homogeneity in students' familiarity with group work and the content may cause effects, such as overwhelming other students. For this purpose, the proper level of preparation for students is very critical. Such prep work has to be offered regularly with the right challenge level and amount of work. The activities and the after-class activities should be in the same direction with the prep work in more depth. Frequent repetition of the course materials and the main course objectives is necessary to remind students of critical concepts and also of the relationship of the materials with each other. The integration of continuous reflections into the course will direct students into the generation of knowledge and conceptualizing the main contents. In addition, it provides necessary feedback to the instructor to track student progress and possible struggling points in their learning, either individually or in small or large groups.

References

Adams, R. S., Turns, J., & Atman, C. (2003). Educating effective engineering designers: The role of reflective practice. *Design Studies, 24*(3), 275–294. doi:10.1016/S0142-694X(02)00056-X

Armbruster, P., Patel, M., Johnson, E., & Weiss, M. (2009). Active learning and student-centered pedagogy improve student attitudes and performance in introductory biology. *CBE Life Sciences Education, 8*(3), 203–213. doi: 10.1187/cbe.09-03-0025

Bonwell, C. C., & Eison, J. A. (1991). *Active learning: Creating excitement in the classroom* (ASHE-ERIC Higher Education Report No. 1). Washington, DC: The George Washington University, School of Education and Human Development. Retrieved from https://files.eric.ed.gov/fulltext/ED336049.pdf

Boud, D., & Falchikov, N. (1989). Quantitative studies of student self-assessment in higher education: A critical analysis of findings. *Higher Education, 18*(5), 529–549. doi: https://doi.org/10.1007/BF00138746

Boud, D., Keogh, R., & Walker, D. (1985). *Reflection: Turning experience into learning.* New York, NY: Nichols Publishing Company.

Bruffee, K. A. (1995). Sharing our toys: Cooperative learning versus collaborative learning. *Change: The Magazine of Higher Learning, 27*(1), 12–18. doi: 10.1080/00091383.1995.9937722

Deslauriers, L., Schelew, E., & Wieman, C. (2011). Improved learning in a large enrollment physics class. *Science, 332*(6031), 862–864. doi: 10.1126/science.1201783

Dorodchi, M., Benedict, A., Desai, D., Mahzoon, M. J., MacNeil, S., & Dehbozorgi, N. (2018). Design and implementation of an activity-based introductory computer science course (CS1) with periodic reflections validated by learning analytics. *2018 IEEE Frontiers In Education Conference,* 1–8. doi: 10.1109/FIE.2018.8659196

Dorodchi, M., & Dehbozorgi, N. (2017). Addressing the paradox of fun and rigor in learning programming. *ITiCSE '17 Proceedings of the 2017 ACM Conference on Innovation and Technology in Computer Science Education,* 370. doi: 10.1145/3059009.3073004

Dorodchi, M., Dehbozorgi, N., & Frevert, T. (2017). "I wish I could rank my exam's challenge level!": An algorithm of Bloom's taxonomy in teaching CS1. *2017 IEEE Frontiers in Education Conference.* doi: 10.1109/FIE.2017.8190523

Duderstadt, J. J. (2008). *Engineering for a changing world: A roadmap to the future of engineering practice, research, and education.* Ann Arbor, MI: The Millennium Project, University of Michigan.

Fink, L. D. (2003). *A self-directed guide to designing courses for significant learning.* Retrieved from https://www.deefinkandassociates.com/GuidetoCourseDesignAug05.pdf

Freeman, S., Eddy, S. L., McDonough, M., Smith, M. K., Okoroafor, N., Jordt, H., & Wenderoth, M. P. (2014). Active learning increases student performance in science, engineering, and mathematics. *Proceedings of the National Academy of Sciences, 111*(23), 8410–8415. doi:10.1073/pnas.1319030111

Guzdial, M. (2015). Bringing evidence-based education to CS. *Communications of the ACM, 58*(6), 10–11. doi: 10.1145/2754947

Kinnunen P., & Malmi, L. (2006). Why do students drop out of CS1 courses? *ICER '06: Proceedings of the second international workshop on International Computing Education Research,* 97–108. doi: 10.1145/1151588.1151604

Kohavi, R. (1995). A study of cross-validation and bootstrap for accuracy estimation and model selection. *IJCAI '95 Proceedings of the 14th International Joint Conference on Artificial Intelligence,* 1137–1145. Retrieved from https://dl.acm.org/citation.cfm?id=1643047

Kolb, D. A. (1976). Management and the learning process. *California Management Review, 18*(3), 21–31. doi: https://doi.org/10.2307/41164649

Kolb, D. A. (2015). *Experiential learning: Experience as the source of learning and development.* Upper Saddle River, NJ: Pearson Education Inc.

Kolb, A., & Kolb, D. A. (2013). *The Kolb learning style inventory 2013 technical specifications, version 3.1, 3.2.* Retrieved from https://learningfromexperience.com/research-library/klsi-3_1-3_2-technical-specifications/

McCarthy, J., & Anderson, L. (2000). Active learning techniques versus traditional teaching styles: Two experiments from history and political science. *Innovative Higher Education, 24*(4), 279–294. doi: https://doi.org/10.1023/B:IHIE.0000047415.48495.05

Mezirow, J. (1990). *Fostering critical reflection in adulthood: A guide to transformative and emancipatory learning (pp. 1–20).* San Francisco, CA: Jossey-Bass.

Millis, B. J., & Cottell Jr., P. G. (1998). *Cooperative learning for higher education faculty.* Pheonix, AZ: Oryx Press.

Panitz, T. (1999). *Collaborative versus cooperative learning: A comparison of the two concepts which will help us understand the underlying nature of interactive learning.* Retrieved from https://files.eric.ed.gov/fulltext/ED448443.pdf

Pellegrino, J. W., Chudowsky, N., & Glaser, R. (Eds). (2001). *Knowing what students know: The science and design of educational assessment.* Washington, DC: National Academy Press.

Pierce, R., & Fox, J. (2012). Vodcasts and active-learning exercises in a "flipped classroom" model of a renal pharmacology module. *American Journal of Pharmaceutical Education, 76*(10), 196. doi: 10.5688/ajpe7610196

Prince, M. (2004). Does active learning work? A review of the research. *Journal of Engineering Education, 93*(3), 223–231. doi: https://doi.org/10.1002/j.2168-9830.2004.tb00809.x

Sanders, K., Boustedt, J., Eckerdal, A., McCartney, R., & Zander, C. (2017). Folk pedagogy: Nobody doesn't like active learning. *ICER '17 Proceedings of the 2017 ACM Conference on International Computing Education Research,* 145–154. https://doi.org/10.1145/3105726.3106192

Shekar, A. (2007). Active learning and reflection in product development engineering education. *European Journal of Engineering Education, 32*(2), 125–133. doi: 10.1080/03043790601118705

Silver, D. (2012). Using the "zone" help reach every learner. *Kappa Delta Pi Record, 47,* 28–31. doi: 10.1080/00228958.2011.10516721

Slavin, R. E. (1983). *Cooperative learning: Research on teaching monograph series.* New York, NY: Longman Inc.

Smith, B. L., & MacGregor, J. T. (1992). What is collaborative learning? In B. L. Smith & J. T. MacGregor (Eds.), *Collaborative learning: A sourcebook for higher education* (pp. 9–22). University Park, PA: National Center on Postsecondary Teaching, Learning, and Assessment.

Stahl, R. J. (1994). The essential elements of cooperative learning in the classroom. *ERIC Digest.* Retrieved from ERIC database (ED370881).

Turns, J., Sattler, B., Yasuhara, K., Borgford-Parnell, J., & Atman, C. J. (2014). Integrating reflection into engineering education. *Proceedings of 2014 American Society of Engineering Education Annual Conference.* Retrieved from https://www.asee.org/public/conferences/32/papers/9230/view

U.S. Department of Education. (2002). *What is EBE? Evidence-based education.* Retrieved from https://www2.ed.gov/nclb/methods/whatworks/eb/edlite-slide003.html.

Watson, C., & Li, F. W. B. (2014). Failure rates in introductory programming revisited. *ITiCSE '14 Proceedings of the 2014 Conference on Innovation & Technology in Computer Science Education*, 39–44. doi: http://dx.doi.org/10.1145/2591708.2591749

Xinogalos, S. (2016). Designing and deploying programming courses: Strategies, tools, difficulties and pedagogy. *Educational Information Technology, 21*, 559. doi: https://doi.org/10.1007/s10639 -014-9341-9

CHAPTER 3

A Fully Flipped Active Learning Course

CELINE LATULIPE

In this chapter, I present a case study description of a large, fully flipped active learning (FFAL) class in computer science. The class, a sophomore-level core course that combines both theory and programming, is required for all students in our major. The FFAL section of this course has been taught for five semesters. Research on how this class has been designed for more inclusive success was presented at the Institute of Electrical and Electronics Engineers (IEEE) Frontiers in Engineering Education conference and is published and available for reference (Latulipe, MacNeil, & Thompson, 2018). There are many details on how to make such a large and critical class work, and this chapter will cover the details. I hope that by writing this chapter and describing how the whole class runs, others may be inspired to try something similar in their own large core courses.

Data Structures: A Core Course in Computer Science

The Data Structures class is a core course in computer science programs at most institutions, known as CS2. Data structures (lists, queues, arrays, graphs, and trees) are crucial building blocks in computer programming. Most applications and digital systems make use of at least one data structure to store information. At a minimum, computer science students need to learn how the most common data structures work, their relative efficiencies, and which data structures are appropriate for different types of problems or applications. This is the theory of data structures. In the application/implementation part of the Data Structures class, students learn to implement data structures from scratch, rather than just learning to use the data structures that are already built into high-level programming languages such as Java, Python, or C++. Students commonly complete at least some programming assignments as part of a CS2 curriculum.

CS2 courses vary widely in their focus on theory versus programming. Some professors focus on deep mathematical theory and ignore the applied programming aspects of the course. Instructors who put significant focus on the applied programming aspect of data structures vary in how much of the programming they require of students to be from scratch versus making use of built-in data structures. These variations occur across computer science programs at different institutions and sometimes across sections of the same class within a program.

Many CS2 curricula assume students already know how to program, and so the programming assignments are designed for students to complete outside of class without any help. Thus, many CS2 classes do not have a separate programming lab, and this is the case at UNC Charlotte.

Data Structures classes at UNC Charlotte have historically been taught in a traditional lecture format, with instructors sometimes adding code demonstrations to help show the programming application. Students are given homework assignments that may or may not involve programming, and they are assessed based on those assignments. This course is seen as a gateway course and typically has high rates of students who are not successful and either receive Ds, Fs, or withdraw (DFWs). dAt UNC Charlotte, this course is where we often lose students from groups underrepresented in computer science (students who are female and/ or minorities).

Goals for Reworking the Class

In the summer of 2016, I worked to create a new FFAL section of the Data Structures course. My aim was to make the course a mix of theory and application but focused more heavily on the application. I treat the course as essentially the third programming course for our majors. My reason for doing this is based on data that show that the majority of students coming into our computer science program did not learn any computer programming prior to entering UNC Charlotte. This is not surprising, given that only 18% of high schools in North Carolina offer an Advanced Placement Computer Science class. Students who have taken two semesters of introductory programming usually are still not proficient or comfortable with programming. Like learning a foreign language, learning to program takes time and practice. Many of our students are economically marginalized and working multiple part-time jobs, so they struggle to find the time to practice programming outside of class, which often makes the learning process slow. That does not mean that these students are not capable, but it does mean that instructors need to have realistic expectations about what students are capable of doing in the first semester of their second year in a computer science degree.

It is also worth noting that the vast majority of our computer science undergraduate students get jobs in the industry right after graduation doing some type of software development or information technology (IT). Few go on to graduate school because there is high demand for skilled IT workers, and the salaries are very competitive. This points to the necessity to focus on the application of data structures more heavily than on the theory.

Given this context, I had a few specific objectives in mind when designing the fully flipped version of the Data Structures course. These are broken down into three professional development goals:

1. To help students continue on their journey of learning how to program.
2. To help students become resilient programmers, willing to work through bugs and use standard software testing methods to help discover issues with their own code.

3. To help students become collaborative team players and learn how to communicate effectively about computing and programming concepts because the software industry is very team-based.

I also had four subject-specific goals:

1. To help students learn which data structures to use for different types of problems.
2. To help students learn how to use the built-in data structures in Java.
3. To teach students how to build their own data structures from scratch.
4. To teach students to interpret data structure implementations built into a programming language by understanding abstract data types (ADTs).

FFAL Essential Class Components

I chose an FFAL structure to follow the restructuring I had already applied to the first two programming classes in our college. A flipped (or inverted) class is one in which the students consume the course content to gain facts, knowledge, and understanding on their own before coming to the class. These are the lowest order elements of learning in Bloom's taxonomy (Adams, 2015). When they attend class, they can actively engage with the material in higher-order cognitive learning activities that involve Bloom's theory of application, synthesis, evaluation, and creation. There are a variety of challenges to the flipped class approach (Maher, Latulipe, Lipford, & Rorrer, 2015), but most research shows significant benefits for student learning outcomes (Thai, De Wever, & Valcke, 2017).

The four main components to the overall structure of my FFAL class are:

1. **Structured Prep Work:** Students absorb content through watching videos and reading the textbook before coming to class, with a prep work quiz due before class starts.
2. **Lightweight Teams:** During class sessions, students sit at an assigned table with a team, and this seating plan and team stays the same all semester long.
3. **Active Learning:** During class sessions, students engage in peer instruction quizzes with their teams and pair programming activities.
4. **Varied Assessment:** Students are assessed across a wide variety of activities, including prep work, peer instruction quizzes, in-class programming labs, individual programming assignments, and individual tests.

These four components integrate together to form a very structured learning experience (Eddy & Hogan, 2014) that helps students stay on track as they learn to become programmers and learn the theories and application of the data structures content. I illustrate this case study with data collected from detailed, anonymous, end-of-class surveys that I give students time to complete on the last day of class every semester. Table 3.1 below shows various aspects of the course and how they have evolved over the first five semesters, including the enrollment, classroom setting, resources used, and the decreasing DFW rates, shown in the last row.

Table 3.1 Evolution Over Five Semesters of the FFAL Data Structures and Algorithms Class

	Fall 2016	Spring 2017	Fall 2017	Spring 2018	Fall 2018
Enrollment at census/ end	88/77	51/49	124/115	74/68	126/123
Classroom	KENN 236 Large active learning class. 14 large round tables seating nine students each	BINF 210 Medium active learning class. 14 small round tables seating four to five students each	KENN 236 Large active learning class. 14 large round tables seating nine students each	WOOD 135 Medium active learning class. 75 individual rolling chairs with under-chair storage	KENN 236 Large active learning class. 14 large round tables seating nine students each
Teaching team	Two professors (1F, 1M), two graduate students (1F, 1M)	One professor (F), one graduate student (M), one undergraduate student (M)	One professor (F), two graduate students (2F), three undergraduate students (1F, 2M)	One professor (F), one graduate student (F), three undergraduate students (1F, 2M)	One professor (F), one graduate student (M), six undergraduate students (2F, 4M)
Peer instruction quizzes	Turning Technologies clickers	Turning Technologies clickers	Poll Everywhere with word cloud warm-up questions	Poll Everywhere with word cloud warm-up questions	Poll Everywhere with word cloud warm-up questions
Discussion forum	Canvas Discussion Forum	Canvas Discussion Forum	Piazza, allowing anonymous posting	Piazza, allowing anonymous posting	Piazza, allowing anonymous posting
Textbook	Lewis & Chase, *Java Software Structures*	Lewis & Chase, *Java Software Structures*	zyBooks interactive textbook	zyBooks interactive textbook	zyBooks interactive textbook
Final course feedback response rate	43%	76%	90%	91%	92%
DFW rates	27%	24%	13%	13%	9%

Note. DFW = "D," "F" (fail), and withdraw; F = female; FFAL = fully flipped active learning; M = male. My final course feedback survey (given through Canvas) has higher response rates in later semesters because I give students time in class to complete it.

Structured Prep Work

In an FFAL class, the students are to consume the main content before class, typically through some combination of reading and watching videos. A major challenge with flipped classes is ensuring that students actually complete the prep work, which I called the forcing function. Both components (prep work content and prep work forcing function) are important.

Prep Work Content

I have assigned two different textbooks as reading for the Data Structures course. In the first few semesters, I assigned Lewis and Chase's *Java Software Structures*, a book that explained things well and focused on both the implementation and use of data structures and provided a lot of sample code. While I really like this book, I found that students were not always reading it.

For the last three semesters of the class, I have used an interactive, online textbook as part of the prep work in the class. This book intersperses the reading content with multiple-choice questions, animations, fill-in-the-blank questions, and other short activities designed to help students test their learning (Figure 3.1).

The zyBooks interactive textbook integrates with the Canvas platform. This enables me to assign sections or chapters of the textbook and grade for participation and challenge activities that the students do as they complete the reading. Because there is a grade associated with the reading, the grade transfer happens before they come to class each week, and this acts as a forcing function. The built-in activities make the reading active and engaging, as shown in Figure 3.2 and Figure 3.3. Results in these figures represent feedback from the fall 2017 semester and come from an end-of-semester anonymous feedback survey. Students were given time in class to respond, and the response rate was 93%.

Videos are another critical component of prep work. The current generation of students generally respond really well to learning by watching videos, and there are so many advantages to the format. Students can watch the videos as many times as they need to. They can pause, scroll back to things they have missed, and take a break and finish a video later. They also have the ability to slow down the video if they have trouble understanding the speaker or watch it at double-speed if they find the video goes too slow or if they just want a brief refresher on the topic. This level of flexibility just is not possible in a classroom lecture. But there are a number of challenges to address with respect to videos, specifically the challenge of creating them yourself or curating from the videos available online. I have done some of both, and I have some best practices to share.

If there are good videos available on a topic, then why reinvent the wheel? For a core topic like data structures, many videos are available on YouTube, and finding a few to use in my class is a massive curation task. One of the best ways to manage this is to involve some undergraduate students in independent studies. I set up a weekly meeting time and define a set of tasks related to the curriculum development for the class. One of the main tasks is video curation. I set up a Google sheet with all the topics and subtopics, and ask the students to add video links, along with comments and descriptions about the videos they find. During the weekly

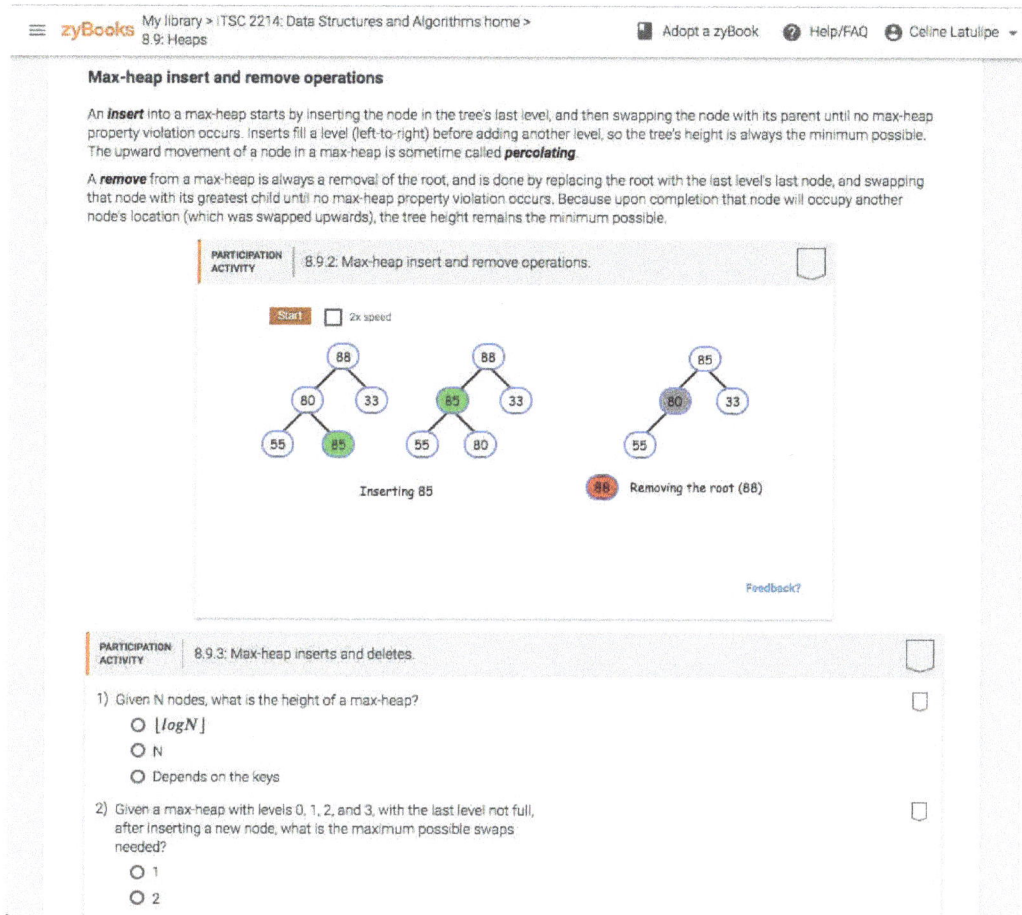

Figure 3.1. Active reading through zyBooks interactive textbook. Grades for participation and challenge activities are automatically submitted to the Canvas gradebook prior to class, so students have the incentive to complete the reading on time.

meetings, we go through the best videos and decide which ones are most suitable for the class. I also involve these students in creating weekly prep work quiz questions and testing out lab exercises or class assignments. The benefit to the students is that they get to revisit material and deepen their learning in the topic while earning credit. They also get exposure to the other side of the classroom—the prep work and planning that goes into course development.

Sometimes there may not be a suitable video on a topic, and that is when I create my own. I have found that students respond well to videos that I have made, and it sends the message that they are learning from me. (Some students may feel that if they only watch videos on YouTube made by other people, they are not getting their money's worth.) I am not capturing videos of me, but rather videos of my screen as I do voice-over and explain things. Some of my videos are of me explaining concepts using animated PowerPoint slides. I try to keep these videos under

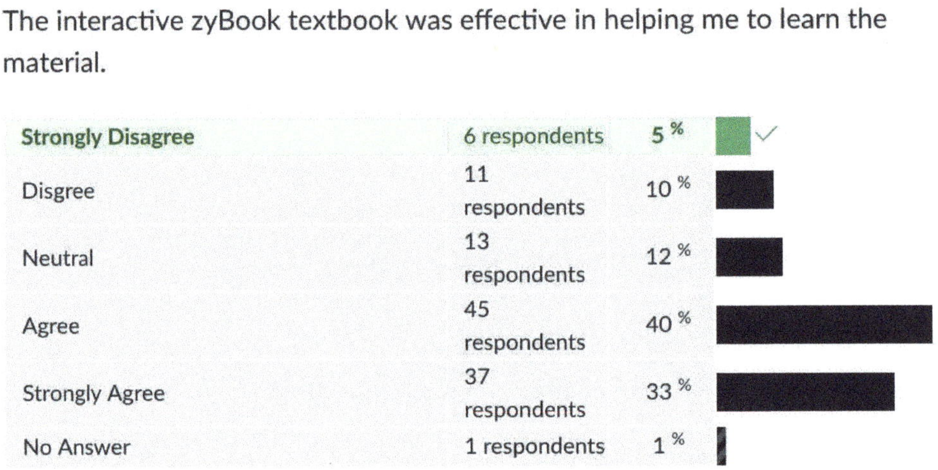

The interactive zyBook textbook was effective in helping me to learn the material.

Strongly Disagree	6 respondents	5 %	
Disgree	11 respondents	10 %	
Neutral	13 respondents	12 %	
Agree	45 respondents	40 %	
Strongly Agree	37 respondents	33 %	
No Answer	1 respondents	1 %	

Figure 3.2. Students' perceptions about the effectiveness of the zyBooks.

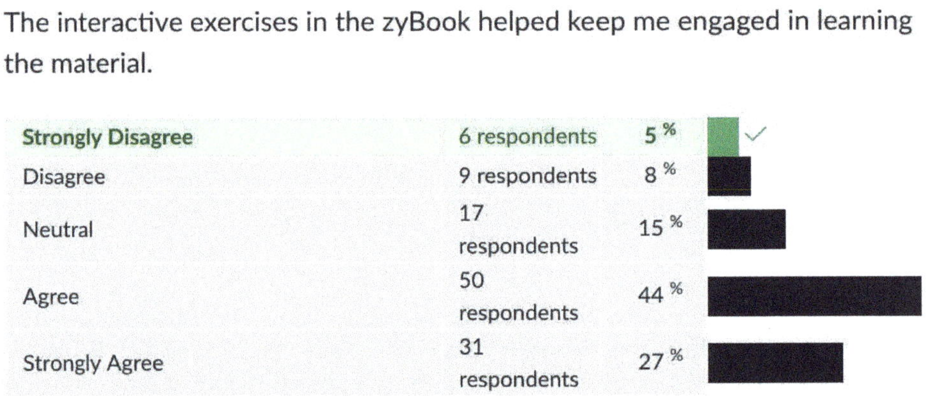

The interactive exercises in the zyBook helped keep me engaged in learning the material.

Strongly Disagree	6 respondents	5 %	
Disagree	9 respondents	8 %	
Neutral	17 respondents	15 %	
Agree	50 respondents	44 %	
Strongly Agree	31 respondents	27 %	

Figure 3.3. Students' perceptions about how well zyBooks keeps them engaged in the reading prep work.

10 minutes, as research shows students do not finish long videos. Some of my videos show me programming something by typing in an editor and running the code. These videos are slightly longer (15 to 20 minutes), but they are intended as reference rather than something to watch for conceptual understanding. I also have used a program on my iPad called ShowMe that is a recorded whiteboard session. With ShowMe, I might create some diagrams ahead of time and load them on different pages, and then walk through annotating and illustrating, while the software records my drawings and my voice (see Figure 3.4).

Two major notes: First, I have never had someone come in and record me giving a full-length class lecture and then just put that online. Research shows that is not effective. A 75-minute lecture tends to put students to sleep, even when they are physically in the same room as the lecturer. We fill those 75 minutes with many examples, and we ramble on trying to relate the

Figure 3.4. Screenshot of a ShowMe video created for the class using the iPad software.

concept to other concepts. Lectures are not typically efficient in terms of content. So breaking up what was communicated into smaller chunks makes way more sense when people are going to be watching the content on video. Second, I do not fret about production quality. It is just me talking to the students, and I think it is more personal that way.

Prep Work Forcing Function

Because the in-class active learning activities will assume the students have been exposed to (and hopefully have absorbed) the material, it is critical to ensure the prep work is being completed. The class activities are meant to actively engage the students with the material, tease out any misunderstandings, and help apply the content. None of that can happen if students have not done the prep work. The most effective way that I have found to get students to do the prep work is to have a quiz completed before class. The quiz has to be challenging enough that they cannot just guess the answers. It also needs to be worth points toward their final grade. I typically make prep work quizzes worth about 10% of the grade. Each quiz is worth less than 1%, so it is not enough to incentivize cheating, but it is enough to incentivize them to do the work. It is not 100% perfect. The impact of social structure of the class also tends to act as an implicit forcing function. That is one of the benefits of the lightweight teams structure, which is the second major component of the class and the topic of the next section.

Lightweight Teams

FFAL classes provide an excellent opportunity to leverage social learning. While you could have a fully flipped classroom where students do the prep work and then come to class to silently work alone on active learning activities, this would offer little benefit over the non-flipped classroom. The only benefit in this case would be that the teaching assistants (TAs) and professors are available to help students if they struggle. The real benefit of the fully flipped classroom stems from the social learning that happens when the classroom is structured so that student–student interaction is the expected norm. While this could happen to some extent naturally, the lightweight teams approach (Latulipe, Long, & Seminario, 2015; Latulipe, Mac-Neil, et al., 2018; Latulipe, Rorrer, & Long, 2018) is designed to promote and facilitate social learning, and it is particularly useful in medium and large classes.

Lightweight teams are teams of four to nine students who sit together all semester long and work on activities that are worth very little toward their final grades. This lack of emphasis on graded work is what makes these teams lightweight and very different from traditional student project teams. I devise a seating plan for the classroom, specify where each team sits, and display this on the first day of classes. I do not care which seat a student sits in, as long as the student sits with their team. The main idea with lightweight teams is that the students get comfortable with each other and are given activities that will benefit them from discussing the work with each other.

Team Logistics

The size of the teams is somewhat dependent on the classroom layout, but I believe that five in a group is the best team size. In the Kennedy active learning classrooms, the round tables seat nine students, so when I first taught there, I created teams of nine. However, a team of nine students leaves a lot of room for students to fade into the background and not participate. In that classroom, I now create teams of four or five students, with two teams at each table. In classrooms that have really small tables, I create teams of four. In more traditional classrooms with rows of tables and chairs, I go with teams of five and use a layout that alternates two in front, three behind with three in front, two behind, as shown in Figure 3.5 for one of the CHHS classrooms:

There are various ways to form lightweight teams, but the general approach is to let the learning management system (LMS) randomly create them, only making adjustments to fit the situation. In computer science, there is a lack of female students. I do not allow a lone female to be on a team with four males, so I will pair the female students up. This means there are a bunch of teams with no female students at all, but it also means the female students are less likely to feel isolated. I also try to do the same with underrepresented minority students. Determining student gender identity and racial identity is tricky and typically requires down-loading institutional reports as this information is not available in Canvas or Banner. In more recent semesters, I have asked students to provide their preferred pronouns on an introductory background survey and use that to help with the team formation.

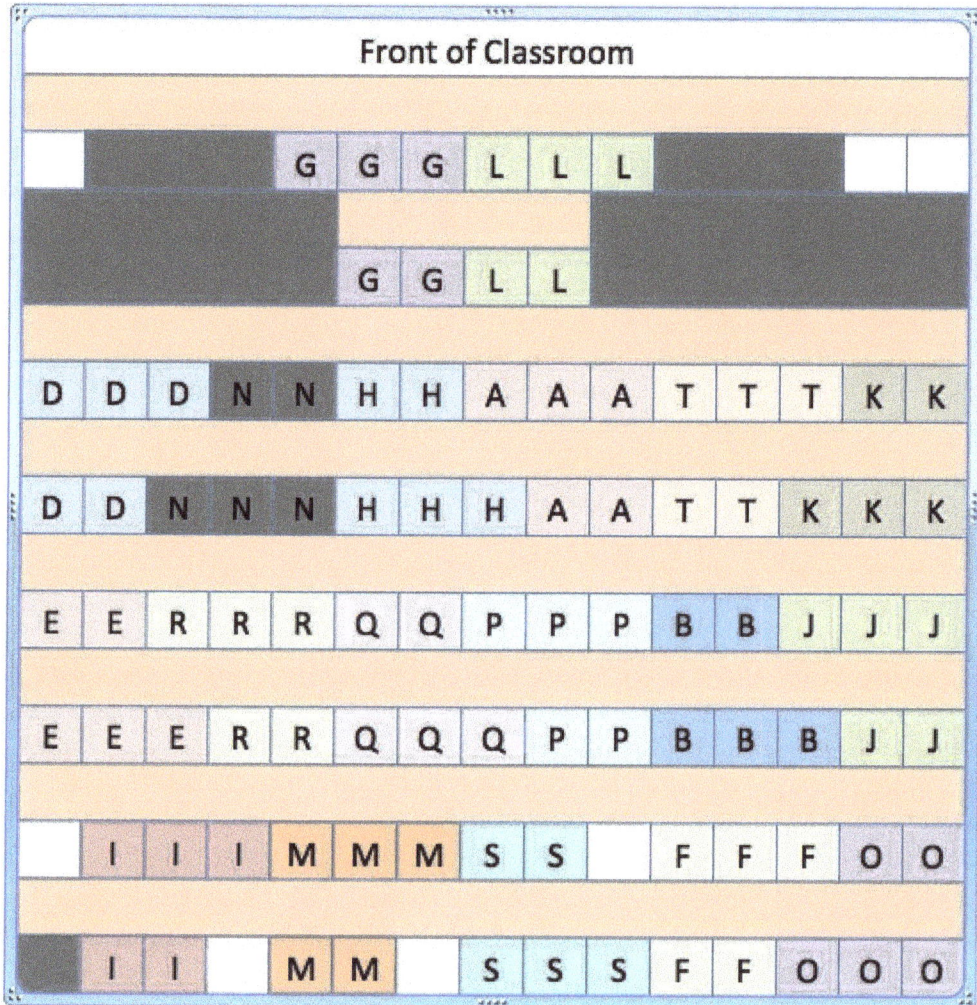

Figure 3.5. A classroom with rows of tables and chairs, set up to accommodate 18 teams with five students each (total of 90 students). Teams are denoted by letters, with Teams G and L at the front of the classroom.

Another consideration might be skill or background level. In classes with heavyweight projects, this type of balance is critical. In first- and second-year classes with lightweight teams, skill balance is somewhat less critical. However, I have experienced semesters where there are some teams full of great students and other teams full of students with much less background preparation, and mixing these students up ensures that there are well-prepared students on every team. In recent semesters, I have given students a programming assessment test on the first day of class so that I can plan for there to be a mix of levels of programming experience on each team.

It sometimes feels like a lot of effort to try to balance teams across gender, race, and background preparation. And even after all this balancing, there are occasionally teams that just do not work well together. It is amazing how much one or two extraverts at a table can make a difference, and I have not yet found a way to ensure that I do not end up with an entire team of extreme introverts. There are a lot of introverts in the computing major, so this does happen. Introverts often end up becoming great team members once they get comfortable. But I have seen a team full of introverts stay fairly quiet all semester long because there is not someone on the team to get them started talking.

Benefits of Lightweight Teams

Lightweight teams enable us to really leverage the power of social learning. When a student hears other students' perspectives on a concept, it gives that student new ways to think about and relate to that concept. By working and talking with others, students get to practice all of the crucial skills needed in the professional world: socializing, talking, working together, and communicating within the discipline. It also works to reinforce their own knowledge by explaining what they know to other students. By having students communicate with each other, we are allowing them to become more engaged in the topic than they would be if they sat silently listening to a faculty member lecture.

In sociology, the contact hypothesis (McKeown & Dixon, 2017) explains that working together with others who are different from us actually helps mitigate prejudice. This is important in computer science where there are domain-specific prejudices, namely that boys are better at programming and technical work, that layer on top of the standard prejudices prevalent in U.S. society. In addition to helping students realize that they have more in common with "others" than they think, I have come to believe that the lightweight teams approach is also beneficial for moderating student confidence. Students who come in thinking that they know nothing find out that there are others who also do not have a lot of previous experience, and over time, they realize that they can, in fact, contribute to the conversation. On the other hand, students who come in thinking they know everything will soon realize through the team-based peer instruction quizzes, that they do not know everything. Those who have significant prior experience (such as taking programming classes in high school) may come to realize that not everyone was as privileged and that in fact many high schools do not offer any programming courses at all. None of these insights can be gained by students who sit silently in a lecture hall.

Lightweight Team Results

Every semester I survey students anonymously to get feedback about their experience in this class, and I find that most students in Data Structures are generally happy to be on a team. When I first started teaching this way, I thought that students put on a team without choosing their own teammates would hate being told where to sit. But results show that the students do see the benefits of this approach, as demonstrated by Figure 3.6, Figure 3.7, and Figure 3.8. I am forcing them to meet new people and make new friends while also allowing them to learn together and from each other. Creating a social environment in the class makes the learning more enjoyable.

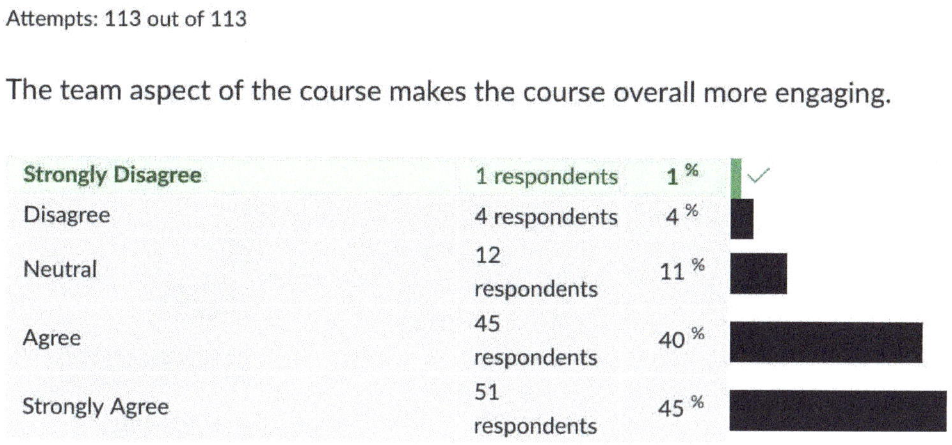

Attempts: 113 out of 113

The team aspect of the course makes the course overall more engaging.

Strongly Disagree	1 respondents	1 %
Disagree	4 respondents	4 %
Neutral	12 respondents	11 %
Agree	45 respondents	40 %
Strongly Agree	51 respondents	45 %

Figure 3.6. Students' perceptions about how being on a team impacts engagement with the course.

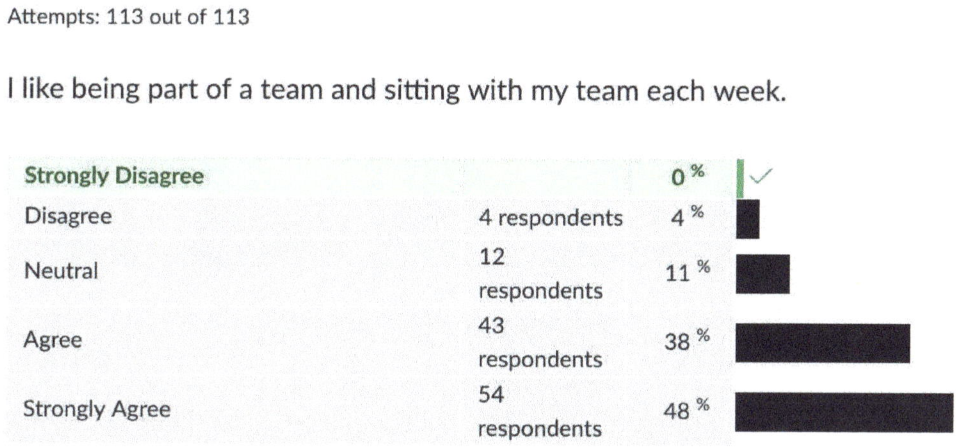

Attempts: 113 out of 113

I like being part of a team and sitting with my team each week.

Strongly Disagree		0 %
Disagree	4 respondents	4 %
Neutral	12 respondents	11 %
Agree	43 respondents	38 %
Strongly Agree	54 respondents	48 %

Figure 3.7. Students' perceptions about being on a team and the fixed seating plan.

I also asked students how many new friends they made as a result of taking this class. The results can be seen in Figure 3.9. Now, this may seem like a bizarre thing to measure because, after all, are they not here to learn? But this is when we must think about the bigger picture: retention within the program and within the university and helping our students become better global citizens. Helping students to develop interpersonal relationships is an important aspect of the college experience. Many of our students have part-time jobs, which means that they do not have a lot of time to spend on campus engaged in extracurricular activities. For these students, the socioacademic integrative moments (Deli-Amen, 2011) that we can provide in the classroom are critical in helping them feel like they are part of the campus community.

Attempts: 113 out of 113

Being on a team has helped me develop skills that are useful when I do teamwork in my other classes.

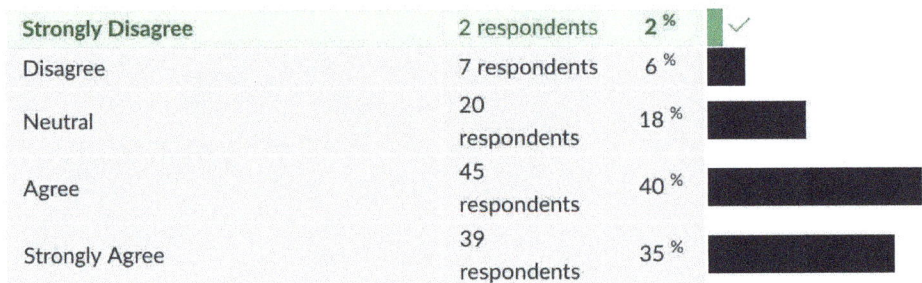

Figure 3.8. Students' perceptions about how being on a team impacts their teamwork skills.

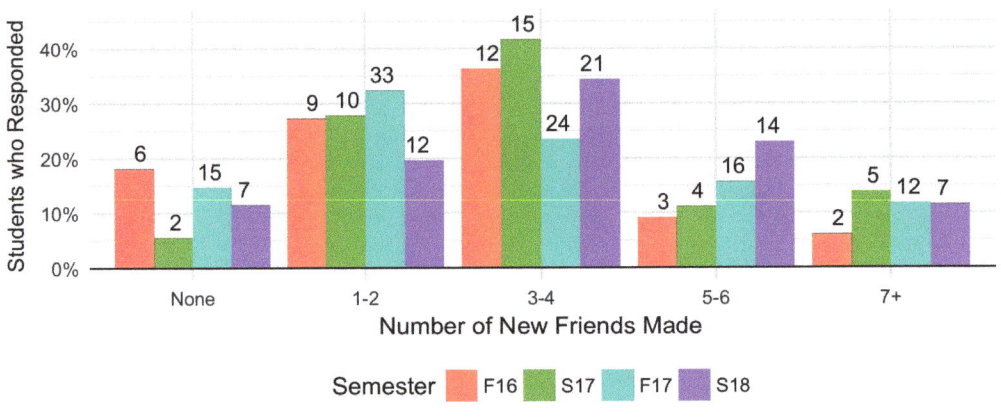

Figure 3.9. Histogram showing how many new friends students made each semester as a result of taking this class. For example, in the spring 2018 semester (purple), 14 students reported making five or six new friends.

Active Learning

In the classroom, my aim is to engage students in active learning activities that get them to move up Bloom's taxonomy from simple information recall to understanding, synthesis, application, and evaluation activities. With three hours per week of instruction, I divide the time between peer instruction quizzes and programming activities. Peer instruction quizzes focus on understanding, synthesis, and evaluation activities while programming activities require those types of cognition as well as application.

Peer instruction quizzes with Poll Everywhere are the anchor activity in my FFAL classes.

1. What does **extends** do in the first parameter type in this method?

```
public int myMethod(<T extends Number<T>> t1, int i) {…}
```

A. It allows any object passed in to be treated as a Number
B. It ensures only objects from classes that implement/extend Number can be used for this parameter
C. It ensures that all the following parameters in the method header are class types that extend Number
D. It allows returns of generic type

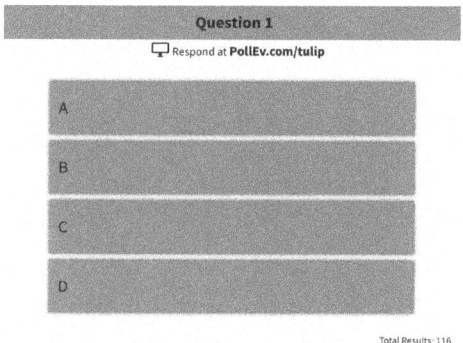

Figure 3.10. A sample PowerPoint slide showing a question and the Poll Everywhere poll. Student responses are hidden, although the number at the bottom right indicates 116 students have answered.

I have created PowerPoint slide decks with my questions that allow me to type in formatted code, show screenshots of programming environments, etc. Each slide has the question and the Poll Everywhere poll inserted (see Figure 3.10), and the students use their smartphones or laptops to log in to respond.

I encourage students to talk to each other before answering to stimulate communication between students. I do not consider this an assessment activity, so I am not worried that students might get the answer from others. Instead, I treat this as a learning activity and continually remind them that they need to not just say to their teammates, "the answer is B," but also to explain to each other *why* they think that B is the correct answer. I repoll questions if the histogram of responses shows that students are not in agreement about the correct answer (as in Figure 3.11).

When these disagreements arise, I encourage students to talk to students on other teams before taking a second shot at answering. My instruction in this situation is "Get up and walk around—find someone who has a different answer than you and convince them that you are right."

When there is this level of confusion about a topic, as evidenced by the answer distribution, I take this as a sign of a general misconception and will use this time to launch into an impromptu minilecture to clear up the misconception. This typically involves me using Sharpie pens and a sketchbook under the doc cam so that my explanation can be broadcast to screens around the room. The beauty of such impromptu, on-demand explanations is that the students are fully tuned in. They have just lost points in the Poll Everywhere quiz and know there is something that they do not understand, so they are fully primed to listen to the explanation.

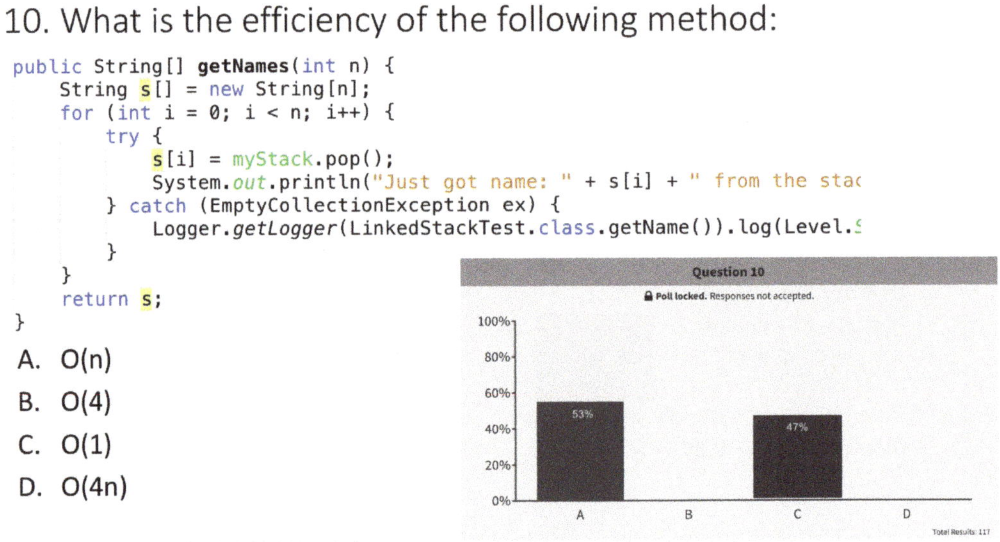

10. What is the efficiency of the following method:

```
public String[] getNames(int n) {
    String s[] = new String[n];
    for (int i = 0; i < n; i++) {
        try {
            s[i] = myStack.pop();
            System.out.println("Just got name: " + s[i] + " from the stac
        } catch (EmptyCollectionException ex) {
            Logger.getLogger(LinkedStackTest.class.getName()).log(Level.S
        }
    }
    return s;
}
```

A. O(n)

B. O(4)

C. O(1)

D. O(4n)

Figure 3.11. In this slide, student responses are shown and indicate that there is a split, with half the students thinking A is correct and half the students thinking C is correct. This shows a misconception and would lead to a five-minute minilecture explanation.

These short explanations usually last no more than four minutes, so the students do not have a chance to get bored and tune out.

Varied Assessment

One of the most important aspects of the FFAL class is that the grading is as structured as the rest of the course. In a traditional Data Structures class, students might be assigned a few programming assignments and have a midterm and final exam. This format gives students no feedback on their understanding of the material or their mastery of requisite skills until the midterm or first assignment is graded. It gives students the impression that nothing major is required of them until the midterm or the first assignment deadline. In FFAL classes, especially at the freshman and sophomore levels, providing a lot of structure to help students do all the things required for successful learning is key. Research has shown that providing such structure is especially beneficial to students without a lot of social capital—students coming from lower socioeconomic status (SES) backgrounds, who are first-generation college students, etc. These students often do not get a lot of help or guidance from their families and home communities about what it means to succeed in such an environment. Providing significant structure helps scaffold these students toward success while also helping them understand what activities they need to be successful at university classes. By encouraging early successes, we can build up their social capital and self-efficacy so that they have a better chance of succeeding in later

Table 3.2 Weighted Grading Scheme

Activity	Grade weight
Prep work quizzes	10%
zyBooks interactive textbook reading	10%
Poll Everywhere peer instruction quizzes	5%
In-class programming labs	10%
Tests	20%
Individual programming assignments	40%
Reflections and sketchbooks	5%
Each unexcused absence	(–2%)
Total	100%

Note. In this class, almost everything counts toward a student's final grade.

classes even when the structure is reduced. One form of structure is the forced prep work discussed in the last section. Another form of structure is in varied grading, which is discussed next.

In my Data Structures class, everything a student does counts toward their final grade in some way. Table 3.2 shows the weighted grading scheme for the class.

Some of the components that are graded are items that students do in groups or pairs such as the Poll Everywhere quizzes and in-class programming labs, but these are only worth 15% of the final grade. Yes, it is possible some students could completely rely on other students to do well in these portions, but it would not be enough to pass a student who is otherwise completely failing to do any work because 60% of the final grade is based on tests and assignments that each student must complete individually.

The effect of this varied grading scheme is that it forces students to put in the work that is necessary for success. They get points for reading the interactive textbook and completing the questions that are embedded in the book; these questions are designed to help students check their understanding while forcing them to be actively engaged in the reading. Getting points for completing their prep work and the associated quiz before coming to class means they are more likely ready to be engaged for the in-class active learning. Because they have put in this study time and are prepared for the in-class work, they get more out of the in-class active learning activities, which helps prepare them for their tests and individual assignments.

I apply the low-stakes testing philosophy to this class. Rather than two high-stakes exams, I have students take four noncumulative tests throughout the semester. This reduces the amount of test anxiety and allows students to focus more on learning a smaller amount of material rather than trying to simply cram in a large amount of material. High-stakes exams typically lead to surface learning.

There is a negative grade weight associated with unexcused absences in the class. While I feel that it does not make sense to give a student points "just for showing up," missing class means they are losing valuable learning opportunities. Thus, I impose a −2% penalty for unexcused absences. This ensures that students are punctual. If a student has a medical excuse, reasonable documentation, or an excuse approved by the dean of students, I do not deduct these points.

Finally, there is also a hidden performance incentive related to attendance and tests. If a student has no unexcused absences at the end of the semester, they are given the opportunity to retake one of the first three tests after taking Test 4 during the final exam period session. This is a win–win situation; students go back and revisit the material that they struggled with the most, thereby enhancing their learning. The chance to raise their grade provides students with even more incentive to make sure they attend every class.

Supporting Technologies

In addition to the four structural elements I have covered, it is also important to note that I made heavy use of various technologies to run this FFAL class. While some of those technologies have been explained in the sections above (Poll Everywhere, zyBooks), there are other technologies that played an important supporting role and are worthy of mention. Below I briefly describe how and why I consider each to be critical.

Canvas

The Canvas LMS is my organizational go to. I structure the Canvas page using weekly modules that show students the flow of work in the class. Figure 3.12 shows what a typical week looks like.

I often make use of the dependencies built in to Canvas, which allow you to specify that certain elements are not accessible to students until they complete other items. This ensures students cannot have access to in-class lab materials until they have completed prep work, forcing them to stay on top of the work.

Piazza

In an FFAL class, where there are many moving parts, students may have lots of questions about expectations and the varying tools being used. In order to prevent my email inbox from being overwhelmed, I have a strict communications policy. Questions about the class, content, assignments, etc. must be posted on the class discussion forum on Piazza. I have chosen to use Piazza for a number of reasons. First, Piazza is a much faster system than the built-in discussion forum in Canvas, which has a poor user interface and is typically slow to load. Second, Piazza allows students to post questions anonymously (though the posts are only anonymous to other students, not to the TAs or professors). This is very important because many students are afraid that if they ask a question they will "look dumb" in front of their peers. Allowing anonymous posts gives them the opportunity to post without unnecessary anxiety. Third, Pi-

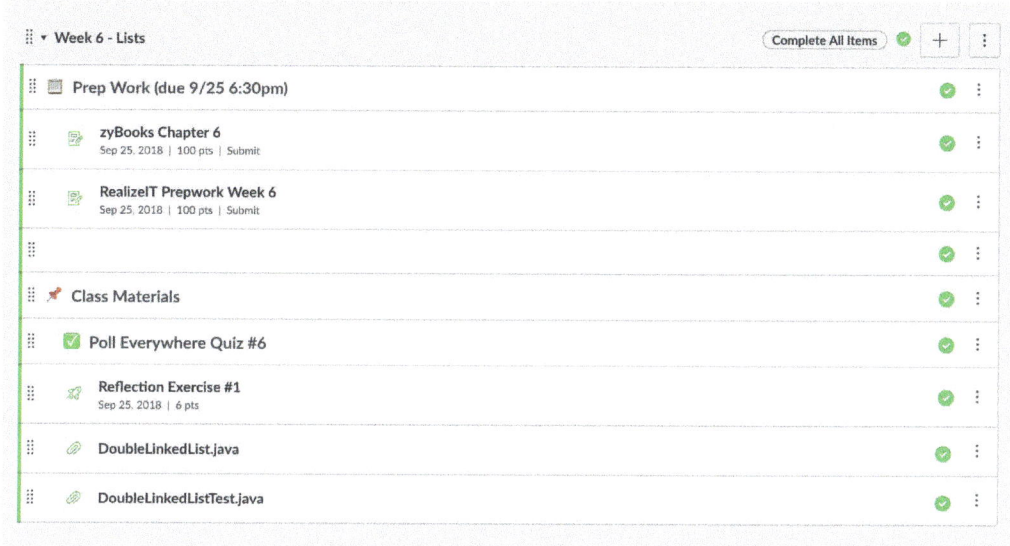

Figure 3.12. A typical weekly module in Canvas, with separated sections for prep work and class materials.

azza allows up-voting of questions so the teaching team can see which questions or comments the students agree are important. Finally, the homepage of the Piazza forum tells me at a glance what is happening in the course discussion (see Figure 3.13).

To come back to the communications policy, this ensures that all students have access to information provided in response to questions about course content, policies, assignment clarifications, etc. This information transparency helps to ensure equity, so that the information is available even to those students who do not have the social capital to know that they could be asking those questions at all. The only exceptions to this communication policy are for when students need to email me about their personal grades, an illness, or other personal issues.

RealizeIT

In the fall 2018 semester, I embarked on a new adventure with the class by moving most of the prep work content into an adaptive learning platform called RealizeIT. In the RealizeIT platform, students enter each week's module and immediately take a "determine knowledge" quiz. This then populates a learning map with varying levels of mastery, depending on how much a student already knows about the concepts covered in the module. The learning map not only provides a visual indication of how the concepts they are learning link together, but also shows students how much they have grasped each concept and what the mastery level of everyone else in the class is. Based on the determine knowledge quiz results and the student's prior learning, the system personalizes the learning by pointing students to appropriate starting points. From there, they work through each node consuming material through video or text content. The learning map could be considered a gamification of the learning experience as it encourages students to work hard to get all green stars across the learning map.

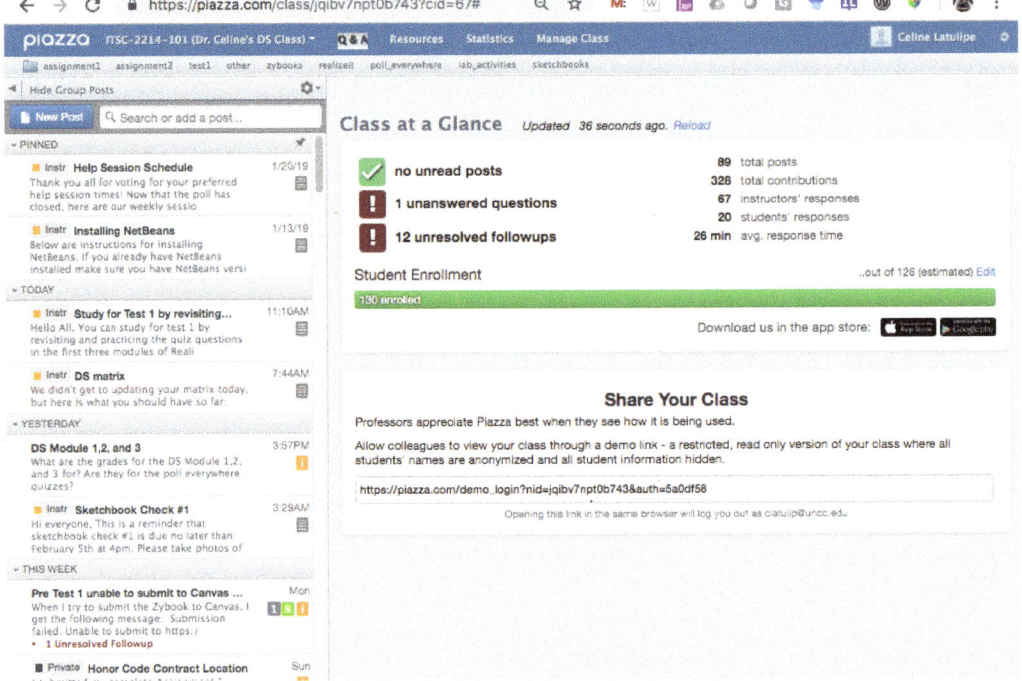

Figure 3.13. The Piazza course discussion interface. The homepage shows me at a glance the number of new posts and unresolved questions. Each post also has icons showing whether other students or instructors have responded.

There were some bumps in the road during the first semester use of RealizeIT and mixed feedback from the students, but it does appear that students are spending more time on their prep work in order to reach mastery. I have even been able to increase the difficulty of the in-class Poll Everywhere questions as a result. In the spring 2019 semester, the RealizeIT platform provided integration with zyBooks, and the adaptive learning experience is something that we will continue to expand on. Measuring the effectiveness of this platform and how it impacts student learning is important. The DFW rates dropped from 13% to 9% when the course switched to the adaptive learning platform (see Table 3.1), and while we cannot say for sure that it was because of RealizeIT, the delta shows a positive correlation.

In addition to the three technologies described above, I also made use of numerous domain-specific technologies to help teach programming and data structures concepts. The Web-Cat system for autograding programming assignments proved to be a crucial tool for programming classes. Students submit their code that is then run against a set of test cases. Students receive feedback on what test cases their code did not pass and have the chance to resubmit their programs up to 30 times for each assignment. This allows them to learn how to make robust code that does not break when odd inputs are applied.

Other programs I use are the MOSS system, which is like plagiarism detection for code. I

Figure 3.14. The learning map shown to students for a module in the RealizeIT adaptive learning platform.

make use of a Code Workout server that provides students with small practice programming assignments, and CodingBat, which similarly provides programming practice assignments. And finally, the website visualgo.net provides step-through animations of data structures and online quizzes to test student understanding.

Conclusion

In this chapter, I have described in detail the workings of an FFAL class in the College of Computing and Informatics. Every detail of this class has been engineered, designed, and tweaked in an attempt to create a rich learning experience for students. The goals are not only to make sure students learn about data structures and develop their programming skills, but also to ensure that they develop their social, communication, and teamwork skills by developing relationships with other students in the computing major. There are many moving parts, and as seen by the staffing row in Table 3.1, it takes more than just one person to run this course. The course depends on a dedicated set of TAs who care deeply about the class and the learning experiences of the students coming up behind them. A later chapter in this book focuses on how a stepping stone mentorship model is an important element in making such complex classes work well.

References

Adams, N. E. (2015). Bloom's taxonomy of cognitive learning objectives. *Journal of the Medical Library Association, 103*(3), 152–153. https://doi.org/10.3163/1536-5050.103.3.010

Deil-Amen, R. (2011). Socio-academic integrative moments: Rethinking academic and social integration among two-year college students in career-related programs. *The Journal of Higher Education, 82*(1), 54–91. https://doi.org/10.1353/jhe.2011.0006

Eddy, S. L., & Hogan, K. A. (2014). Getting under the hood: How and for whom does increasing course structure work? *CBE—Life Sciences Education, 13*(3), 453–468.
https://doi.org/10.1187/cbe.14-03-0050

Latulipe, C., Long, N. B., & Seminario, C. E. (2015). Structuring flipped classes with lightweight teams and gamification. *Proceedings of the 46th ACM Technical Symposium on Computer Science Education,* 392–397. https://doi.org/10.1145/2676723.2677240

Latulipe, C., MacNeil, S., & Thompson, B. (2018). Evolving a data structures class toward inclusive success. *2018 IEEE Frontiers in Education Conference (FIE),* 1–9. https://doi.org/10.1109/FIE.2018.8659334

Latulipe, C., Rorrer, A., & Long, B. (2018). Longitudinal data on flipped class effects on performance in CS1 and retention after CS1. *Proceedings of the 49th ACM Technical Symposium on Computer Science Education,* 411–416. https://doi.org/10.1145/3159450.3159518

Maher, M. L., Latulipe, C., Lipford, H., & Rorrer, A. (2015). Flipped classroom strategies for CS education. *Proceedings of the 46th ACM Technical Symposium on Computer Science Education,* 218–223. https://doi.org/10.1145/2676723.2677252

McKeown, S., & Dixon, J. (2017). The "contact hypothesis": Critical reflections and future directions. *Social and Personality Psychology Compass, 11*(1), e12295. https://doi.org/10.1111/spc3.12295

Thai, N. T. T., De Wever, B., & Valcke, M. (2017). The impact of a flipped classroom design on learning performance in higher education: Looking for the best "blend" of lectures and guiding questions with feedback. *Computers & Education, 107,* 113–126. https://doi.org/10.1016/j.compedu.2017.01.003

CHAPTER 4

Converting a Traditional Class to Active Learning

MOLLY REDMOND AND CELINE LATULIPE

Creating an active learning classroom can be done all at once, when creating a new class, or it can be done slowly, changing an existing traditional lecture course over time to embed increasing amounts of active learning. The first approach works well if a faculty member can devote an entire summer to course development and be compensated for the effort. However, that is not always an option. In this chapter, we present some strategies and advice related to the second option: incorporating more active learning into a classroom over time.

The main goal is to have students more actively engage in the course material, ideally getting them to the higher levels of Bloom's taxonomy: synthesizing, applying, evaluating, and creating. These higher-level cognitive processes require that students have consumed the basic contents and facts needed before class. While there are a variety of ways to adopt and increase active learning, the flipped classroom or partial flipped classroom approach is ideal because it provides a structure in which students consume some or all of the course content at home by reading and/or watching videos (Auster & Wylie, 2006; Gannod, Burge, & Helmick, 2008; Gehringer & Peddycord, 2013; Lockwood & Esselstein, 2013; Moravec, Williams, Aguilar-Roca, & O'Dowd, 2010; Toto & Nguyen, 2009). This practice replaces some or all of the traditional lecture and provides the time in class needed for active learning activities. The learning activities may be completed individually, in pairs, or in groups, depending on the goals and setup of the class. Creating such classes brings about challenges in four areas:

- Course Selection: Which classes work well with this approach?
- Content Creation: How do you make/find video content for out-of-class consumption?
- Activity Design: How do you design effective active learning techniques for in-class?
- Group Formation & Incentives: How do you encourage students to work together effectively to form productive groups for active learning? How do you set up an incentive structure to ensure students do all of the work?

These types of questions are asked when designing a brand-new, fully flipped classroom from the ground up. But in this chapter, we look at how to address these questions when engaged in the slow game of converting an existing class to active learning over the course of several semesters.

Course Selection

Whether the goal is to improve the learning outcomes or to create a more satisfactory teaching experience by adding active learning, one of the first decisions is with which course to begin. In almost any discipline, there are courses that lend themselves more clearly and easily to active learning. For instance, a course that has obvious hands-on activities or obvious skill development goals is optimal. These courses often already have a few active learning activities built in, and so in some sense already have a transition to active learning. Taking such a course and migrating it to a fully flipped active learning course may take time, but it is more likely to be successful. If the first experience is successful, your confidence will increase as an active learning instructor. In addition, this will provide the opportunity to see what works well and what does not for students in a specific discipline and teaching environment. This chapter showcases several examples of slow migrations toward active learning, starting with an easier class in which to incorporate change.

Dr. Celine Latulipe took this approach when she first began her active learning journey. She slowly transformed the Rapid Prototyping and Design Patterns course in the College of Computing and Informatics into a fully flipped active learning (FFAL) course. This process took place over three semesters. There were hands-on activities that could be conducted in class, but to make time for these, the theoretical content had to be delivered outside of class.

Dr. Molly Redmond initially taught her introductory ecology class as a mostly lecture-based class, but over several semesters, she began to increase the active learning components each time she taught the class. She started by using clickers and has been increasing the number and length of other class activities each semester. Redmond is using a similar, though greatly accelerated, approach in her genetics class this semester.

Content Creation

One of the biggest challenges in moving toward an FFAL course (or even a partially flipped course) is the amount of work involved in creating video content for students to consume outside of class to deliver the facts and knowledge students need, so class time can be spent on active learning activities. The split here reflects Bloom's taxonomy, with the students doing the cognitively easier, lower-level activities on the taxonomy (gaining facts, knowledge, and understanding) at home, and then coming into class ready to engage in the more challenging, higher-order learning activities (synthesis, application, evaluation, and creation). In the past, students were expected to read the textbook before coming to class, and that is still often part of the preclass prep work in active learning. However, for many courses, faculty have found it most effective to create or source videos for content delivery. Modern students are of a media generation: They prefer videos, which can be watched while multitasking, and want the flexibility to watch at any pace, multiple times if necessary.

Thus, the challenge for the faculty member is creating or sourcing the videos. There are four approaches to this part of the course transition.

- Extra Credit Video Curation: In one semester, offer an extra credit project to students in which they find videos that present the topic being covered, and write a summary of why that video works well to present and/or reinforce the material. Ask students to create a few quiz questions that test a student's basic understanding of the material. The videos can then be reviewed and assigned to students the following semester in place of a lecture, allowing more time in class for active learning.

- Summer Credit/Independent Study Curation: Have one or two students work over the summer or as an independent study to gather video materials and develop quiz questions that help move a class toward a flipped structure. Be sure to assign students who have just taken the course so they are familiar enough with the material. The project will help the students solidify their own learning of the topic as well. Having a few students engaged in the project together allows them to test the quiz questions on each other. These videos can be worked into the course the following semester when the instructor has been able to develop an active learning module for the class.

- One Video Per Week: In a typical class with two lecture periods per week, choose one of the lectures each week to make into a video or a series of short videos that cover the material. Then, use those videos in the present semester, freeing up one period per week for active learning. The next time the same course is taught, the material from the second lecture period each week can be converted to videos. This strategy can be stretched out over three or four semesters. By the end, the instructor has an entire series of videos that solve the content delivery challenge and is free to focus on developing challenging in-class learning activities.

- Student Video Creation: Add a project to the end of a course asking students to produce high-quality video that explains a core course concept. It may be likely that only some of the videos will be good enough for use in future semesters, but doing this repeatedly over several semesters will generate enough quality videos. And in this case, the students will be watching their peers explain concepts, which might be more fun and engaging for them.

Activity Design

Clickers/Poll Everywhere

One of the simplest ways to introduce active learning techniques into a large lecture class is by using clickers (Caldwell, 2007). UNC Charlotte currently contracts with Poll Everywhere, a software platform that can be used on mobile phones, tablets, or any device with a web browser and Wi-Fi connection. This simplifies use, as students no longer have to purchase a standalone device and remember to bring it to class. Additionally, clickers can be used just once or many times during a class period and can be used in several different ways:

- Recall Questions: These are often used at the beginning of class to remind students of material discussed during the last class period or a concept introduced earlier in the semester that they need to remember to make sense of that day's topic.

- Surveys: Clickers are useful for surveying on matters relevant to course administration (e.g., What topics should I review before the exam? How much progress have you made on the assignment?). They can also provide insight into student experience and opinions about the course material (e.g., How concerned are you about climate change?) and be used as a prompt for students to defend a particular point of view when discussing a controversial topic where student opinion will reasonably differ (e.g., Should pandas get priority for conservation?).
- Concept Questions: This is the type of question Redmond uses most frequently in her biology classes. Many of these questions are designed to address common misconceptions (e.g., plants take up carbon from the soil). She designs these questions based on personal experience with the class and studies on common misconceptions in ecology and genetics (Wilke, D'Avanzo, Anderson, Schramm, & Hartley, 2011; Parker et al., 2012; Smith & Knight, 2012; Briggs et al., 2017).
- Problems: Genetics problems can be posted with multiple-choice or open-answer options. Problems can be worked on the board by the instructor or a student after the students respond, but when explaining the answer, it helps to have a sense of how many students were able to get the correct answer on their own.
- Clicker Case Studies: These involve a series of clicker questions applied to an interesting example and are usually a mix of the types of questions mentioned above. They can be custom designed, pulled from a textbook, or modified from examples available online.

For all types of questions, students can be encouraged to consult with their classmates before answering. In Redmond's classes, students receive credit solely for participation, and they are allowed to miss 10% of the points with no grade penalty. Redmond also allows students to leave a note at the end of class if their clicker malfunctioned or they were not able to get an answer in on time, which happens to about 5–10% of students each class period. Those policies reduce stress associated with not being able to figure out the correct answer quickly enough and inevitable technical mishaps.

Mixing Activities and Lecture

If not moving to an FFAL course, faculty members can intersperse activities and lecturing. Redmond has used a mix of short (2 to 10 minutes), medium (10 to 30 minutes), and long (30-plus minutes) group activities, gradually increasing both the number and length of the activities. The short activities are informal and almost always of her own design, and they are usually group discussion questions followed up by whole-class discussion. The medium length activities are completed in class and may be turned in for a small amount of credit. Some of these activities require students to complete an individual component in advance, like calculating their carbon footprint, participating in a citizen science bird count program, or reading an article on the costs of climate change. Students turn in the individual component on Canvas before the group activity in class. Then they share the results of their individual activity to come up with a group synthesis. The longer group activities take more time to develop and can be a mix of activities designed by the instructor and activities modified from other sources. Some of the sources useful in biology courses include the textbooks, the InTeGrate Project (In-TeGrate Project, 2019), and the National Center for Case Study Teaching in Science (National Center for Case Study Teaching in Science, 2019).

Wrap Around a MOOC

One way to ease the burden associated with developing a fully flipped class is to make use of full-scale resources that are online and freely available. With the advent of massive open online courses (MOOCs), it is possible to structure a face-to-face or blended class around existing MOOCs, augmenting and personalizing the learning experience with content that is relevant to your students. This strategy has a name: the small, private, online course, or SPOC, and it is growing in popularity as institutions of higher education attempt to leverage the power of great lectures available for free on MOOC platforms (Fox, 2013).

This technique of wrapping around a MOOC has been used in the Human–Computer Interaction (HCI) class in the College of Computing and Informatics (CCI) at UNC Charlotte, making use of the HCI class MOOC offered through Coursera. The videos on this MOOC were created by Dr. Scott Klemmer, a professor who was at Stanford University at the time, but is now at the University of California, San Diego. Klemmer gave permission to the computing faculty at UNC Charlotte to use his videos for their flipped, active learning HCI class (Russell et al., 2013). These videos have been supplemented with a handful of other videos created by the faculty in the CCI to augment the material and to highlight areas of the topic that Klemmer did not cover. Students watch these videos before coming to class and then engage in active learning design activities in class, applying the principles of HCI design to a variety of design problems.

The benefit of the SPOC model is that companies like Coursera have poured resources into creating high-end video lectures covering entire course curricula. Often the lectures are even interspersed with interactive questions. Importantly, the lectures are often given by preeminent scholars in the field. Thus, by wrapping a course around such a set of videos, a faculty member can save time and still be reasonably assured that the students are getting a good presentation of course content. The faculty member can then devote time to creating supplementary video material and to designing effective active learning activities to engage the students in the topic in the classroom.

Group Formation and Incentives

One of the strategies that can be used to slowly phase in active learning is short group activities or discussion questions interspersed with lecturing. While this is effective at breaking up lecturing, the transitions can sometimes be difficult. It is important to differentiate a transition to group work, as opposed to just asking questions generally. This can be accomplished both verbally and by notation on lecture slides. It is also necessary for these activities or questions to be written very clearly since there is usually not enough time to go around the room to take questions. If students cannot figure out what the instructor is asking, they do not engage in discussion. After a successful discussion, it can also be difficult to get the class to quiet down for the return to lecture. Using a clicker question to survey group responses is one good way to get everyone's attention and signal that group discussion time is over.

Dealing with expectations for group work when it is a relatively small portion of the class time or of students' grades can be challenging. When group activities are short enough to be completed in one class period, it generally makes more sense to form new groups for each activity, as different students are in attendance on different days. However, students generally form groups with the students sitting near them, so group composition often remains similar, but not identical, from activity to activity. While a student who was not happy with the efforts of their fellow group members certainly could join another group, many students appear to decide that it is not worth appearing rude when the stakes are fairly low. Many groups function well, but there are always some in which students are not participating; therefore, there are complaints from the students who feel that they did a disproportionate amount of the work. Capping the group size at four students appears to reduce the number of students who join a group but do not fully participate. Assigning permanent groups where the students are accountable to each other over the course of the semester might also help, but this could be problematic when students miss class on the day of an activity. Permanent groups are essential as group work becomes a larger portion of the class grade, and activities extend over longer time periods.

Conclusion

For faculty members new to active learning, gradually adding active learning components into their lecture-based classes will be more manageable than developing an FFAL course all at once. For students unaccustomed to active learning approaches, it is less overwhelming to take a hybrid approach and may lead to greater student acceptance. We encourage those interested in trying active learning to use these strategies to make the transition over multiple semesters or to simply increase the amount of active learning in a class that retains traditional lecture components as well.

References

Auster, E. R., & Wylie, K. K. (2006). Creating active learning in the classroom: A systematic approach. *Journal of Management Education, 30*(2), 333–353. https://doi.org/10.1177/1052562905283346

Briggs, A. G., Hughes, L. E., Brennan, R. E., Buchner, J., Horak, R. E., Amburn, D. S. K., ... Stevens, A. M. (2017). Concept inventory development reveals common student misconceptions about microbiology. *Journal of Microbiology & Biology Education, 18*(3). https://doi.org/10.1128/jmbe.v18i3.1319

Caldwell, J. E. (2007). Clickers in the large classroom: Current research and best-practice tips. *CBE Life Sciences Education, 6*(1), 9–20. https://doi.org/10.1187/cbe.06-12-0205

Fox, A. (2013). From MOOCs to SPOCs. *Communications of the ACM, 56*(12), 38–40. https://doi.org/10.1145/2535918

Gannod, G. C., Burge, J. E., & Helmick, M. T. (2008). Using the inverted classroom to teach software engineering. *2008 ACM/IEEE 30th International Conference on Software Engineering, 777–786.* https://doi.org/10.1145/1368088.1368198

Gehringer, E. F., & Peddycord III, B. W. (2013). The inverted-lecture model: A case study in computer architecture. *Proceeding of the 44th ACM Technical Symposium on Computer Science Education, 489–494.* https://doi.org/10.1145/2445196.2445343

InTeGrate Project. (n.d.). *InTeGrate Teaching Materials.* Retrieved from https://serc.carleton.edu/integrate/teaching_materials/index.html

Lockwood, K., & Esselstein, R. (2013). The inverted classroom and the CS curriculum. *Proceeding of the 44th ACM Technical Symposium on Computer Science Education, 113–118.* https://doi.org/10.1145/2445196.2445236

Moravec, M., Williams, A., Aguilar-Roca, N., & O'Dowd, D. K. (2010). Learn before lecture: A strategy that improves learning outcomes in a large introductory biology class. *CBE Life Sciences Education, 9*(4), 473–481. https://doi.org/10.1187/cbe.10-04-0063

National Center for Case Study Teaching in Science. (n.d.) *Case Collection.* Retrieved from https://sciencecases.lib.buffalo.edu

Parker, J. M., Anderson, C. W., Heidemann, M., Merrill, J., Merritt, B., Richmond, G., & Urban-Lurain, M. (2012). Exploring undergraduates' understanding of photosynthesis using diagnostic question clusters. *CBE Life Sciences Education, 11*(1), 47–57. https://doi.org/10.1187/cbe.11-07-0054

Russell, D. M., Klemmer, S., Fox, A., Latulipe, C., Duneier, M., & Losh, E. (2013). Will massive online open courses (MOOCs) change education? *CHI '13 Extended Abstracts on Human Factors in Computing Systems, 2395–2398.* https://doi.org/10.1145/2468356.2468783

Smith, M. K., & Knight, J. K. (2012). Using the genetics concept assessment to document persistent conceptual difficulties in undergraduate genetics courses. *Genetics, 191*(1), 21–32. https://doi.org/10.1534/genetics.111.137810

Toto, R., & Nguyen, H. (2009). Flipping the work design in an industrial engineering course. *2009 39th IEEE International Conference on Frontiers in Education Conference, 1–4.* https://doi.org/10.1109/FIE.2009.5350529

Wilke, B. J., D'Avanzo, C., Anderson, C. W., Schramm, J. W., & Hartley, L. M. (2011). College students' understanding of the carbon cycle: Contrasting principle-based and informal reasoning. *BioScience, 61*(1), 65–75. https://doi.org/10.1525/bio.2011.61.1.12

CHAPTER 5

POGIL Learning Cycle as a Model for Active Learning

KATHY ASALA

Introduction

The types of active learning strategies implemented in college classrooms are varied. Determining which active learning strategies fit your teaching philosophy and learning goals for your students involves researching available strategies and trying them. After investigating the myriad of evidence-based teaching practices reported in the last several years, we settled on Process Oriented Guided Inquiry Learning (POGIL) as the student-centered teaching strategy to implement in introductory chemistry courses for the following reasons:

- POGIL is a research-based pedagogy that is well established in undergraduate chemistry courses (Simonson, 2019).
- Published materials are available in general chemistry (Wiley and Flinn Scientific).
- Professional development opportunities are available through regional workshops, national conferences (National Conference for Advanced POGIL Practitioners), and writer's retreats.

Theoretical Framework

POGIL activities are based on a learning cycle model (Figure 5.1) that is consistent with the constructivist theory of learning: the idea that knowledge and understanding must be constructed in the mind of each individual learner. Additionally, the format of POGIL activities builds meaningful learning: Ideas learned meaningfully are interconnected within the cognitive structure of the learner and are memorable and recallable. Karplus and Their (1967) were the originators of this learning cycle model as a teaching strategy for elementary school science. Research by Abraham and Renner (1986) further demonstrated that a learning cycle sequence of exploration, then invention, then discovery is optimal for developing content knowledge.

The Guided Inquiry Learning (GIL) aspect of POGIL is based on a learning cycle of exploration, concept invention, and application phases (Figure 5.1) and forms the foundation for the in-class activities that learners use to guide them to construct new knowledge.

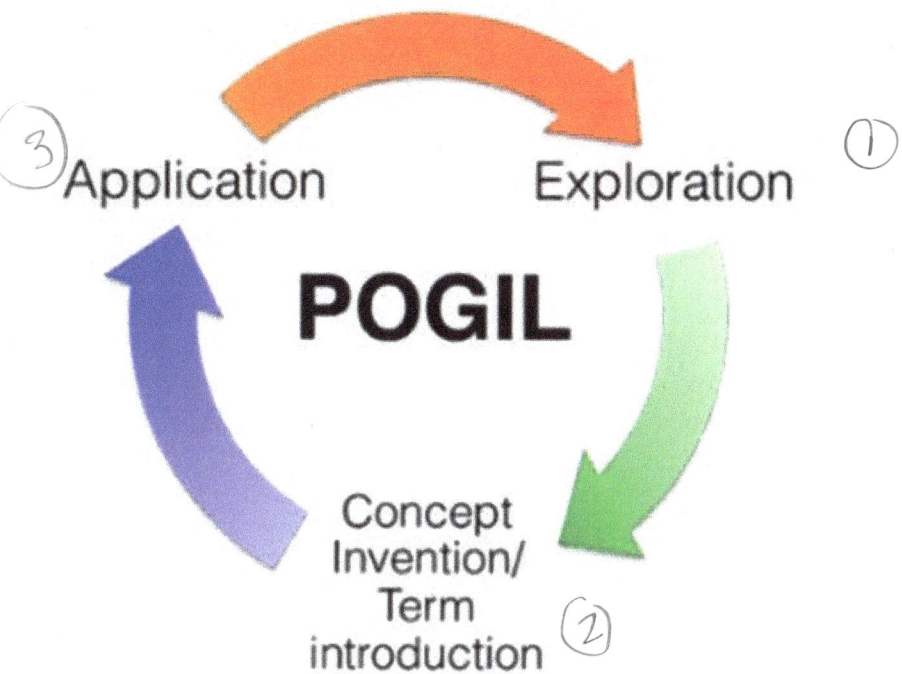

Figure 5.1. POGIL learning cycle.

Bauer, Daubenmire, and Minderhout (as cited in Simonson, 2019, p. 9) describe the learning cycle steps as follows:

During the exploration phase, students examine a model, which can be data, a figure, text, or other suitable material. The model is a critical feature of a POGIL activity and is carefully crafted. The model is interrogated using specially designed (guiding) questions to direct students' attention to the salient features of the model and may include questions that prompt recall of relevant prior knowledge. The student team discusses responses to the questions, and their conversations lead them to recognize a relationship or pattern in the information provided in the model and to link that with prior knowledge. The questions and model combine so that students recognize and "invent" the idea that is the focus of the learning cycle activity. Once the concept is invented, the standard name of the concept is provided. The POGIL activity concludes with an application segment in which questions are posed that apply the newly learned concept to new contexts.

The POGIL classroom structure also incorporates Vygotsky's idea that constructing knowledge and gaining understanding happen in a sociocultural context (Newman & Holzman, 1993). Classrooms designed to incorporate communication between peers or between instructor and learners is a critical component of developing understanding. Cooperative learning is fundamental to the implementation of POGIL. Students work in small teams of three or four students and hold individual roles to ensure that all students are fully engaged in the learning process.

Benefits of POGIL

The POGIL pedagogy has been validated in a variety of educational settings (high schools, two-year and four-year institutions) and in a variety of science, technology, engineering, and mathematics (STEM) disciplines (chemistry, biology, clinical and health sciences, engineering, mathematics, and computer science) over the last 20 years (Simonson, 2019). The benefits include helping students better grasp the concepts of the discipline, improve student success, and prepare students for the workforce.

National reports published by the American Association for the Advancement of Science (2009), National Research Council (2012), and the ABET Engineering Accreditation Commission (2016), for example, discuss the importance of students graduating from college ready for the workforce in skills such as problem-solving, management, creative thinking, leadership, communication, teamwork, and learning how to learn. An important aspect of POGIL activities is the development of process skills. Learners cultivate essential professional skills such as communication, critical thinking, information processing, management, problem-solving, and teamwork as they work through each POGIL activity.

Lo and Mendez (as cited in Simonson, 2019) completed a literature review of 43 studies selected based on their criteria of POGIL being identified as the intervention method in the study and as the primary data aimed to demonstrate potential efficacy of POGIL. The data collected was broadly categorized as performance or survey data. Performance data included exam scores, quizzes, or questions from these summative assessments, grade distributions for courses, and pass/fail rates. Survey data pertained to the student's experience or effect on motivation/interest. The results from the survey data showed a positive (79%) or neutral effect (19%) from the POGIL method. The results from the performance studies (pretest vs. posttest scores, grade point average [GPA], course grades, and completion rates) demonstrated that students in POGIL courses had higher GPAs by 0.57 on a four-point scale and a 14% higher completion rate, on average (Simonson, 2019).

POGIL Implementation in Introductory Chemistry Courses at UNC Charlotte

Why POGIL?

The first semester of transitioning from lecture-based instruction to student-centered instruction involved trying a few different active learning strategies. What emerged from these trials was that some techniques were met by students more favorably than others. Many active learning strategies require students to obtain foundational material on their own before it is discussed in class. Students must watch a video or read the textbook to learn some of the basic terms and concepts before they use them in class activities. Students in introductory chemistry courses often struggle with the language and information presented in written or graphical format. Asking students to read or watch a video before knowing the terms or thinking about the concepts is often confusing to them. Yet these are skills that students must develop to continue to learn beyond the classroom environment.

POGIL is designed to have students learn terms and develop concepts through guided inquiry activities during class, as previously described. Students are introduced to the topic and construct knowledge of the underlying principles in class, and then practice applying this new knowledge before they are asked to read the textbook or see further explanations. The concept invention/term introduction and application phases of the POGIL learning cycle allow students to gain the fundamental knowledge and apply it before leaving class. This approach gives students the opportunity to ask questions for clarification as they are learning the material for the first time. Then, when they read the explanations in the textbook or watch videos that present more complex information or problems, they have a basic understanding of the key terms and concepts.

Instructional Time

The instructor's role in a POGIL classroom is a facilitator of learning instead of a deliverer of content. The instructor circulates throughout the classroom and observes teams as they interact and attempt to answer the guided inquiry questions. The instructor intervenes only as needed, which may occur when teams need clarification or to further guide their thinking toward a comprehensive response. The instructor controls the classroom flow in that they must decide when teams need to continue working to grasp a key concept or when a whole class discussion is required to ensure the class is practicing scientific reasoning in their explanations as they present to their peer teams. There may be moments when the instructor decides that a brief lecture presentation to the entire class is needed if a majority of students are not grasping the important underlying concepts being developed in the POGIL activity.

The student's role in a POGIL classroom is to actively engage in the topics for the day by reading, thinking, writing, and discussing with their peers the guided inquiry questions in the activity and to develop a team consensus to gain conceptual understanding. Students may be asked to present to the class their team's response to a key question in the activity. Students are doing the cognitive lifting for a majority of the class period.

Team Assignments and Roles

Forming teams that foster contributions from all team members effectively and equitably is necessary for collaborative learning environments. It is not an easy task to get introductory-level college students to work together toward a shared goal of learning. The educational literature provides ample discussions of how to form effective teams and can be used for guidance. Teams of three were formed in the implementation of POGIL in introductory chemistry courses. Each team was designed to have a range of academic ability, but not too large of a range, and with an awareness of diversity and inclusion issues. For example, teams in which an underrepresented student is isolated as the lone representative in the group were avoided. The first team assignments were made based on limited information about each student, as they were made right after the add/drop deadline. Academic abilities were determined based on results from the prerequisite quiz given at the end of the first week of class. Academic behaviors that foster student success are not established until about a month into the course. For these reasons, and to address conflicts that have occurred between team members, new teams are assigned about halfway through the course.

A true POGIL practitioner will assign each student in the team a role. Roles are designed to ensure the team works effectively, and all members contribute as they help each other construct new knowledge. Common roles assigned in POGIL settings are manager, recorder, presenter, and reflector, or a similar variation. The manager keeps the team working collaboratively and makes sure everyone is participating and staying on task. The recorder writes the consensus response developed by the team on the activity worksheet, or as designated by the instructor, which may be collected or used by the presenter. The presenter reports the team's findings to the class. The presenter is responsible for articulating the team's response and its reasoning as to how they determined their response in oral or written form to the class. The reflector observes interactions among team members and provides feedback to the team on what they are doing well and where they need to improve. The reflector role is a challenging role for younger students, as it requires the ability to contribute to the learning activity and to how the team is interacting.

The primary roles we have used in introductory chemistry courses are a reader and recorder. The reader helps get the team started on each set of questions in the activity by reading the information and question out loud. The reader serves as a facilitator of the team's discussion by asking others for a response or rebuttal to another student's response. The recorder is responsible for writing the team's response to the key questions as designated by the instructor.

Peer-Assisted Leaders

The implementation of POGIL as an instructional strategy in larger enrollment courses (more than 50 students) requires additional facilitators beyond the instructor to be present. We have incorporated peer-assisted leaders (PALs) into the interactive classroom to provide the additional support needed. PALs are undergraduate students who successfully completed the course recently. They help facilitate discussion among teams and field questions from the teams as students work through the activities. PALs are trained as learning facilitators during a weekly meeting led by the instructor. Topics discussed during this weekly meeting were centered around how to get students to work together as a team and group dynamics, as well as the POGIL activity and its content. Some PALs also held weekly review sessions for students to attend to get extra help outside of class. The PAL-led review sessions, like traditional supplemental instruction sessions, were available through a partnership with the University Center for Academic Excellence (UCAE). The UCAE trained the PALs for their review sessions at a biweekly meeting.

Outside of Class Time

Students are assigned readings from their textbook that correspond to the activity completed in class immediately following the class meeting and before the next class. In addition, three to five traditional textbook problems are assigned as homework to further practice the key concepts discovered in the most recent activity completed. Instructor-written problem sets are assigned at the end of a chapter to give students the opportunity to practice the topics for a given chapter in a comprehensive way. Students can request examples from the assigned homework be worked by the instructor in the weekly problem session or through a video posted in Canvas. Weekly assessments are given to ensure students receive additional feedback on their learning gains.

Challenges

Implementing active learning strategies in introductory chemistry courses presents a few challenges. Students new to actively participating in their learning during class are initially resistant. Most students expect to sit quietly and take notes during class as the instructor presents information to them, since this scenario is the typical setting found in high school and college classrooms. A student may be asked an occasional question about the information being presented, but often they do not have to answer the question at all, or they do not need to answer the question out loud to anyone else in the class (they may answer through use of personal response systems, for example). Many students are not used to a social constructivist approach to learning. Asking students to answer questions in a collaborative team setting makes some students disengage. They fear being wrong in front of their peers, they may be shy, or they may lack a personal stake in the team's progress, to name a few reasons why students choose to not engage with their group members. There are strategies an instructor can use to help students understand the benefits of collaborative group learning to try to get students to buy in to the approach. The instructor can insist that team members follow their respective roles and provide explicit instructions on teamwork on cue cards for students to follow. In large lecture settings, it is especially challenging to enforce all of the team roles and to make sure the roles rotate among team members, so all members have the opportunity to experience each role and see their value in team contributions.

It is also difficult to train the PALs adequately. PALs are just beyond novices themselves in terms of content knowledge. They do not always recognize legitimate answers from students if the concept is explained in a different way from how they know it, nor do they know how to adjust misguided thinking from a team in some situations. Training PALs takes additional time by the instructor as well as additional resources.

An additional challenge is keeping a large number of teams working through an activity at approximately the same pace. Some teams work through the activity quickly while others struggle through the questions and take longer. One technique used to keep teams moving forward at about the same pace is to use a personal response system to have occasional check-in points in the activity where teams must ensure they are to a certain point in the activity when the check-in question is posed. Having additional application problems for students to practice after completing the activity is another method used to ensure faster-paced teams are still engaged in the activity topics.

Summary

POGIL is a pedagogy based on cognitive science and educational research in which students collaborate by working in teams on carefully designed activities. The learning cycle on which POGIL activities are based involves exploring a model and answering guided inquiry questions that lead students to discover the underlying concept of the topic. Students then apply their new knowledge gained to new situations, which reinforce the concepts.

References

Abrahm, M. R., & Renner, J. W. (1986). The sequence of learning cycle activities in high school chemistry. *Journal of research in Science teaching, 23*(2), 121-143. https://doi.org/10.1002/tea.3660230205

ABET Engineering Accreditation Commission. (2016). *Criteria for accrediting engineering programs, 2016–2017.* Retrieved from https://www.abet.org/accreditation/accreditation-criteria/criteria-for-accrediting-engineering-programs-2016-2017/

Association for the Advancement of Science. (2019). *Vision and change in undergraduate biology education: A call to action.* Retrieved from http://visionandchange.org/finalreport/

Bauer, C. F., Daubenmire, P. L., & Minderhout, V. (2019). Not just a good idea, POGIL has a theoretical foundation. In S. R. Simonson (Ed.), *POGIL: An introduction to process oriented guided inquiry learning for those who wish to empower learners* (pp. 3–22). Sterling, VA: Stylus Publishing LLC.

Karplus, R., & Their, H. D. (1967). *New trends in curriculum and instruction.* Chicago, IL: Rand McNally & Co.

Lo, S. M., & Mendez, J. I. (2019). Learning—The evidence. In S. R. Simonson (Ed.), *POGIL: An introduction to process oriented guided inquiry learning for those who wish to empower learners* (pp. 85–110). Sterling, VA: Stylus Publishing LLC.

National Research Council. (2012). *Education for life and work: Developing transferable knowledge and skills in the 21st century.* Retrieved from https://doi.org/10.17226/13398

Newman, F., & Holzman, L. (1993). *Lev Vygotsky: Revolutionary scientist.* London, England: Routledge.

Simonson, S. R. (2019). *POGIL: An introduction to process oriented guided inquiry learning for those who wish to empower learners.* Sterling, VA: Stylus Publishing LLC.

CHAPTER 6

Addressing Access in Active Learning

DONNA SACCO, MOLLY REDMOND, AND CELINE LATULIPE

This chapter addresses strategies for ensuring access to instruction in the unique settings of active learning classrooms. By using a proactive, flexible approach to deliberately planning instructional goals and assessment, the needs of all learners can be met. More specifically, this chapter will examine the Universal Design for Learning (UDL) model as a means of eliminating a one-size-fits-all approach to instruction. It will also examine a framework for identifying and removing barriers by using multiple means of representation, expression, and engagement with UDL.

Figure 6.1. Clearing a path for people with special needs clears the path for everyone! From Giangreco (2002).

Vignette: It is the beginning of a new semester, and Dr. Hathaway is excited to begin using a flipped learning model for student engagement in her introductory-level education course. Leading up to the first day of classes, she watches the enrollment climb. She wonders how active learning will be manageable given the large class size. In addition, she has begun to receive documents from the Disability Services Office regarding accommodations for students in her class. As she looks back over past semesters and the students she taught, she remembers that several of her students experienced difficulty staying engaged within the large classrooms. Some fell behind. Others admitted to having learning disabilities or attention deficit hyperactivity disorder (ADHD) and not wanting to use the Disabilities Services Office. As she plans the course, she decides that she is going to utilize new methods of interaction this semester. But where does she start, and how does she ensure that she will not lose students along the way?

Each year thousands of students enter college classrooms bringing with them great diversity in cultural and linguistic backgrounds, ages, prior knowledge, prior educational experiences, and learning differences. Accommodating all students' diverse needs can be difficult. At the same time, it is incumbent upon faculty to provide access for all learners in their classrooms, and, most particularly, those students protected by Section 504 of the Rehabilitation Act, the Americans with Disabilities Act (ADA) of 1990, and the ADA Amendments Act of 2008. Some of the categories of disabilities that may be encountered in a university classroom include a specific learning disability, traumatic brain injury, physical/mobility-related disability, blindness or vision impairment, deafness or hard of hearing disability, psychological disability, medical impairment, and attention deficit hyperactivity disorder (ADHD). How might faculty ensure that they are meeting students' needs?

Certainly, the university's Office of Disability Services (ODS) will provide documentation for students for whom they have processed the appropriate paperwork. They will also provide faculty with assistance in meeting the needs of these students. Some of the typical classroom accommodations are flexible classroom attendance, permission to record classes, alternative testing, class notes provided by a notetaker, alternative texts, access to PowerPoint presentations, breaks, preferential seating, use of a laptop, frequency modulation (FM) system, video captioning, or American Sign Language (ASL) interpreters. There may also be accommodations specific to assessments. These include extended time, a testing environment with reduced distractions, screen readers, calculators, and computers.

The Hidden Disabilities

However, some disabilities might be considered hidden disabilities, a disability not apparent to the observer that most people would be unaware of it unless the student decided to disclose the presence and/or nature of the disability. Some of these hidden disabilities are learning or attentional disabilities. There are also a number of medical disabilities that may include Crohn's disease, epilepsy, and lupus, to name a few. Students with these disabilities might receive accommodations; however, there are many students who do not seek the support.

In their most recent executive summary, the National Center for Learning Disabilities (NCLD; Horowitz, Rawe, & Whittaker, 2017) explained that many students with learning and attention issues who enroll in four-year colleges are not getting the support they need. Only 24% of college students with learning and attention issues have gone through the process of receiving services from their college ODS. Seven percent, although they identify as having a learning disability, did not inform their college. Another 69% did not register with the ODS because they decided they no longer had disabilities, or they were afraid they would be perceived as less intelligent. The fact is that a learning disability is not something a person grows out of once he or she graduates from high school. The same can be said of attention issues such as ADHD and attention deficit disorder (ADD). People learn strategies for managing the disability, and so it may appear that they have "outgrown" it. At the same time, many students who graduate from high school do not advocate for themselves and utilize the services that they are entitled to receive.

Once a student does register with the ODS, the student may not want or need to utilize all of the accommodations included in the disability services agreement. Yet, it is critical to provide the accommodations as required. Students might determine that certain accommodations, such as note takers, are not needed given the format of instruction. This may be especially true within a fully flipped active learning (FFAL) class. Faculty must understand that it is the student's prerogative to determine what is or is not necessary, but the faculty member should stay in contact with the student about the accommodations and let the student determine the degree to which they utilize the necessary accommodations. It is in the best interest of students to have the accommodations in place even if they choose not to use them in case their conditions change and they realize the accommodations are needed.

Some students, whose disabilities are medical in nature, may experience unexpected exacerbations related to the condition. The accommodation letter may ask the professor to provide flexibility with the attendance policy while signaling to the student that it is their responsibility to make up the missed work. In an FFAL class, this could be difficult. Much of the learning is experiential and relies on collaboration during the class period. Some possible solutions for university professors could be found in the paradigm shift that many businesses have made with workers telecommuting from home or holding business meetings via such services as Skype, Zoom, GoToMeeting, and WebEx. Mobile robotic telepresence solutions have begun to provide connections from hospital rooms to classrooms. Perhaps university professors could allow a student with a medical diagnosis, who is occasionally unable to attend class, to attend class remotely thereby allowing the student to participate and learn from interactions with peers. In those cases, students can still work together on a document simultaneously by using Google Docs. Students can even present as part of a group by using a platform such as WebEx and having the presentation projected on a classroom screen.

Another disability that is not always evident is when a student is hard of hearing or deaf. The student may be able to hear with hearing aids that are not noticeable; however, this does not mean that the student can hear everything even with hearing aids. For a professor to say "I will use my teacher voice" and put aside the microphone is not acceptable. This is true for students within the class as well. Each student would need to use a microphone so that the person with the hearing impairment receives the accommodation. If the student's paperwork requires a microphone or FM system, it must be used for all oral communication. It also helps to have the student seated close to the professor to be able to see facial expressions and read lips if possible. Also, subtitles are still required for any classroom videos. The very end of class might be particularly difficult for students with hearing disabilities. As a professor is making announcements and students begin to pack up, the background noise could make it impossible for a student with a hearing loss to differentiate the sounds and hear the professor. A professor can ask students to wait to pack up so that all can hear important announcements, announcements can be made at the beginning of class, and/or announcements can be made online.

Something to keep in mind is that students do not have to disclose their disability to their professors. The paperwork from ODS describes the accommodations in place but not the particular disability. The best way to begin working with a student who has paperwork from ODS is to arrange to meet. Open communication with the student is critical. The student can usually describe what they need in order to access the course fully. They will often have suggestions. By initiating open conversations with students early in the semester, professors can develop a plan for moving forward and a system for checking in when there are concerns by either party about course instruction, work, or assessments. It is also helpful to meet with a counselor from the ODS to seek assistance. The population of students who register with the ODS in any university is ever changing. Currently, the UNC Charlotte ODS reports that there has been a recent increase in the number of students with autism spectrum disorder (ASD) and other disabilities with associated behavioral challenges. Determining the best course of action to address the students' needs can sometimes be difficult, and ODS counselors may have helpful suggestions based on the specifics that they know about the case.

Proactive from the Start

One of the ways to be proactive is to begin problem-solving before the semester starts. Take some time to investigate the classroom itself. What are the strengths and weaknesses of the setting? How might you utilize what is there and provide enhancements to enrich learning experiences? What barriers might be integral to the setting, and how might you address these barriers before classes begin? It is sometimes a couple of weeks into the semester before faculty receive accommodation letters from the ODS, but surveying the room in advance may help mitigate any possible access issues.

The next step is to learn more about your students. "Getting to Know You" student surveys are a useful tool. An online survey provides a safe format for students to share important information about themselves as learners. By asking, "What would you like me to know about you?" students are able to share their learning difficulties and fears. These surveys can also help faculty discover which students speak other languages and those for whom English is not their first language. Faculty can use what they learn in these surveys about students' strengths and interests to help promote engagement. This type of survey could also be useful in arranging working groups. If the classroom is designed in such a manner as to have flexible seating, the professor can be very intentional about who is in each group, even if those groups change over the course of the semester.

Paying close attention to the classroom setting, the students, and their unique needs are important factors in determining instruction. The course design, goals, assignments, and assessments may all be in place, but looking back to Dr. Hathaway, how might she approach the active learning classroom in a manner that removes barriers for all students?

Active Learning with Universal Design for Learning

Universal Design for Learning (UDL) was born out of the concepts from universal design in architecture. When the ADA was passed in 1990, it delivered the guarantee of greater accessibility for all people with disabilities. This required some strategic planning and new architectural design ideas. Many of the changes made to everyday living are common now. Cuts in curbs to allow for access, ramps, universal symbols, crosswalks with auditory indicators, wide doorways with low thresholds, and automated doors are a few new design features that address access issues. These architectural designs not only provide access to people with disabilities, but they also make tasks easier for us all.

In keeping with the architectural design features, there are many adaptations to instructional materials that remove barriers and provide access for all learners. By designing instruction that considers and addresses possible barriers, even students without disabilities benefit. For instance, to be in compliance with the ADA, all videos used at the university setting require closed-captioning for the hearing impaired. Most universities are able to provide resources that will provide captioning for all videos. At the same time, a transcript for any audio should be supplied. These features are useful and benefit many students, even those without disabilities.

There is assistive technology software and hardware available at universities to assist faculty in working with the technology required for students with disabilities. Most universities and their students have access to the JAWS screen reader for students with visual impairments or reading disabilities, screen magnifiers for students with visual impairments, and Read&Write Gold for students with reading and writing disabilities. These are just a few of the resources available to students and faculty.

In addition, faculty can make simple adjustments to create text that is easier to read. By using a font such as Verdana or Arial, a size that is appropriate for the medium, and text colors that are most easily read, all students benefit. With the click of a button, a PDF can be converted to an accessible tagged structure that will allow access to a screen reader on an electronic device. These adjustments can help many students. However, UDL applies to an even broader context for teaching and learning that aligns nicely with active learning and/or FFAL classrooms.

Just as the cut in a sidewalk provides a manageable path for a person in a wheelchair, it also eases the effort for someone wheeling a suitcase, backpack, or stroller. Likewise, UDL in the classroom removes barriers to curriculum access for all students and focuses on student learning in a proactive manner. The teacher is responsible for removing the possible barriers that could prevent all students from learning the material.

Although the accessible design features for instruction are important, the teaching and learning practices of UDL are most beneficial to practitioners in active learning and/or FFAL classrooms. Researchers at the Center for Applied Special Technology (CAST) developed the UDL research-based framework to meet the diverse needs of students in today's K–12 classrooms, and postsecondary education is no exception to having a diverse student body. See Figure 6.2 for the UDL guidelines.

> UDL is a framework for teaching and learning. It assumes from the beginning that learners are very different. The design part of universal design is designing a learning environment that is as diverse as the students are. There are many options for how to learn within it. So the idea of Universal Design for Learning is to create good learning environments that work across a wide spectrum of students.

> David Rose, The IRIS Center, (2009)

CAST has developed three guiding principles for teachers as they plan instruction with UDL: (a) to provide multiple means of engagement, (b) to provide multiple means of representation, and (c) to provide multiple means of action and expression (CAST, 2018). UDL emphasizes new technologies to provide more access, such as alternatives to textbooks that introduce barriers to students. But this is not only a framework about technology; it is a framework about teaching and learning and is based on the neuroscience of learning (Hall, Meyer, & Rose, 2012).

Figure 6.2 provides the UDL guidelines with principles explained. It is possible that each lesson developed does not include all three guiding principles; however, the overall intentional instructional design should include learning goals, instructional materials, instructional methods, and the assessment. These four elements are interconnected. The learning goal should always be kept in mind, and each of the elements that lead to the learning outcome should be examined for access for all. Table 6.1 demonstrates the traditional instructional model, the active learning classroom, possible barriers, and a UDL option.

Once students become accustomed to UDL and the multiple modes of representation, expression, and engagement, barriers are minimized or eliminated for all students. The course structure using UDL helps to eliminate any violations of student privacy with regard to a disability area. All students receive the choices, and many without disabilities find that they are better able to engage with the content in a meaningful way. Remember, if the goal is to remove possible barriers to student learning, the multiple modes will benefit students who have decided not to take advantage of disability services, students who are English learners, and students who have not been identified with a disability but may have one. Perhaps there are students in the class who struggle for any number of reasons. They may be first generation college students. They may be gifted and would prefer to add some extensions to the learning. Utilizing UDL principles allows the professor to meet a variety of student needs.

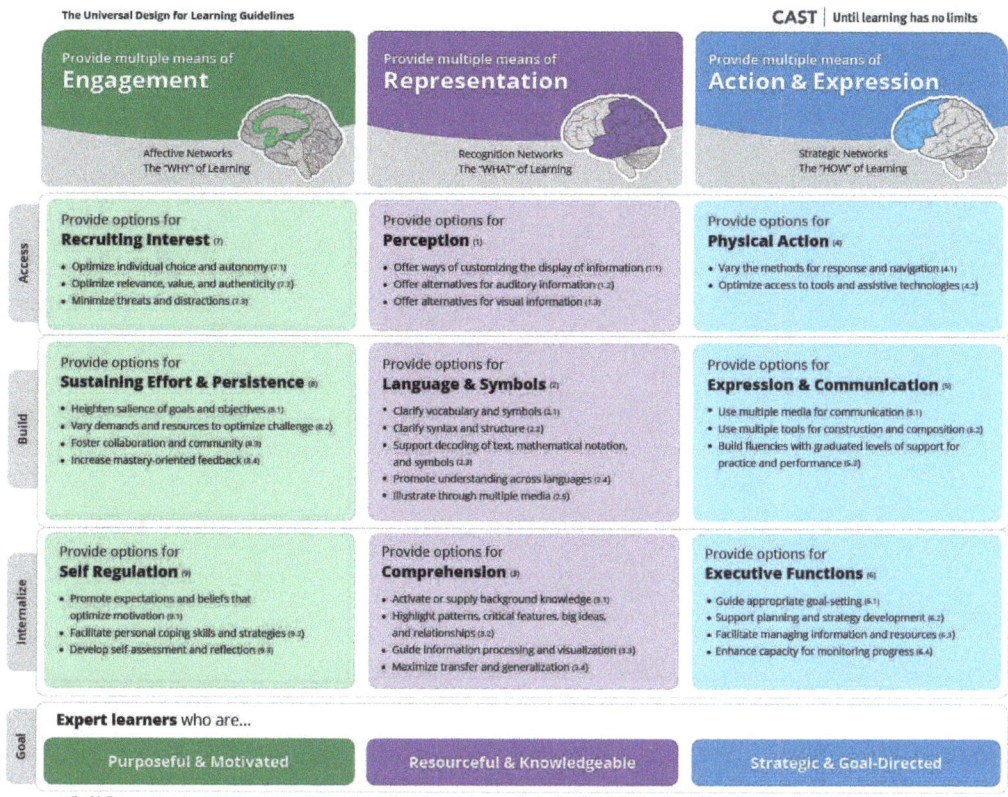

Figure 6.2. Universal Design for Learning Guidelines, version 2.2 (CAST, 2018).

This does not happen by magic, however. And the goal is not merely to provide students with choices. The intent is to produce high performance with curriculum that is not only accessible but also engaging. There should be sustained engagement in learning tasks by increasing the complexity (Edyburn, 2010). Again, by focusing on the course objectives, the professor is able to determine critical concepts and means of providing enduring understanding for students.

Take a look at some of the following vignettes and think about what you would do if you were presented with these scenarios in your classes. Remember, think outside the box. It is your class, and you can develop creative solutions that provide a more engaging environment for all students, not just those with access issues. The key is to be proactive, reflective, open, and willing to change.

Absences Due to Disabilities

Emma has a chronic illness that sometimes causes her to miss class, usually without much warning. In her biology class, students are working in groups to interpret figures in a paper from the primary

Table 6.1 *Planning for UDL Strategies*

Instructional strategy in traditional lecture class	Instructional strategy in active learning class	Possible barriers	UDL option
Students read text	Students read text	Students may have: • reading difficulties • vision issues • reading comprehension difficulties	Provide: • multiple forms of text such as digital format • speech-to-text option • book on tape
Professor lectures	Students engage in group work	Students may have: • attention issues • receptive processing disorder • hearing issues • social anxiety	Provide: • multiple modes for working • allowance for students to work remotely • utilization of a microphone or PA system • low interaction roles
Professor demonstrates and begins a class discussion	Professor demonstrates and begins a class discussion	Students may have: • social anxiety • frequent absences • difficulty hearing demonstration	Provide: • alternative methods to respond, such as active response cards • allowance for remote access • polling program that is anonymous (such as Poll Everywhere or Kahoot!) • augmented sound
Students write essays	Students write quick responses	Students may have: • fine motor issues • poor typing ability • poor handwriting • processing issues • organizational planning issues	Provide: • speech-to-text option • drawing • movie • PPT • diorama/poster

Note. PA = public address; PPT = PowerPoint; UDL = Universal Design for Learning.

scientific literature. They spend one class period studying their figure and putting together a short presentation. The next class period they will be presenting their figure to the class. The presentations are short, informal, and ungraded. The primary purpose is to help prepare them for the more formal presentations later in the semester. Emma is unable to attend class on the first day when the groups are formed and they prepare their presentations. She emails the instructor a few days later stating that she missed class because of her disability. What is an appropriate accommodation? The presentation is ungraded, so she will not be penalized if she just sits in the audience and does not present, but she has missed out on the opportunity to practice interpreting figures, the hands-on learning experience, and presenting. All of the figures in the paper have already been assigned, so she cannot simply be assigned another figure to present on her own. This particular class does not have regular groups. If it did, she could check in with her regular group members and still participate in the presentation on the second day. Are there other ways to manage this scenario?

Certainly, students with disabilities are not the only students who miss classes. On any given day, there may be absences from a class, and having procedures in place for accessing class work when absent would benefit everyone. Most colleges utilize a learning management system (LMS) platform such as Canvas or Blackboard. Perhaps the professor could have selected two to three extra figures to add to the LMS for additional practice for students that could be used by anyone missing class. If there are systems in place that allow students to refer to the LMS when they have missed a class, then everyone benefits. The professor can post class PowerPoints, quizzes, and assignments to the LMS along with options for participation. If the class had a buddy system in place, any student missing class could learn from their buddy. If a student needs to miss multiple days, it is now possible to attend class remotely using any number of virtual meeting systems. Using Google Drive, a student could participate in class simultaneously with peers in real time. There is also no need to miss a presentation. An absent student can easily be available on any one of the many video conference calling systems that most universities have subscriptions to and present on the monitor or screen while the rest of the team is in the classroom.

In cases where the student has missed so many classes that it seems impossible to catch up, a conversation with the student and the ODS counselor will begin a process to develop solutions. Sometimes the student has to take an incomplete or take the class again. These things can be negotiated with the team in place. Communication is always key in situations such as this.

Privacy Issues

In a computing class, Jack and Radhu are expected to work together each week to do in-class pair programming exercises. These are learning exercises that help the students practice some of the new programming concepts being introduced. Pair programming is a specific paradigm in which the students take turns in two roles: driver and navigator. The driver is the person who has the key-

board and who actually types in the code; the navigator has the lab instructions and is in charge of figuring out what to do step-by-step. In an ideal world, the two students discuss and agree on each step before it is typed in. A typical lab may have two to four different parts, and the students are supposed to switch roles for each part.

Jack has dyslexia and is registered with disability services. He has accommodations on his computer for reading the online textbook. The lab instructions are typically handed out on paper so that the students only have one laptop open. This ensures that the navigator has to play an active role. Jack expresses to the instructor that he really prefers to just stay in the driver role at the keyboard and have his partner be the navigator. However, he does not want his partner to know about his disability. This poses a real dilemma for the instructor. First, should the instructor agree to this request for Jack to always be driver and Radhu to always be navigator? That disadvantages Radhu, and takes away an educational opportunity for him, since he also needs practice being at the keyboard. An alternative might be to give Jack the instructions ahead of time so that he can look them over before class, and/or to let him view them online, where he might be able to use accommodation software that helps with the dyslexia. Regardless of the course of action, it is unclear how to provide any accommodation in such a situation without Radhu becoming aware that an accommodation is being provided to Jack.

Once again, there are many students without disabilities who may also have difficulty following the instructions when presented on paper. If all students were able to view the instructions online in advance then Jack would not stand out as having a disability. All students would have the option of reviewing instructions in advance. Alternatively, utilizing a read-aloud program could help many in the class. This is a feature that is available on any document, and a student could easily use a cell phone or tablet with headphones and have it be seen as socially acceptable. Confidentiality about the ODS accommodations is essential, yet when all students know that there are multiple means of accessing the material, it does not stand out as being related to a disability. It just seems to be a natural course of action.

With regard to the student's request to only be in the driver role, that is certainly an example of a request that can be denied. These two roles require the students to develop specific skills. Many students prefer to work alone and may even request working alone. In each case, the professor must determine whether working cooperatively is key to the instructional design and/or a critical skill within the particular field. For instance, preservice teachers must learn to work cooperatively in order to be effective in a school setting. This is also a 21st-century skill that is important for people within the workforce. University settings can provide excellent opportunities to develop these skills.

Noise Levels

Aditya teaches a large active learning class in a large active learning classroom. She uses a team-based learning approach, online polling/quiz platforms, and a variety of other active learning activities. She regularly has students get up and move around the room. The teams are assigned at the beginning of the semester and have lots of opportunities for collaborative, peer learning. All in all, this creates a climate that Aditya is very proud of—the classroom is lively, and the students are highly engaged throughout the class. She gets rave reviews from her students saying that the class is fun and that it is a great learning environment. Unfortunately, at the end of last semester, Aditya received feedback in an anonymous survey from a student who said he wished he had not taken her class because he has ADHD and auditory processing issues. He said that he consistently found it really hard to focus and concentrate because of the high levels of noise that are part of the classroom environment. Now Aditya feels awful that this student had such a bad experience. At the same time, she is frustrated that he did not come to her earlier in the semester when she might have been able to do something about it. Even so, she is not sure what she would have done about it if she had known.

Not all students are going to enjoy being in an active learning classroom. For some it takes some reflection after the fact to realize how much the format promoted deeper learning. Instructors can also take some steps to make their class activities more accessible and less stressful for all students. For example, online polling questions can be ungraded or based on participation, rather than accuracy, and students should be given adequate time to answer them (Cooper, Downing, & Brownell, 2018). Activities can be posted online in advance so that students have time to prepare before class. Nevertheless, there will always be students for whom this is not the best choice of class format. To avoid a mismatch in learning styles, universities could flag courses that are active learning classes or that use an FFAL approach. If that is not possible, it is important to explain how the active learning or FFAL class will function and provide examples of activities and expectations at the beginning of the course. That provides students with the opportunity to transfer to a different class. Midsemester surveys can be useful for determining how students feel they are managing in the setting. This is a good time to meet with students for whom the setting is not working and try to develop a plan to improve the situation. Even so, students may not realize that this style does not fit their needs until it is too late. Students need to make these decisions for themselves and be responsible for their learning. It is never appropriate to tell a student with a disability that the class would not be appropriate for them. That would be a violation of the ADA.

Social Interaction Issues

Students in an electronics lab have to work together in class each week to complete active learning lab activities that count toward the students' final grades. One of the students in the class, Aaron, exhibits a lot of social awkwardness, but he has not registered with disability services. He approaches Professor Atkins and asks if he can work alone instead of with a partner. He is very insistent that he can only work alone. Professor Atkins feels really strongly that the students need to talk with one another as they do the work so that they can practice communication in the discipline and so that they can hear other perspectives on the activity. Plus, each lab is a lot of work and would be hard for a student to complete on his/ or her own. He really does not want to let Aaron work alone, but he does see that Aaron really struggles with social interaction. He guesses that Aaron is probably somewhere on the autism spectrum. He eventually decides to let Aaron work alone, but he asks him to work next to another pair and instructs him to ask the pair of students next to him questions if he runs into any issues. Professor Atkins is also concerned that this sets a bad precedent and that other students are going to also ask to work alone.

There are many students who exhibit social phobias. Whether or not a student has registered with disability services, a professor could look at this as an opportunity to employ UDL. What are the barriers to students in the class? How can the professor offer multiple modes of expression in the course? If it is critical to develop an ease of expression using content-specific language, perhaps a PowerPoint with voice-over or an audio presentation could be used as a means of presenting the lab results. This is also an opportunity to speak to the student about possible scaffolding that could be used as a means of building the student's ability to interact with peers. This would be a case where the professor would have to determine what the course objectives are and whether the student was unable to access course objectives because of this inability to work with others. Also, the professor could determine how much additional scaffolding and training would be required for the student to develop an ease of working with others. There is a lot to be considered, and each situation may be very different. The likelihood of everyone wanting to work alone is small; sometimes one has to be willing to just take a chance. As mentioned in the previous vignette with Jack, each case is individual, and all factors must be considered.

The vignettes and suggestions in this chapter are suggestive only. If nothing else, perhaps they have provided the reader with a new lens for addressing access in a university-level course. Each situation that presents itself will be unique. The best way to approach access is to be open-minded and creative, and to ask for help when faced with a challenge. The ODS in any university is designed to serve as a resource for faculty as much as it is meant to provide services for students. Most offer training, tutorials, and consultation for faculty. This is especially helpful when it comes to learning about assistive technology, various accommodations, and methods for making documents accessible.

References

Center for Applied Special Technology (CAST). (2018). *Universal Design for Learning guidelines, version 2.2* [graphic organizer]. Wakefield, MA: Author. Retrieved from http://udlguidelines.castorg/

Cooper, K. M., Downing, V. R., & Brownell, S. E. (2018). The influence of active learning practices on student anxiety in large-enrollment college science classrooms. *International Journal of STEM Education, 5,* 23. doi: 10.1186/s40594-018-0123-6

Edyburn, D. L. (2010). Would you recognize Universal Design for Learning if you saw it? Ten propositions for new directions for the second decade of UDL. *Learning Disability Quarterly, 33,* 33–41. doi: 10.1177/073194871003300103

Giangreco, M. F. (2002). *Absurdities and realities of special education: The best of ants . . . , flying . . . , and logs . . .* (full color ed.). Thousand Oaks, CA: Corwin.

Hall, T. E., Meyer, A., & Rose, D. H. (2012). An introduction to Universal Design for Learning. In T. E. Hall, A. Meyer, & D. H. Rose (Eds.), *Universal Design for Learning in the classroom* (pp. 1–8). New York, NY: The Guilford Press.

Horowitz, S. H., Rawe, J., & Whittaker, M. C. (2017). *The state of learning disabilities: Understanding the 1 in 5.* New York, NY: National Center for Learning Disabilities.

The IRIS Center. (2009). *Universal Design for Learning: Creating a learning environment that challenges and engages all students.* Retrieved from https://iris.peabody.vanderbilt.edu/udl/

CHAPTER 7

A Learning Analytics Approach to Assessing Student Risk in Active Learning

MOHSEN DORODCHI, MOHAMMAD J. MAHZOON,
MARY LOU MAHER, AND AILEEN BENEDICT

Introduction

Learning analytics is an emerging discipline within data science. It is analytics that is concerned with developing methods for exploring the unique and increasingly large-scale datasets collected from educational settings, including the collection, analysis, and visualization of such educational data. The goal of the analyses and visualizations is to understand and improve students' learning and their learning environments. These methods are developed and applied in the same way as general data analytics, including exploiting statistical and machine learning for prediction, clustering, outlier detection, knowledge discovery with models, text mining, knowledge tracing, relationship mining, etc. to search for unobserved patterns and underlying information in learning processes (Agudo-Peregrina, Iglesias-Pradas, Conde-Gonzáles, & Hernandez-García, 2014).

Learning analytics of a course includes the gathering and analysis of data about a course and its students with the goal of improving its learning environment. The tracking of a student's progress and potential factors for success and failure can be valuable for the evaluation of the course. Coursework could then be redesigned by exploring these factors and learning more about student patterns, such as examining how student attitude and motivation can affect their success. These insights could then help create a better learning environment for the students over time. By using computer science techniques and creating visualizations for these factors, we are able to discover and understand patterns more easily, something that could be much more difficult to accomplish by simply looking at the raw data itself.

Learning analytics has been used in many situations. For example, Cherenkova, Zingaro, and Petersen (2014) explored which student difficulties arise within beginning computer science courses by mining data from CodeLab, a "web-based interactive programming problem system," finding that conditions and loops are the main challenges for students. They also encourage the use of large data from many institutions to lead to greater insight. Agudo-Peregrina et al. (2014) have applied learning analytics, specifically bivariate correlation analysis, to find the correlation between interactions (i.e., student-to-student interactions within the learning management system [LMS], student interactions with LMS content, and student interactions with the professor) and student performance. In another study, learning analytics was used to identify significant behavioral indicators of learning. Results showed that students' regular study, times of assignment submission, number of login sessions, and proof of reading course information were all significant factors in predicting course achievement (You, 2016).

Agudo-Peregrina et al. (2014) extracted different data from the LMS, such as student-to-student interaction inside the LMS, student interactions with LMS and content of the LMS, and student interactions with the professor within the LMS. Furthermore; they applied statistical methods, such as bivariate correlation analysis, to find the correlation between such interactions and student performance for an online as well as a face-to-face class. The results showed some correlation from mid-to-strong for the online class; however, for the face-to-face class, they found a no-to-weak correlation. The differences between the course structures and LMS structures are not very clear.

Learning Analytics for Student Risk Analysis

Research is drawn from various areas that view analytics in different perspectives or dimensions. Gašević, Dawson, and Siemens (2015) identified three common dimensions in learning analytics research: design, theory, and data science. For example, action research (McNiff & Whitehead, 2011) and personalized adaptive learning best fit into design or theory categories because their research focuses on improving teaching practice. However, our research contributes to learning analytics from a data science perspective and uses research in theory and design dimensions to make sense of data.

From the data science perspective, we focus on the issue of predicting student success/risk using analytical methods. Research in student risk analytics helps instructors keep track of student performance, and given the prediction results, policymakers can plan for improving retention by helping at-risk students.

Depending on the goal of the research, student risk analytics employs one of two general ways to define success and risk. The first method is to consider a student's final grade. For example, a student with an acceptable final grade for a course (usually C and above) is deemed successful in the course while others are considered at-risk. Other studies use course completion rather than the final grade to determine success. This definition of success is often best used when analytics is done at a micro level by looking at individual key courses and focusing on student success in those courses. Analytics in this area contributes to better student performances by identifying issues that students may have while taking courses and by providing insights to create interventions to help fix those issues. The second method is to look at student graduation. For example, a student graduating "on-time" is successful, while one who does not is at-risk (of dropping out). This definition of success and risk can be useful for academic leaders and executives who need to check the health of the education system from the macro level. Analytics in this domain analyzes student behaviors to identify issues, such as flaws in curriculum design.

Regardless of how success and risk are defined, research in student risk analytics needs to be confirmed with some data source, such as the LMS, to obtain granular and meaningful data from students. For example, Macfadyen and Dawson (2010) used Blackboard Vista LMS to extract 15 features correlating with students' final grades. These features include the total number of discussion messages posted, mail messages sent, and assessments completed. Macfadyen and Dawson (2010) used logistic regression to classify students as successful or at-risk with 81% accuracy. As another example, Wolff, Zdrahal, Nikolov, and Pantucek (2013) used click behaviors in the virtual learning environments as the data source to identify students at-risk using a decision tree model. Moreover, Jayaprakash, Moody, Lauría, Regan, and Baron (2014) combined the log data from student interactions within Sakai Learning Management System with student demographics, aptitude data, course grades, course-related data, and partial contributions to students' final grades such as individual assignment grades.

In terms of the models used in student risk analytics, we refer to surveys done by Romero and Ventura (2007) and Romero, Ventura, and García (2008) showing different approaches taken in the learning community to discern student behavior using machine learning or statistical methods. Generally, the data mining approaches discussed in their surveys used statistics or machine learning techniques operating on a feature vector representation of each student having data such as demographic information, course grades, and LMS logs. Several others, such as Mohamad and Tasir (2013) and Peña-Ayala (2014), review approaches that used different analytics with similar feature sets for their vector representations.

When it comes to the analyses of student learning, the major question is what student-related features can be used to accurately analyze performance, such as study patterns, exhibited emotions, and temporal features. By analyzing these features, it is possible to extract crucial information, such as identifying at-risk students to improve the course or to intervene on their behalf. In a study of 350 college students, a learning analytics model was used to predict course achievement as measured by their activities inside a LMS (You, 2016). The study demonstrated that their pattern of study, late submissions, and whether they reviewed the materials was predictive of performance. In another study, students' emotional reactions were correlated with student performance on programming assignments (Lishinski, Yadav, & Enbody, 2017). This work influences our use of sentiment to identify risk.

In this chapter, we look at learning analytics methods, particularly the sequence analytics method, a temporal approach to analyzing data. In particular, we look into course-related data that can be extracted from the LMS and/or student reflections pointing directly or indirectly toward their learning in the classroom.

Learning Analytics Using Time

During the last decade, increasing research in the data mining and machine learning communities have produced many approaches to analyze time-related raw data to identify trends and unexpected behaviors over time. However, these approaches still have not been widely adapted for learning analytics, and state-of-the-art approaches in student success and risk analysis do not consider temporal aspects of data.

Molenaar (2014) argues that temporal aspects of student data deserve more attention, and temporal analysis yields a paradigm shift addressing new research questions in learning analytics. Similarly, previous work in computer-supported collaborative learning (CSCL) and self-regulated learning (SRL) emphasizes the importance of temporal features in student data (Kapur, 2011; Bannert, Reimann, & Sonnenberg, 2014).

There are potentials in time series analysis, data stream mining, and sequence pattern mining that can contribute to analyzing student data while preserving the temporal dependencies. However, for each of these approaches to be used with student data, there are potential obstacles as described below.

Time Series

Time series analysis aims to arrive at a mathematical or statistical model to describe a series of observations over time, and it has applications from the stock market to weather forecasting. Various methods have been proposed in time series analysis literature to solve prediction, classification, and regression problems. All of these models were built on the same assumptions that (a) the data are in a numerical format, and (b) a significant number of data samples are available. Neither of these assumptions is necessarily true for student data because it is highly heterogeneous, containing ordinal and categorical features in addition to numerical features. Even though some data items such as grades and other performance features can be converted to numerical data, many features such as reflection data and quiz answers cannot be represented in numbers while preserving meaning.

The data we have for each student are limited and uniquely different from that of other students. The data about a single student cannot be generalized to a format that reconciles it with the data on all students without significant information being lost. The amount of data available for each student is also unique and can vary widely. Additionally, time series analysis usually looks for recurring patterns or regularities within a time period. In contrast, student data are temporal but not periodic. Students' progress each week as they acquire knowledge and prepare for the next activity. While time series can still be applied to student data to identify periodic patterns for numerical features, our sequence data facilitate detecting trends and irregularities in sequences having heterogeneous and variable length data items.

Data Stream Mining

Data stream mining is a subdomain of data mining that presents methods to efficiently process continuous massive sequences of data items called streams. These methods can watch for "concept drift" (Widmer & Kubat, 1996) when the general statistical properties of the target prediction change. Methods in data stream mining adapt to the changes in the stream to produce better prediction for new instances of data. For example, Hulten, Spencer, and Domingos (2001) present a model to maintain and update a decision tree for concept-drifting data streams. The model is always up-to-date with the latest instances of the stream while discarding old concepts that were changed over time. Adapting data stream mining ideas to the student data analytics faces several challenges. In student data analytics, we are not dealing with massive continuous data streams. Student sequences have a clear starting point and a duration of several weeks, and therefore the streams are not massive and content is sparse. Furthermore, data stream algorithms do not keep track of changes in data since they discard the changed concepts to account for the newest ones. To interpret students' behavior and investigate what it means to be at risk, we need to capture changes in trends and identify unexpected patterns.

Sequence Pattern Mining

Another subdomain of data mining that works with sequences is sequence pattern mining used to identify frequent sets of items or patterns in data or strings (Agrawal, Imielinski, & Swami, 1993). This domain is generally used for identifying behavior patterns of consumers in the business domain. One such approach detects frequent items bought together from a dataset of all transactions. For example, Padmanabhan and Tuzhilin (1999) propose an interestingness measure to filter all frequent items to obtain interesting items that happen to be unexpected transactions, contradicting beliefs.

We can make an analogy to transfer ideas from sequence pattern mining to student sequence data mining. If we treat each student sequence as a transaction, then the task becomes frequent events happening together in student sequences. However, there are certain assumptions in sequence pattern mining that make it hard to continue the analogy further. For instance, in sequence pattern mining, it is assumed that we know beforehand about all potential items in transactions (i.e., all items being sold in a store). This assumption holds in business and marketing because the number of items is finite and known. However, student data sequences have a wide range of possibilities such as quizzes taken, assignment grades, forum participation, and other academic and nonacademic activities. It is a daunting task to generate all potential events for a student sequence.

Sequence Data Model

We define a student sequence as data items that are grouped into temporally ordered structures called "nodes." For example, a node may represent a semester and may contain a student's data items related to that semester: courses taken, grades received, extracurricular activities, and so on. This grouping gives context to the data items and allows for analysis at the level of both data items and nodes.

Figure 7.1 illustrates the structure of the sequence data model in which information about a student is grouped by semester. The sequence starts with an initial node that captures attributes outside of the node-based temporal sequence, such as demographics and prior academic achievement. A node is then included for each semester the student is enrolled and finishes with an outcome node. The properties that characterize a sequence data model include time dependency, contextualization, segmentation, and storytelling.

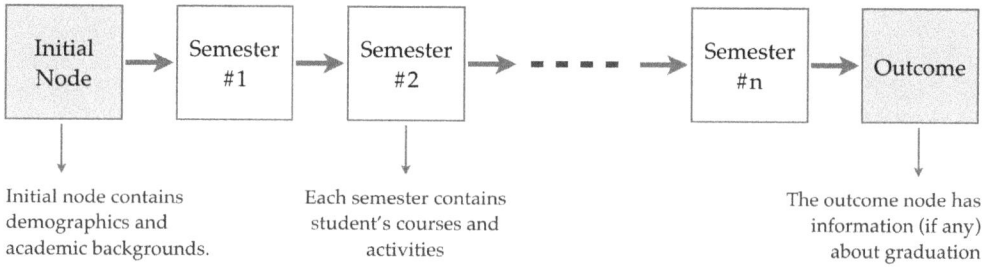

Figure 7.1. The structure of the sequence data model in which information about a student is grouped by semester.

Time Dependency. The sequence data model explicitly represents that the later data items can depend on former data items. This allows the explicit representation of temporal dependencies, such as the correlation between final grade and student assignment grades. In comparison, a vector representation assumes that data points are independent of each other, and features (independent variables) do not have a correlation with each other.

Contextualization. The grouping of data items into nodes gives context to salient features that are selected for analysis. For example, if each node groups different information throughout the course mostly coming from the LMS for a given week within the semester, then data can be identified as salient features within each node, such as grades of the activities, while other features, such as student activities, are the context of the salient feature.

Segmentation. The nodes in a sequence allow us to represent the data in segments. Different choices for the beginning and end of each node define a principle for a window of time and allow the data model to capture a different granularity for the segments, for example, semesters versus weeks. Access to LMS data makes finer-grained node segmentation possible, which may lead to more timely assessments of academic risk.

Storytelling. A sequence of information expresses a student's learning events throughout a particular course. This property enables us to view each node as a collection of student data from course events happening during a particular week in a semester. Moreover, there is an opportunity to infer a narrative from the nodes to tell a story about a specific or typical student in order to hypothesize about success or risk.

Applying Learning Analytics to a Course

To verify the effectiveness of our active learning course, learning analytics methods are applied to a course as explained in the following sections (Dorodchi et al., 2018).

Data Collection

The data were collected from the LMS from 91 university students enrolled in the Introduction to Computer Science (CS1) course in the spring semester of 2017. The course demographics consisted of 21.9% female students and 72.5% computer science (CS) majors. The data have three main categories per student:

- Student background information
- Student performance scores
- Student reflections and self-assessments

Each of the above three categories includes specific attributes used in our algorithm as features. More specifically, student background includes attributes such as age group, gender, and major. Student performance scores are numerous as is typical in an active learning classroom in which students are submitting items for preparation, in-class and in-lab activities, and assignments outside the classroom. In the example in this chapter, we include grades for all quizzes (18 total), pre- and postlabs (16), long assignments (four), lecture tests (four total, including three during the semester and one final), lab tests (four), lab/lecture activities (37), and extra credit activities (four) for a total of 87 different columns per student. Reflections are informal surveys students take regularly after class (both labs and lectures) activities, assignments, quizzes, and tests for a total of 23 reflections per student. Students reflected on their learning of different course topics, as well as on the learning processes, group activities, or the tests and assignments. Some of the reflections, therefore, were mandatory as a part of the activity while others were optional extra credit activities. We ended up with a heterogeneous dataset for different reasons: (a) we have both numerical and textual data; (b) data items' frequency of occurrences are different such as weekly, biweekly, or monthly; and (c) the data included objective and subjective measures, as well as self-assessment or group assessment by students.

All the 110 different grades and quantified reflections are spread over our dataset, based on the date of the activity, which highlights their strong temporal dependencies with each other. Therefore, these data are a good candidate for using temporal data analysis models. It should be emphasized that the temporal dependency of the data items comes from the fact that students must do different types of activities in the lab and lecture as explained while providing reflections over time. The activities are all dependent on and build on each other. In addition, students were reflecting on their learning and outcomes of activities that suggest the strong dependency as shown in Figure 7.2.

In other words, it is possible that a student who received low grades for the first few weeks of the course might change their study pattern to make up for the low performance. Consequently, we have dependencies in activities themselves as well as dependencies in the time between reflections and activities.

Student Data Model

Our goal was to discover the trends of students' activities throughout the semester, predict the student outcome (success or fail), and discover the impact of reflections on the prediction. To do so, we built a temporal data model, called the "student sequence model" (Mahzoon, Maher, Eltayeby, Dou, & Grace, 2018). In this model, we put all the data for one week into one node as shown in Figure 7.2. Next, we connected the nodes to form a sequence. The sequence was then

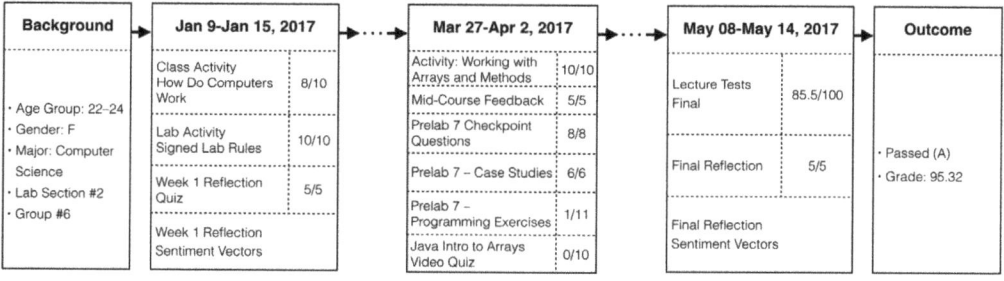

Figure 7.2.

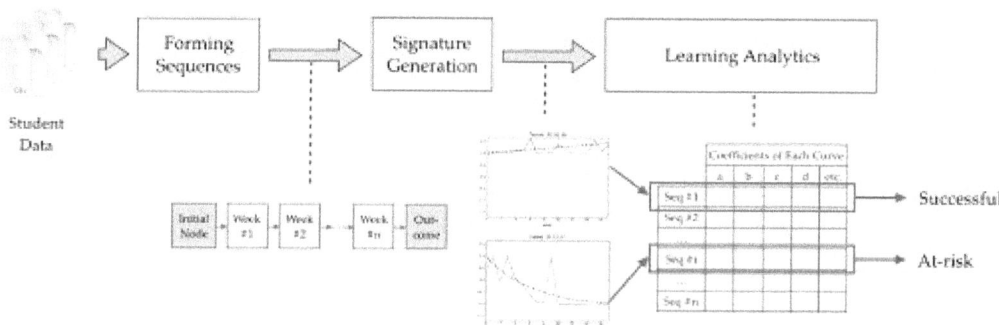

Figure 7.3.

passed to a signature generation submodule followed by the learning analytics submodule for final determination, as shown in Figure 7.3.

Analysis: Sequence Model versus Feature Vector Model

While the student sequence model uses nodes to sort and group data items temporally, a more common method uses feature vectors to represent data items. Feature vector representation in knowledge discovery and data mining constructs features vectors for data items in which each data item is represented by one vector with a fixed set of features or dimensions. For example, in student data, each data item could contain a vector of one student's performance in a certain course or program. The features of the vector could then include the student's background information (e.g., demographics and course information) and the student's performance (e.g., grades, assignments, and activities).

Feature vector representation makes strict assumptions about data dependencies that enable the use of conventional machine learning tools. This representation assumes that vectors are independent of each other and features are independent of other features. These independency assumptions, as well as the fixed length of the vectors (i.e., the number of features), make the application of machine learning tools widely available.

However, having that strict assumption for data dependencies in vector representations ignores the temporal correlations in student data—something we wanted to emphasize. A typical example of such temporal correlation is the correlation between the final grade and different types of grades (e.g., class activities, lecture tests, assignments) over time for the same course. The order in which these grades occur provides important information for predicting success or risk. However, that order is discarded in feature vector representation due to its inability to represent temporal correlations.

Structure of the Sequence Model

Our sequence model consists of 19 nodes: one node at the beginning of the semester for student background data, 17 intermediary weekly nodes that include grades and reflection responses, and one outcome node containing the overall course grade. There are four background features in the first node. The 110 grade scores and maximum of 23 reflection responses (depending on the individual student) are then spread out over the intermediary weekly nodes. We converted reflective surveys from text to numbers using the commercial linguistic sentiment analytics tool called Linguistic Inquiry and Word Count, or LIWC (Tausczik & Pennebaker, 2010). LIWC generates 93 sentiment features as numbers for every input text. Many of these features were highly correlated with each other. For this reason, we only chose 18 sentiment features with the least correlation to each other. This also improves computational efficiency. Therefore, each reflective survey's text was converted to a vector of 18 sentiment features.

Analysis

One of the benefits of our sequence data model and analytics is its capability to repeat the analysis with different salient features in the data model to identify the predictive impact of each data category. Based on the model by Mahzoon et al. (2018), salient features are involved in the analytics while contextual features are used for interpretability after the analysis. Our three main salient features were tests, activities, and reflections. We then experimented with these features both individually and together to evaluate their relative predictive impact to help us understand the effectiveness and importance of each feature as predictors of success. For each salient feature, we ran sequence analytics to classify students at risk of obtaining at-risk grades of D, F, or W in the course. Figure 7.4 shows two examples of individual student signatures that were generated for successful grades of A, B, or C and at-risk (DFW) students.

Figure 7.5 shows the averages of all the student signatures in the class grouped by final grade category.

Figure 7.6 shows the averages grouped by successful (ABC) or at-risk (DFW). In all three figures, the data include tests, activities, and reflections used to generate the signatures.

The classification is performed in two phases: training and validation. In the training phase of classification, we use the 10-fold cross-validation method (Kohavi, 1995) to split our data into training and validation sets. After training, the system output will be validated by repeating the validation set 10 different times. The performance measures of the analytics were then averaged over the 10-fold cross-validation.

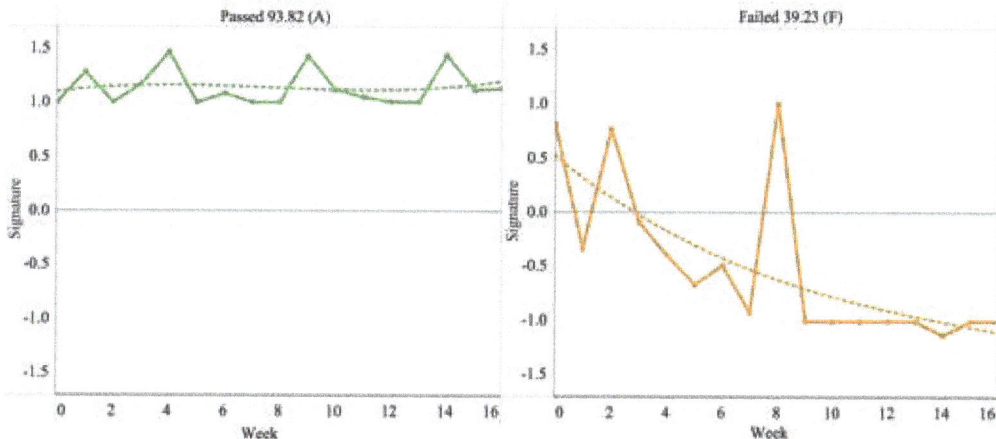

Figure 7.4. Two examples of individual student signatures that were generated for successful grades of A, B, or C and at-risk (DFW) students.

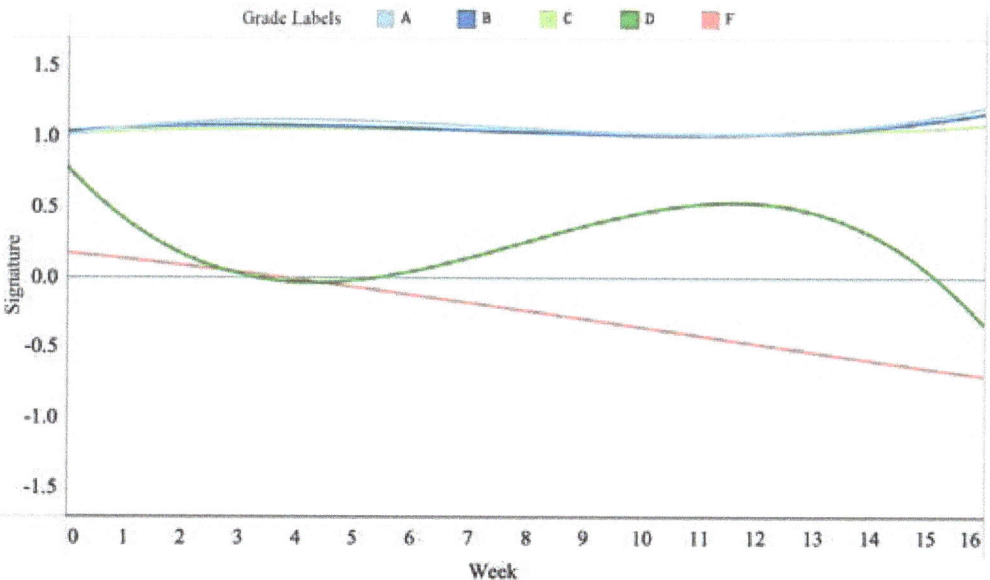

Figure 7.5. The averages of all the student signatures in the class grouped by final grade category.

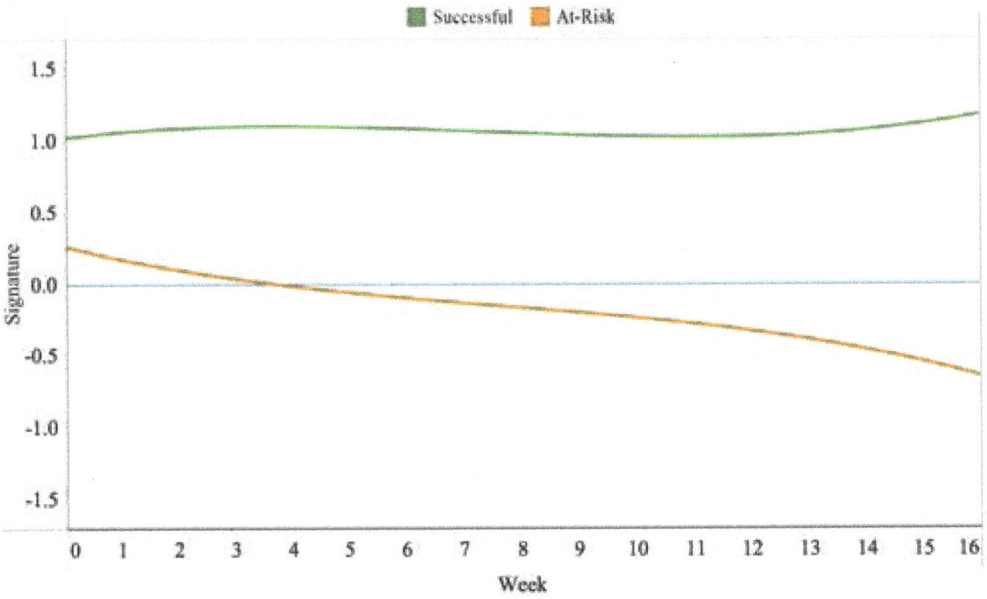

Figure 7.6. The averages grouped by successful (ABC) or at-risk (DFW).

We evaluated the sequence model incrementally at multiple points in time to assess how the temporal model's accuracy changes over time. Figure 7.7 reports the model's accuracy for the following three salient features: tests, activities, and reflections.

These features were plotted over time to show how the accuracy improved as more data were included. In this figure, the horizontal axis shows the number of weekly nodes included in the model, and the vertical axis shows the accuracy of the model as a percentage. For example, from Figure 7.7 we can conclude that if we only use one week of the data (e.g., tests, activities, or reflections), we are able to accurately classify the risk status of 70% of students. This accuracy increases as we include more nodes (i.e., more weeks into the semester) in the sequence model. However, the trend of increasing accuracy is not the same for different salient features. For instance, having tests as the only salient feature will improve accuracy but only up to the four-week point in the semester; on the other hand, having activities as the only salient feature produces models with higher accuracies in comparison with tests after five weeks of activities. Reflections as the salient feature perform even better than activities or tests and can predict at-risk students with 90% accuracy even after having only five weeks of reflections. In all cases, the additional benefit for including more information diminishes at the halfway point of the course. It is important to try to maximize earlier prediction rather than overall accuracy after the middle of the semester. At this early point, there are still opportunities to intervene on behalf of the student. Some examples of interventions include: helping the student understand patterns of the active learning class and how to prepare, working with other students, and learning materials by practicing. It is worth noting that the

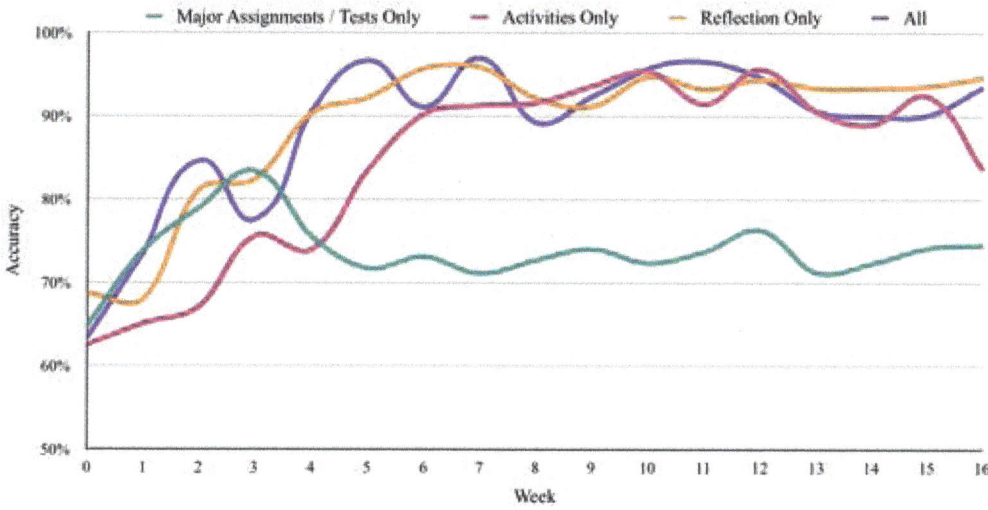

Figure 7.7. The model's accuracy for the following three salient features: tests, activities, and reflections.

closest individual salient feature compared to including all features together in Figure 7.7 is a reflection-only plot.

Based on our results, we observed that including reflections as a feature improves the accuracy of our risk classification model. This shows that including student reflection in a course proves to be useful, as we can use them in a predictive model to improve both accuracy and time-to-classify student success and risk. Having an improved time-to-classify is important, as interventions need to be made early enough to help the at-risk students adjust and make improvements toward success. Thus, using student reflections provides additional motivation for instructors as they not only improve our risk classification model but can serve as an effective learning tool for students.

Our findings are encouraging for integrating reflections into the curriculum. Previous research has investigated reflections as a tool for learning and has cited many different potential benefits, such as the development of metacognitive skills (Turns, Sattler, Yasuhara, Borgford-Parnell, & Atman, 2014). What we have shown in this work is that, in addition to previously explored benefits affecting students, there are also benefits for instructors and administrators. For example, they will have the ability to predict the students who may be at-risk early on. With that knowledge, instructors can intervene to aid the at-risk students. Furthermore, it is crucial that these predictions be accurately made early on so that it is not too late for the student to make improvements when those interventions are implemented.

Although our results suggest that reflections were predictive of student success on their own, they were most effective when used with traditional features such as tests, activities, and assignments. While most features performed well after the first six weeks of the course, reflections served as the earliest predictors of success for students. Hence, it also suggests that infusing student reflective practices between activities and throughout the course is effective as an early predictor of success. Reflection in CS has the ability to help students think more deeply about the course material and make broader connections to other courses and aspects of computing. Our work has shown that in addition to these benefits, there are also administrative benefits that help instructors and teaching staff identify at-risk students sooner and more accurately. Our results provide another compelling reason to integrate reflections into engineering and CS courses.

Conclusions

Learning analytics provides a broad range of tools to analyze and predict student progress as a whole and individually. This provides an opportunity for the course instructors to detect the at-risk students in the early weeks of the semester and to intervene in different forms before it is too late. Accuracy of learning analytics algorithms significantly increases by infusing more feedback points from students. This is in line with the notion of activity-based active learning that provides students with many different forms of activities throughout a week. By analyzing such data, we are able to predict with some level of accuracy the students who are at-risk of failing the course.

Acknowledgments

This work is supported by NSF-1820862: EAGER: An Interactive Learning Analytics Framework Based on a Student Sequence Model for Understanding Students, Retention, and Time to Graduation.

References

Agrawal, R., Imielinski, T., & Swami, A. (1993). Database mining: A performance perspective. IEEE transactions on knowledge and data engineering, 5(6), 914-925. http://dx.doi.org/ 10.1109 /69.250074

Agudo-Peregrina, A., Iglesias-Pradas, S., Conde-Gonzáles, M. A., & Hernandez-García, Á. (2014). Can we predict success from log data in VLEs? Classification of interactions for learning analytics and their relation with performance in VLE-supported F2F and online learning. *Computers in Human Behavior, 31*, 542–550. https://doi.org/10.1016/j.chb.2013.05.031

Bannert, M., Reimann, P., & Sonnenberg, C. (2014). Process mining techniques for analysing patterns and strategies in students' self-regulated learning. *Metacognition and Learning, 9*(2), 161–185. http://dx.doi.org/10.1007/s11409-013-9107-6

Cherenkova, Y., Zingaro, D., & Petersen, A. (2014). Identifying challenging CS1 concepts in a large problem dataset. *Proceedings of the 45th ACM Technical Symposium on Computer Science Education, 14*, 695–700. https://doi.org/10.1145/2538862.2538966

Dorodchi, M., Benedict, A., Desai, D., Mahzoon, M. J., MacNeil, S., & Dehbozorgi, N. (2018). Design and implementation of an activity-based introductory computer science course (CS1) with periodic reflections validated by learning analytics. *Proceedings of Frontiers in Education, 1,* 1–8. https://dx.doi.org/10.1109/FIE.2018.8659196

Gašević, D., Dawson, S., & Siemens, G. (2015). Let's not forget: Learning analytics are about learning. *TechTrends, 59*(1), 64–71. http://dx.doi.org/10.1007/s11528-014-0822-x

Hulten, G., Spencer, L., & Domingos, P. (2001). Mining time-changing data streams. *Proceedings of the Seventh ACM SIGKDD International Conference on Knowledge Discovery and Data Mining,* 97–106. https://doi.org/10.1145/502512.502529

Jayaprakash, S. M., Moody, E. W., Lauría, E. J. M., Regan, J. R., & Baron, J. D. (2014). Early alert of academically at-risk students: An open source analytics initiative. *Journal of Learning Analytics, 1*(1), 6–47.

Kapur, M. (2011). Temporality matters: Advancing a method for analyzing problem-solving processes in a computer-supported collaborative environment. *International Journal of Computer-Supported Collaborative Learning, 6,* 39–56. https://dx.doi.org/10.1007/s11412-011-9109-9

Kohavi, R. (1995). A study of cross-validation and bootstrap for accuracy estimation and model selection. *Proceedings of International Joint Conference on Artificial Intelligence, 14,* 1137–1145.

Lishinski, A., Yadav, A., & Enbody, R. (2017). Students' emotional reactions to programming projects in introduction to programming: Measurement approach and influence on learning outcomes. *Proceedings of the 2017 ACM Conference on International Computing Education Research, 17,* 30–38. https://dx.doi.org/10.1145/3105726.3106187

Macfadyen, L. P., & Dawson, S. (2010). Mining LMS data to develop an "early warning system" for educators: A proof of concept. *Computers & Education, 54,* 588–599.

Mahzoon, M. J., Maher, M. L., Eltayeby, O., Dou, W., & Grace, K. (2018). A sequence data model for analyzing temporal patterns of student data. *Journal of Learning Analytics, 5*(1), 55–74. https://doi.org/10.18608/jla.2018.51.5

McNiff, J., & Whitehead, J. (2011). *All you need to know about action research* (2nd ed.). London, England: Sage Publications.

Mohamad, S. K., & Tasir, Z. (2013). Educational data mining: A review. *Proceedings of Procedia—Social and Behavioral Sciences, the 9th International Conference on Cognitive Science, 97,* 320–324. http://dx.doi.org/10.1016/j.sbspro.2013.10.240

Molenaar, I. (2014). Advances in temporal analysis in learning and instruction. *Frontline Learning Research, 2*(4), 15–24. https://doi.org/10.14786/flr.v2i4.118

Padmanabhan, B., & Tuzhilin, A. (1999). Unexpectedness as a measure of interestingness in knowledge discovery. *Decision Support System, 27*(3), 303–318. http://doi.org/10.1016/S0167-9236(99)00053-6

Peña-Ayala, A. (2014). Educational data mining: A survey and a data mining-based analysis of recent works. *Expert Systems with Applications, 41,* 1432–1462. http://dx.doi.org/10.1016/j.eswa.2013.08.042

Romero, C., & Ventura, S. (2007). Educational data mining: A survey from 1995 to 2005. *Expert Systems with Applications, 33,* 135–146. http://dx.doi.org/10.1016/j.eswa.2006.04.005

Romero, C., Ventura, S., & Garcia, E. (2008). Data mining in course management systems: Moodle case study and tutorial. *Computers & Education, 51,* 368–384. https://doi.org/10.1016/j.compedu.2007.05.016

Tausczik, Y. R., & Pennebaker, J. W. (2010). The psychological meaning of words: LIWC and computerized text analysis methods. *Journal of Language and Social Psychology, 29,* 24–54. https://doi.org/10.1177/0261927X09351676

Turns, J. A., Sattler, B., Yasuhara, K., Borgford-Parnell, J. L., & Atman, C. J. (2014, June). *Integrating reflection into engineering education. Proceedings Presented at ASEE Annual Conference & Exposition, Indianapolis, Indiana.* Retrieved from https://peer.asee.org/20668

Widmer, G., & Kubat, M. (1996). Learning in the presence of concept drift and hidden contexts. *Machine Learning, 23*, 69–101. https://dx.doi.org/10.1007/BF00116900

Wolff, A., Zdrahal, Z., Nikolov, A., & Pantucek, M. (2013). Improving retention: Predicting at-risk students by analysing clicking behaviour in a virtual learning environment. *Proceedings of the Third International Conference on Learning Analytics and Knowledge, Leuven, Belgium,* 145–149. http://dx.doi.org/10.1145/2460296.2460324

You, J. W. (2016). Identifying significant indicators using LMS data to predict course achievement in online learning. *The Internet and Higher Education, 29*, 23–30. https://doi.org/10.1016/j.iheduc.2015.11.003

CHAPTER 8

A Model for Mentoring Faculty
and Teaching Assistants in Active Learning

CELINE LATULIPE AND STEPHEN MACNEIL

Moving to an active learning mode of teaching requires a fair amount of change across a variety of dimensions. There is a mental mindset adjustment, changes to class structure, prep work to develop, new tools to learn, and new ways of interacting with teaching assistants (TAs), who can range from sophomore undergraduates to graduate students. Because this type of teaching can be so different, we propose that a collaborative/ interactive model at multiple levels is the best way to bring faculty and TAs on board for a particular course. For inexperienced instructors, a team-teaching model is employed so that more senior teaching faculty can help scaffold the teaching experience for less experienced faculty members. By sharing the workload, new classes can be created quickly to address emerging needs within the department. At the same time, pedagogies, best practices, and important tacit knowledge can be shared among instructors, a way to apply active learning to the act of education itself.

TAs face the same challenges as they transition into teaching roles. Departments and university systems often do not provide explicit training for new TAs. There is an assumption that new TAs will shift effortlessly from their current role as students to being able to teach, grade, and interact with students effectively. This puts a lot of pressure on new TAs and can reduce their potential effectiveness. Often, through informal mentorship, TAs learn how to perform their roles and then improve over time as they gain experience. By designing the graduate and undergraduate teaching team with formal mentorship, it is possible to ensure a smoother transition for new TAs, reduce the load on the instructor to personally mentor each new student, and provide more senior TAs with valuable mentorship experience.

Both formal and informal mentorship offer an important scaffold to help new teaching team members develop their skills and transition into their new roles. By adopting these two models of mentorship, the stepping stone model (Roberts, Kassianidou, & Irani, 2002) and team teaching, we are able to create a better teaching environment. These models have helped us to reduce the workload, provide opportunities for learning and skill development, and ensure that tacit knowledge is preserved across multiple semesters for all members of the teaching team.

The work described in this chapter represents practices developed in fully flipped active learning (FFAL) courses in the College of Computing and Informatics (CCI) at UNC Charlotte. FFAL is a teaching approach in which students learn the material out of class and then practice and apply the material during class time. This practice is contrasted by partially flipped active learning, where lecture and activities are intertwined, and students learn some material out of class. Examples of the use of the mentoring model are largely drawn from the Data Structures and Algorithms course discussed in a previous chapter as well as in prior published research (Latulipe, MacNeil, & Thompson, 2018). In that class, we evolved a self-sustaining TA mentoring cycle over time that has allowed for a rich and personal learning experience for students, even in large classrooms. All TAs, from sophomore undergraduates to graduate students, learn from each other and stay with the class sometimes up to five semesters. The continuous cycle of new undergrad TAs coming in and learning from the more senior TAs helps with continuity. The faculty member, Dr. Latulipe, strives to empower all of the TAs with responsibility over various aspects of the course and welcomes ideas for course improvement from all involved. The TAs get a much richer experience than if they were just grading assignments, and they experience a cycle of being mentored by more senior TAs and then mentoring the junior TAs coming in.

A Case for Mentorship

Developing a professional identity is challenging across majors and disciplines. Students' reasons for choosing to major in computer science (CS) and for staying in the program are complex; however, there is some evidence that their interactions with other students strongly affect these decisions (Bean, 2005). To help students feel more comfortable in their major, it is important for them develop their self-efficacy (Barker, McDowell, & Kalahar, 2009) and their identity as a computer scientist (Lewis, Yasuhara, & Anderson, 2011). Students with self-efficacy believe that they can accomplish their goals, and self-efficacy is related to the concept of growth mindset (Dweck, 2008) and students' ability to bounce back from failures. This resilience is an important predictor of academic persistence and the ability to do well in difficult programs, especially important in science, technology, engineering, and mathematics (STEM) fields like computing, where some students are significantly more prepared and have more prior experience than their peers (Latulipe et al., 2018). The other important aspect to consider is students' identity as a computing professional. Identities are socially constructed based on our interactions with others. Stereotype threat and intended or unintended microaggressions can serve to undermine this identity. Students may look around the classroom or at big technology companies and see a lack of diversity and internalize this as a message that they are not welcome in the field. Similarly, students may assume behaviors consistent with their gender to fit in with their peers. Finally, microaggressions are not uncommon in science classrooms. Many classes promote competition over collaboration based on the ways that students are graded or on the way interactions between students are designed (accidentally or otherwise). These classrooms can lead to "negative stereotypes about CS, such as it being competitive, singularly-focused, asocial, and primarily male" (Lewis, Anderson, & Yasuhara, 2016).

These challenges can be addressed through mentorship in the classroom. We propose using a combination of faculty and student mentors from our teaching team. If students have multiple sources of mentorship in the classroom, they are more likely to see someone like them on the teaching team (similar race, age, gender, interests, etc.). At the same time, students are more likely to see a progression of skills between themselves and the teaching faculty. Teaching faculty often teach the same class repeatedly; they have obtained a PhD, and they have decades or more of research experience in the field. Students do not see this progression when interacting with faculty members. Students may become discouraged and feel that they too will need to obtain a similar amount of experience to be successful. This can be overwhelming for students who are new to the field, but this level of experience is not required for all computing professionals. By providing multiple types of mentors (faculty, graduate TAs, and undergraduate TAs), students are more likely to see how developing skills in computing is a long and persistent process. Students can attribute setbacks to that aspect rather than to their perceived intellectual limitations. Finally, multiple levels of mentorship provide students with a balance of technical, emotional, and interpersonal support at multiple levels in the teaching team and even encourage students in the class to engage in informal mentorship with each other. This model is called the stepping stone model of mentorship.

Stepping Stone Model of Mentorship

The stepping stone model of mentorship was introduced by Roberts et al. (2002) who advocate for having different mentors for students at different levels within the university. For example, students can be mentored by faculty or by other students more senior in the department. They suggest that doing so helps students to look "not 20 years to the point at which they might themselves be a professor, but one year to the point at which they might become a section leader" (Roberts et al., 2002). While all students may not intend to become professors, they can see that expertise in computing is a continuum and that through persistent practice they can develop these skills over time. The stepping stone model helps students make short-term, achievable goals. The authors cite this model as being critically important for increasing the participation of women in computing. While we adopt this stepping stone model of mentorship, we also consider how mentoring can happen among the mentors themselves and not just between the mentors and the students. Finally, unlike the original stepping stone mentorship model, we implement this model in individual courses rather than throughout the curriculum and department. In Figure 8.1, we present our model for mentorship that is heavily influenced by the stepping stone model of mentorship. By adding in this aspect of intermentor mentorship, we find that our course runs more smoothly. TAs are exponentially engaged and proud of the work that they do, and they learn many more skills than they would otherwise. In this chapter, we describe this mentorship model and how we implemented it in one of our classes. We close with a brief evaluation to demonstrate its effectiveness as a classroom organization technique.

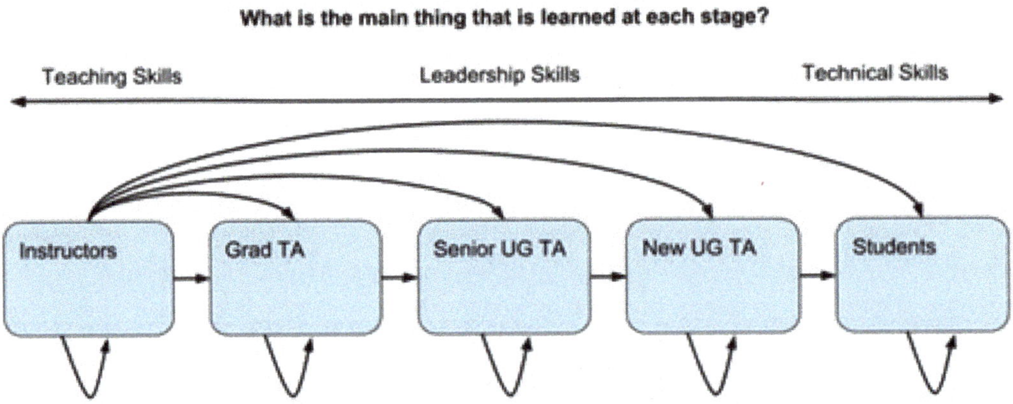

What is the main thing that is learned at each stage?

Teaching Skills   Leadership Skills   Technical Skills

| Instructors | Grad TA | Senior UG TA | New UG TA | Students |

Figure 8.1. A modified stepping stone model of mentoring. The arrows that loop back to the same cells represent the idea that students may mentor each other, and, if you have multiple senior undergraduate (UG) teaching assistants (TAs), they may also mentor and teach one another.

An important aspect of the stepping stone mentorship model is the idea that each individual is mentored by someone who is close to them in terms of the next step they would take in their personal or career progression. So, having a sophomore student mentored by a TA who is a junior or senior undergraduate helps the student not only learn the material but it also allows them to see how students behave and what they know how to do at the next level. A senior TA probably does not need to learn about the higher-level course management from the professor; that is likely more salient to the doctoral-level TA, who is potentially going to move to some other institution and be in charge of their own courses.

Faculty-to-Faculty Mentoring

Mentoring faculty about active learning teaching practices has been a major thrust of effort in the CCI. In this section we highlight two aspects of this: pair teaching and the role of the Center for Education Innovation in creating a supportive community of practice.

Pair Teaching

One of the practices that we have found very beneficial in our college is the use of pair teaching for newly flipped classes. We have three cases of classes that were previously taught in a traditional lecture format but have been completely restructured as FFAL classes. One of these classes is described in detail in Chapter 3: A Fully-Flipped Active Learning Course. The amount of work required to make this major transition is tremendous; typically, a summer is devoted to preparation of materials, creating a structure, and setting up the technology needed for the class. In all three cases, we had two faculty involved the first semester. Involving two faculty in the course transformation process helps split the workload. The two faculty involved also benefit from talking through the design process with each other, generating more ideas and solutions than one faculty member working alone.

A major benefit of this pair teaching approach allows a faculty member with expertise in flipping classes and teaching classes in the flipped style to share that expertise with another faculty member. While this may be seen as expensive in terms of teaching resources, the cost is only for one semester, and it has the effect of increasing the active learning teaching capacity within a department.

In our CCI, an FFAL version was created for the very first programming course, and two instructors (Associate Professor Latulipe and Senior Lecturer Long) were involved in that development and in teaching the initial offering. Both Latulipe and Long then worked to develop a fully flipped model of the subsequent programming class. Long continued to teach the second class as an FFAL class and then cotaught it with an associate professor to help her learn the FFAL approach. The associate professor has since gone on to create an FFAL version of the third programming course at the sophomore level. When developing and teaching it for the first semester, they worked with Associate Dean Perez-Quinones, who had no direct experience with the FFAL approach, but had domain knowledge having taught a similar programming course for many years. Having an associate dean involved also helped the college administration gain a better understanding of the challenges and benefits of active learning. Long continues to teach that class as an FFAL course.

Community of Practice

Our college has also developed a series of Summer Institute for Active Learning programs to help our faculty share how to teach computing courses this way. These summer institutes are run through the Center for Education Innovation within the CCI. This center and the summer workshops and pedagogy luncheons throughout the year have served to create a supportive community of practice in which faculty can mentor each other (Frevert et al., 2018; Maher et al., 2016). Indeed, we have applied the stepping stone model of mentorship to the way the Summer Institutes are run and have assigned faculty members who have previously participated in the workshops to be senior mentors.

Faculty-to-faculty mentoring within our college has helped our faculty learn about the process of flipping a course, about the tools used for supplying appropriate prep work to students and for conducting active learning in the classroom, and about how to structure teams and course work to scaffold student success. However, the mentoring also allows the more experienced FFAL faculty to share their philosophy about teaching and their attitude toward students. The FFAL faculty in our college have engaged in a practice of data-driven responsive teaching. Instead of throwing up our hands in frustration and saying things like: "These students coming in don't know anything! How can I be expected to teach them Z when they don't know X and they can't do Y," our faculty look at the backgrounds of students coming into the classes and then share that aggregate data with the class. They express an attitude that says: "You may not have had the same exposure to this material as someone sitting beside you, but that doesn't mean you are less capable of becoming a good software developer." We believe that this attitude and the exploration of the data around student backgrounds and preparations help our faculty.

All of this faculty mentorship has led to much more collaborative teaching in some of our higher-level core classes. For example, we now have three faculty members teaching three sections of our Networking and Operating Systems class, and all of them are teaching the class as FFAL, sharing resources and even having joint discussion forums for students across the sections. We also have two faculty members teaching sections of Software Engineering and sharing active learning resources and content. Similar arrangements are happening across some sections of our introductory programming courses. This collaborative teaching enhances the student experience because the faculty are able to do more active learning when the activities are jointly created and shared.

TA Mentorship Cycle

While mentorship among faculty can help spread active learning practices, the role of TAs in supporting active learning in classrooms cannot be overlooked. TAs can make a major difference in the student learning experience. In this section, we describe how we have created a cycle of mentoring across various levels of TA (graduate, senior undergraduate, junior undergraduate) experiences.

One of the issues with teaching at the college level is that faculty members might get assigned a new TA every semester and not think that they have any say in the matter. Such a high turnover rate leads faculty members to not consider how best to make use of TAs in their classes and so regard the TAs as simply graders. This means that the work experience for the TA is not engaging and, in fact, is mostly seen as unimportant drudgery. Thus, many TAs do not stay with a course longer than one semester and search for newer and better opportunities. By providing more enriching teaching experiences that allow them room for professional development, we can retain these TAs and ensure better continuity in the course from semester to semester. This continuity is important because a lot of tacit knowledge is hard to document (or is very time consuming to document), especially in courses that are flipped and have extensive active learning components.

TA Team Responsibilities

In the Data Structures class, the TA team typically consists of three to seven undergraduate hourly TAs, depending on the size of the class. Under the guidance of the professor, the TAs are responsible for different aspects of the course. These responsibilities may include testing in-class lab activities before class, reviewing test questions, checking students off as they complete labs, developing or testing the individual programming assignments, grading assignments, setting up assignments in the autograding system, running submitted programming assignments through the plagiarism detection system, answering questions on the class discussion forum, planning and conducting help sessions (especially around the time that assignments are due), and proctoring tests. A TA typically runs the podium laptop with the

Poll Everywhere quiz while the instructor moves around the classroom. The TAs have weekly meetings with the professor to keep the class on track, divide up grading, brainstorm class improvements, and deal with any issues that come up. Because each TA takes charge of a few of these aspects of the class, they feel some ownership in the success of the class as a whole, and that adds to the integrity of the classroom experience.

TAs in the two most recent semesters have developed their own infrastructure. They have set up a code version management repository for managing the testing and refinement of assignments. They have also set up Discord servers with different channels for faculty and TAs to conduct asynchronous discussion of assignments, labs, tests, etc. The Discord server helps manage tasks and facilitate communication, but it also serves as a platform for discussion of new ideas to improve the class. It has become a small online community, and the TAs and faculty end up supporting each other through this medium. At the end of one semester, one of the TAs announced to all on the Discord server that they were having a games day at their place and the other TAs were all invited. This demonstrates that the TA team can become a cohesive community.

Many classes in CCI use a discussion forum to encourage conversations that extend beyond the classroom. We use Piazza as our discussion forum software because it integrates with our learning management system that students use to submit assignments and obtain course material. While the professor and all the TAs generally monitor the Piazza class discussion forum, one of the TAs is typically assigned to decide a schedule for when a TA is going to monitor the Piazza discussion forum for each weekend over the semester so that everyone takes turns. The person in charge of monitoring Piazza on any given weekend is not in charge of answering every question but rather alerting another TA or the faculty member if an issue comes up that they need to address.

One of the most critical roles of TAs in the Data Structures class is running weekly help sessions. These sessions may give more in-depth examples of some of the programming skills needed or how to make use of some of the digital tools that are part of the course. During weeks when assignments are due, the TAs help students understand the assignment requirements, help talk students through approaches to finding solutions, and sometimes help students debug their code. Thus the review sessions not only serve as a source of technical help, but also they often turn into collaborative work sessions for students. Students in the help sessions have been observed to figure out a problem and then go and help other students who are having the same problem. This is an indication of the comfort in the classroom, and it is also an indication that our model for mentorship is adopted informally among students in the class. Students can get to know other students in these help sessions, so they become a source of friendship, in part because the TAs work hard to create a casual, safe space.

TA Mentoring: Instructor to Graduate

Instructors help new graduate TAs move into the position of teaching the class by showing them how to manage the class, generate new material, and guide the teaching staff. They also spend a significant amount of time discussing teaching philosophy, especially why they are teaching the class as an FFAL class. The professor and graduate TAs have informal discussions about the various challenges, how data are collected to make evidence-based improvements, and how the teaching experience differs from a traditional lecture class. These discussions occur because graduate TAs are often involved in codesigning the material and the formative and summative assessments. Fostering the graduate TAs' understanding of these classroom design decisions has a ripple effect: they are able to advocate for these aspects to students and other TAs. This is also helpful for the graduate student TA, especially if the student is a doctoral student who is planning a career in academia. It means the doctoral student can write a much more detailed and sophisticated teaching philosophy statement for their job search.

TA Mentoring: Graduate to Undergraduate

Graduate TAs (GTAs) typically have more experience with course content and more technical skills than undergraduate TAs, and that can be useful. However, finding or training good GTAs can be challenging. They do not typically have a lot of time to invest in their TA work, and they may feel pressure from their research advisor to spend as little time as possible on TA duties to maximize the time they spend on their research. These signals may also inadvertently or purposefully tell doctoral students that teaching is not important. Also, most doctoral students would have taken a core course taught in a traditional lecture style. They may not buy into the active learning approach and may even suffer from typical academic nostalgia: "I had to suffer through boring lectures and hard assignments with no help, so these students should, too." Such GTAs may not be thinking about inclusive education and supporting diverse student success and therefore may not have the appropriate attitude needed for the commitment involved in teaching an FFAL class.

On the other hand, some GTAs are more inclined to consider teaching important, and these doctoral students are often enrolled in the university teaching certificate. They have a more positive attitude about their classroom-based responsibilities and really cherish the opportunities they are given to share ideas and to work directly with students. Finding great GTAs, mentoring them, and providing them with opportunities for growth as teachers can be rewarding, especially as they mentor undergraduate TAs.

There may also be GTAs who fit between these two ends of the spectrum: graduate students who think teaching is important and are interested in pedagogical innovation but are overwhelmed by their other research work and responsibilities. These graduate students could also play a role but may need more mentoring, especially with respect to time management. The ability of these GTAs to be assisted in the workload by the use of undergraduate TAs may help them see the power in the stepping stone teaching mentorship model.

Good GTAs can pass on knowledge about the content and can teach undergraduate TAs how to use the grading systems, the learning management system (including the functionality that comes with the TA role), and various other technologies that might be used in the course. In the Data Structures course, one particularly good GTA helped the undergraduate TAs learn how to set up programming assignments in the Web-Cat autograding system and how to create and share things like lab checkoff Google forms. GTAs can also lead help sessions with senior undergraduate TAs, teaching them the best way to help students. In this case, the undergraduates may actually help the GTAs to ensure they are explaining things at the right level. Sometimes the GTAs are so far removed from having been an undergraduate that they use too much jargon and give too much detail. The undergraduate TAs can check them on that and ensure that the help sessions are at the right level for the undergraduate students.

TA Mentoring: Undergraduate Senior to Undergraduate Junior

Although GTAs are often more knowledgeable and better organized than undergraduate TAs, the undergraduate TAs often have much more time and energy. For instance, undergraduate TAs may be more inclined to stay after class and provide help sessions to socialize with students, helping students feel more comfortable and seeing the teaching staff as personable and approachable. This strength can also be a double-edged sword as they are constantly hungry for new and exciting opportunities. We have designed a progression that continually challenges undergraduate TAs with new and exciting tasks and roles, starting off with well-scoped and highly-structured work to ensure that they are successful and to avoid overwhelming them, each semester assigning more responsibilities and changing the types of roles that they perform.

One of the main roles that junior undergraduate TAs (JUTAs) perform is to debug the labs and test cases before the students in the class attempt them. New TAs are often excited about this kind of work, which would be less exciting for more senior undergraduate TAs and graduate TAs. It also gives them an opportunity to practice the material and prepare for the labs. The JUTAs often challenge themselves to create more elegant solutions than they would have submitted as students. It can be a rewarding experience for these JUTAs to breeze through assignments and labs that used to take them hours and even days. JUTAs are often likely to suggest novel ideas about how to change the class because they have most recently experienced it as a student, and they are less inhibited by "what is possible" in a class. More senior TAs may realize how difficult an idea is to implement before exploring it further. New TAs often do not know how hard it is to make changes, and so they suggest more radical ideas, which can often lead to interesting changes when adapted by more senior TAs and faculty who have a more pragmatic perspective. Finally, the JUTAs are given one important area of responsibility that is overseen by a more senior TA. Having ownership over some aspect of the course gives JUTAs pride about their work, and we have even observed cases of JUTAs bragging to students in the class about something that they implemented, managed, or fixed in the class structure or class material. This is a really good recruitment tool to get new students interested in joining the teaching staff.

The next aspect of our mentorship model involves the senior undergraduate TAs (SUTAs). To maintain undergraduate TAs' enthusiasm and excitement, we have carefully designed a progression for JUTAs to slowly take on new challenges as they become more senior in the teaching team. After a semester or two, the enthusiasm and excitement of being an undergraduate student begins to become a driving force for them to want to try something new. At this point, many undergraduate students leave their TA role to search for new and exciting challenges. While understandable, this can be disruptive for a teaching team. Our mentorship model was designed with this in mind. In our mentorship model, we attempt to provide different experiences for SUTAs. This maintains their enthusiasm and excitement as they begin to develop new skills and have new challenges. The main focus for SUTAs is to train and pass on their knowledge to JUTAs. They also provide supervision to help ensure that JUTAs are successfully developing skills and performing their duties. These management skills are important for when SUTAs start applying for jobs because it is a new leadership challenge for many students. Often the only leadership skills that students have at this point in their careers include group work in class and maybe some leadership roles for student organizations, so being an SUTA is a unique and exciting role for them. SUTAs are typically supervised by the graduate TAs, but they also interact frequently with the faculty members of the teaching team.

We have described how our scaffolding the experience of undergraduate TAs is not only vital for the success of teaching teams but also a mentorship model that focuses on providing balance and progression for students. JUTAs have unique benefits that they provide to the teaching team, and the roles and tasks that they perform help to ensure that they are learning new skills and feeling like an important part of a team. They are afforded opportunities to exercise agency in their role and have their own projects; however, the projects are supervised and structured in a way to ensure success. SUTAs remain engaged in the team, they develop leadership skills, and they start to train their JUTA replacements. Training their replacements ensures continuity in our mentorship process.

Student Mentoring: Teaching Team to Students in Class

The final aspect of our mentorship model is the relationship between the teaching team and the students in the class. Each of the different members of the teaching team has a different relationship with the students that is carefully designed to help the students and leverage the unique aspects of the teaching team. We have already described previously the different aspects of the teaching team; in this section we describe their relationships with the students.

The JUTAs are closest in experience and age to the students in the class. In our mentoring cycle, they often ask to become TAs because they have been in the class and have been helped by JUTAs. JUTAs provide a role model for becoming a TA in the class and the importance of working hard and learning the material. They can provide relatable stories about their own struggles to learn the material and how they overcame setbacks. They can also relate to student misconceptions and misunderstandings with the material. In this way, they are very approachable for students in the class. JUTAs often also stick around after class and after help sessions to socialize and discuss topics outside of the course material. In this way, they can serve as friends to the students in the class. The JUTAs are a very important part of our stepping stone mentorship model. They embody the first step in a progression from student to faculty. Their impartial and imperfect understanding of concepts can actually be a benefit in convincing students to adopt a growth mindset. Students may look at an instructor and think that they have always been experts in the field of computing, but JUTAs give students a relatable example that expertise is developed through hard work and practice.

SUTAs are more removed from the students' experiences; however, they may still serve many of the same roles that JUTAs serve. Because SUTAs are more removed, they can also be more impartial when interacting with students. This can be very beneficial to ensure that all students are being treated fairly. SUTAs are often managing important parts of the course, such as the autograding system and writing test cases and assignments. Thus, they are more familiar with the specifics of the assignments, an impartiality that can be beneficial; at the same time, SUTAs are still very familiar with the challenges that students face. They may be more willing to advocate for students when an assignment is difficult or a deadline should be extended. Finally, as SUTAs begin to search for jobs and other opportunities, they can provide students with important information about what additional skills should be developed, how to frame the work they do in class to impress recruiters, and about different possible careers. Often SUTAs are asked by students to stay after class to give advice about applying for internships and jobs. This is a testament to the respect that students have for SUTAs.

The GTAs are the most experienced and often the most technically sound members of the teaching team. They have completed their undergraduate degrees and are actively doing research. This allows them to solve technical problems in the class that might be too difficult or time consuming for the rest of the teaching team. They can also help students in cases where the SUTAs and JUTAs are unable to figure out a solution on their own. GTAs can also be too removed from the undergraduate students' experiences. They can be overly technical, and they can use a lot of unfamiliar jargon. For some advanced students in the class who have significant previous programming experience, this can be exciting. It is not uncommon for more experienced students in the class to gravitate to the GTAs and to ask them for advice about hobbyist projects, graduate school, and careers in research. These students, who might otherwise be bored by the assignments, can still be motivated to attend class and help sessions to interact with the GTAs.

The instructor oversees and is responsible for all aspects of the course but delegates some of the operational aspects to TAs at various levels. The instructor is able to help students with technical problems but can often also design videos and exercises that present the material in a way that is fun and engaging. They can make the classroom environment enjoyable for students, but they can also be strict and impartial when needed to ensure that all students are treated fairly. The instructor is responsible for communicating to students important aspects at play in the classroom. They can relate the material to real-world examples, but they can also discuss important issues in technology, such as sexism, racism, and bullying and how privilege plays out in the educational system. The instructor can also present concepts from learning sciences research, such as the growth mindset and constructivist theories of cognitive development, to ensure that students have a better understanding of why their learning environment has been designed as a flipped classroom with active learning.

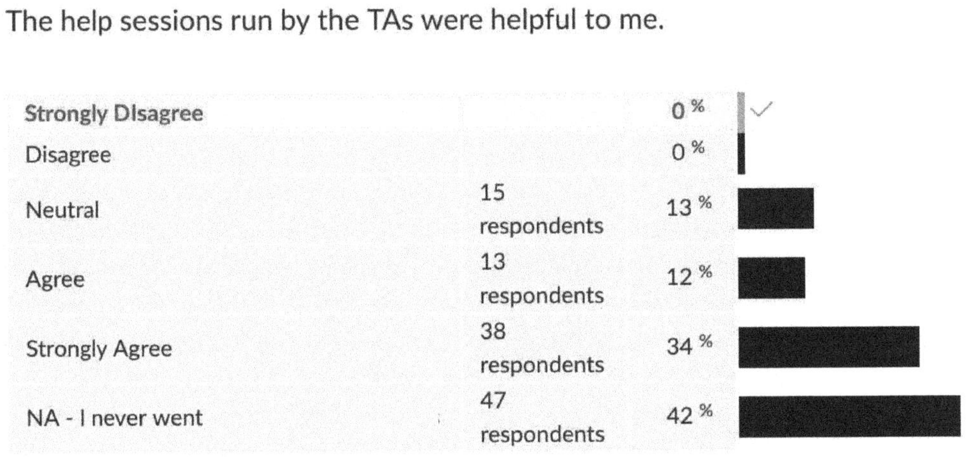

The help sessions run by the TAs were helpful to me.

Strongly Disagree		0 %
Disagree		0 %
Neutral	15 respondents	13 %
Agree	13 respondents	12 %
Strongly Agree	38 respondents	34 %
NA - I never went	47 respondents	42 %

Figure 8.2. Student perceptions about how helpful the TA help sessions were in fall 2018. While some students never attended the help sessions, more than half the class did attend them, and many students found them helpful.

Mentoring Impacts on the Student Learning Experience

When mentoring cycles are effective in active learning classes and in departments or colleges that are investing heavily in active learning, the benefits flow through to students. In our classes, we often ask for detailed anonymous feedback from students both midway through the semester and at the end of the semester. This allows us to continuously improve the classes. Here we present both data from those final class feedback surveys, as well as other sources.

We always end our anonymous feedback surveys with an open question asking students if they have any other comments or suggestions. In more recent semesters, as our mentored TA team has developed, we see this reflected in student comments. Here are comments left by students in the final course feedback surveys in various semesters (edited to show the most relevant parts of the comments):

". . . Also, tutoring sessions were fantastic and your TAs tremendously helped me with the assignments and this class." [Fall 2018]

". . . You were lucky to have such an awesome group of TA's, as was I." [Fall 2018]

". . . The TA's were also super helpful, especially during the assignments." [Fall 2018]

"Dr. Celine, I loved your class so much! It stressed me out right to a healthy level. Basically, it pushed me, but the end goal was possible to achieve. Your TA selection is phenomenal. Brian, Kyle, and Mariah sat down with me for hours individually just to reassure that I understood the concepts. My 1213 class was done outside of UNCC and I was really scared to come into this class, but they helped me every step along the way. I could not have asked for a better semester, thanks!" [Spring 2018]

"I really liked the layout of this class.... The TAs really made this class a lot of fun and I learned a lot during the help sessions." [Spring 2018]

It seems apparent to students that because the TAs have taken the course themselves, they are really invested in helping the students coming into the class after them to learn the material and build their skills. For example, this comment from a student demonstrates how instrumental the TA was in the student's success in the course: "This class was overall a super positive experience for me. I had a 53% in this class in October and e-mailed Brian and he was super helpful and I ended up finishing the semester with a B, which I'm super happy with. More importantly, I feel that I've become a much better programmer than I was at the beginning of this semester." [Fall 2017] One aspect of the mentoring cycle that has developed is that students in our classes see a well-functioning, cohesive team of TAs who appear to be having fun and are really engaged in the entire class experience. This looks different from many other courses where the TAs are simply used for assignment and exam grading. In these cases, the undergraduate students often do not see the TAs at all unless they meet the TA because of a grading complaint. The much more active and visible role of TAs in our course appeals to students so much that at the end of the semester students themselves want to become TAs for the course. It is amusing that in the anonymous feedback survey at the end of the semester, they ask to be considered as TAs for future semesters, as shown by these two comments:

"If there is a position for TA next semester I would love to help. I think that this class is essential to making programs more efficient. So, having a good understanding of all the new data structure we learned is essential. Brian had a big impact on me from the labs, so I would like to give another student the same impact." [Spring 2018]

"I loved this class!!! I think it's perfect just the way it is. If you ever need a TA please let me know I would love to help!" [Spring 2018]

In addition to the final feedback surveys, we also often give students reflection exercises throughout the semester to ask them to reflect on their own learning. In one of these reflections, we asked students to reflect on what they found most surprised them about the course. One student responded this way:

"The effectiveness of the teaching assistants. I have been in a fair amount of classes, many of which have had more TAs than this one; but I've never received help from a TA before beyond just telling me what the correct answer is. I am going to mention this in the course evaluation, also. I really had no idea that a class could actually be accentuated by TAs; I always thought it was only beneficial for the TAs and not necessarily for the students in the class."

This response reflects the fact that the experiences many students have with TAs in other classes are quite limited and possibly even negative. Effective TAing can make for a really positive learning experience for students, and when it happens, students are very appreciative.

We have also seen students comment about the positive experiences they can have in their educational journey when they move through a series of flipped active learning classes taught by faculty who have been mentored in our college. While not every student likes the flipped classroom, many of our students really enjoy the active learning that the flipped class enables, and they comment on how the continuity of flipped experiences across multiple classes is positive. For example, one student left this comment in the end of semester feedback:

"Thank you for making this class in this format. Having this as a similar format to my 1212 (Bruce) and 1213 (Najjar) classes really helped me understand this class better as I was more prepared for the learning curve that comes with this style of teaching." [Fall 2018]

Another student left this comment:

"I really like the teaching style of this class. As someone who used the flipped learning method throughout high school, it was very easy for me to transition from high school, to Prof. Najjar's class, to yours. I hope I can take your class again in the future." [Fall 2018]

Another student in the Data Structures course in spring 2018 sent this email to the professor of the course in the fall of 2018, asking about the common structure he has seen:

"I am curious if you and Professor Ramaprasad (or Dr. Cao or Dr. Najjar) collaborate when designing the structure of your courses' curriculums in any way. I feel as though there are many similarities between the structure of Professor Ramaprasad's ITSC 3146's [Networks and Operating Systems] curriculum and the structure of your ITSC 2214's [Data Structures] curriculum.

"I find that the flipped structure (the focus on videos and prep quizzes and the emphasis on coding and understanding over testing) in your class and Professors Cao's [Discrete Structures], Ramaprasad's, and Najjar's [Intro Programming] classes very conducive to learning." [Fall 2018]

This email demonstrates that some students are noticing the common structure and appreciating how it helps their learning. As more of our classes move toward the FFAL structure, we can expect to see more students who find that this structure provides the support they need to have effective learning experiences.

Limitations

The stepping stone mentorship model for teaching an FFAL class allows support and rich learning experiences for students because there is enough people power to sustain a wide variety of activities and help channels. However, the main limitation to this model is the cost. For a large class, having two faculty involved in the first development semester costs the college or department because one of those faculty members could be teaching something else. However, that is a one-semester cost. Having multiple undergraduate TAs involved in such a class each semester does involve resources. The undergrad TAs are paid $10 per hour. If a class has five undergraduate TAs working five to 10 hours per week, this could impose a significant cost to a department. Thus, this model is most useful for really important core classes. The model could still work scaled down to only one graduate TA and one or two undergraduate TAs. Or the undergraduate TAs could be used for fewer hours per week.

Conclusion

In this chapter, we have presented a case study of creating a self-sustaining, empowered TA team for a large, active learning class as well as a more broadly empowered set of faculty engaging together in active learning pedagogy as a community of practice. We have shown how the stepping stone mentoring model works across multiple levels to empower both faculty and students. We end here with the most salient points for using mentoring to promote and support active learning classes:

- Apply pair teaching to newly flipped classes to minimize workload and allow a faculty member to be apprenticed in the flipped, active learning approach.
- Develop a community of practice within your college or department to allow mentorship among faculty at different points in the active learning pedagogy path.
- Impart the active learning teaching philosophy to the TAs in your course and get them on board.
- Empower TAs to bring forward ideas to improve the class experience.
- Promote mentorship by senior TAs or graduate TAs of more junior TAs and explain the importance of continuity.
- Let TAs interact with students in class and in out-of-class help sessions as much as possible, as this leads to good students asking to join the TA team, creating a self-sustaining cycle.

Some of these practices may be more or less practical depending on resource constraints. We have been fortunate to be able to hire a number of undergraduate TAs for our large active learning classes. These TAs may only work 10 hours a week, and they are not expensive. The investment is worth it, especially for those large core courses where the student learning experience has major impacts on program retention. Having support from the department chair and college dean is critical for these endeavors to be funded and be successful.

References

Barker, L. J., McDowell, C., & Kalahar, K. (2009). Exploring factors that influence computer science introductory course students to persist in the major. *ACM SIGCSE Bulletin, 41*(1), 153–157. doi: 10.1145/1539024.1508923

Bean, J. P. (2005). *Nine themes of college student retention. College student retention: Formula for student success.* Westport, CT: Greenwood.

Dweck, C. S. (2008). *Mindset: The new psychology of success.* New York, NY: Random House Digital, Inc.

Frevert, T., Rorrer, A., Davis, D. J., Latulipe, C., Maher, M. L., Cukic, B., . . . Rogelberg, S. (2018). Sustainable educational innovation through engaged pedagogy and organizational change. *IEEE 2018 IEEE Frontiers in Education Conference (FIE)*, 1–5. doi: 10.1109/FIE.2018.8658491

Latulipe, C., MacNeil, S., & Thompson, B. (2018). Evolving a data structures class toward inclusive success. *IEEE 2018 IEEE Frontiers in Education Conference (FIE)*, 1–9. doi: 10.1109/FIE.2018.8659334

Lewis, C. M., Anderson, R. E., & Yasuhara, K. (2016). I don't code all day: Fitting in computer science when the stereotypes don't fit. *ACM Proceedings of the 2016 ACM Conference on International Computing Education Research, 23–32.* doi: 10.1145/2960310.2960332

Lewis, C. M., Yasuhara, K., & Anderson, R. E. (2011). Deciding to major in computer science: a grounded theory of students' self-assessment of ability. *ACM Proceedings of the Seventh International Workshop on Computing Education Research, 3–10.* doi: 10.1145/2016911.2016915

Maher, M. L., Cukic, B., Mays, L., Rogelberg, S., Latulipe, C., Payton, J., . . . Frevert, T. (2016). The connected learner: Engaging faculty to connect computing students to peers, profession and purpose. *IEEE 2016 IEEE Frontiers in Education Conference (FIE), 1–8.* doi: 10.1109/FIE.2016.7757473

Roberts, E. S., Kassianidou, M., & Irani, L. (2002). Encouraging women in computer science. *ACM SIGCSE Bulletin, 34*(2), 84–88. doi: 10.1145/543812.543837

CHAPTER 9

Active Learning Beyond the Classroom

Community-Engaged Learning Case Studies

COLLEEN HAMMELMAN, TINA KATSANOS, AND BETH AUTEN

Sitting in a classroom is part of the college experience—a necessary and valuable venue for delivering information, ideas, concepts, and theories. But how memorable is this experience? How often does a student recall with great fondness and excitement the bare classroom walls, desks, and overhead projectors? How often does a student exclaim "Wow . . . What a cool classroom!" Probably not often, if at all. Instead many of us remember the field trip—whether, as children, when we boarded a bus for that much-anticipated ride to the state capital or, as college students, when we took the time to visit a community center. Trips to community spaces allow for an embodied education: We navigate new landscapes and people with our bodies and minds, become active agents of our learning through discovery, and thus more effectively memorialize lessons and verbalize our recollections with "Wow . . . What a cool experience!"

Active learning and community-engaged learning are both approaches that are gaining attention and practice as effective university teaching pedagogies. Yet the two fields and literatures do not often engage with each other. In this chapter, we argue for bringing together pedagogy in both active learning and community-engaged learning to improve student outcomes in achieving learning objectives, foster civic participation, and address community concerns in the places we study. We begin this chapter with a brief review of active learning and community-engaged learning literature to identify areas of convergence and gaps. We then provide several case studies of community-engaged active learning projects to demonstrate the impact of this approach on student outcomes and community partners. We conclude by highlighting commonalities across the case studies by discussing possibilities and pitfalls of such an approach.

Literature Review

Active and experiential learning depend on the idea that learning happens through connecting or maintaining a connection between an action and its consequences. The idea of learning by doing and by relating that activity to a learner's existing knowledge and experience emerged from constructivist learning theories developed by Dewey, Piaget, Vygotsky, and others who assume that knowledge is constructed in the mind of the learner rather than wholly acquired from an outside source. The theory of active learning is also linked to the concept of meta-cognition, the learner's awareness of their level of knowledge and understanding—what they already know and what they still need to work on or find out (Bransford, Brown, & Cocking, 1999). Active learning provides an opportunity for a person to direct their own learning, as it depends on their engagement with an activity (Bell & Kozlowski, 2008). This also brings to light what the learner may already know and what they still have to learn, either from the experience gained through the activity they are working on or from another source.

Community-engaged learning, where students actively engage with issues or problems in the community and intentionally reflect on their experiences, is an active learning modality that is different in setting but similar in impact to active learning taking place in the classroom, laboratory, or other, more traditional, settings. However, in practice, the literatures of active learning and community-engaged learning have diverged widely, and there is little overlap between the research on active learning on campus and experiential learning in the world beyond.

Active learning pedagogy is employed in a variety of ways in the classroom. Relying on Bloom's taxonomy, instructors lead students in activities of sharing ideas with peers (i.e., think-pair-share); completing worksheets for films, guest speakers, and other activities; solving problems using new technologies, data sources, and skills learned in class; and addressing current needs in collaboration with community partners. All these approaches to active learning help students apply skills and knowledge gained in class to a hands-on activity to enhance student learning (Gilboy, Heinerichs, & Pazzaglia, 2015). Each skill offers a different level of engagement with current events and stakeholders outside the class. However, much active learning occurs only within the silo of academic space. In this chapter, we provide case studies of how this pedagogy can engage with community partners (and thus build on community-engaged learning pedagogy) not only to enhance student learning of specific skills, but also to increase civic consciousness (Blouin & Perry, 2009).

Increasingly, student engagement beyond the classroom is viewed as effective for providing students with hands-on, practical experience in applying classroom material to real-life contexts, increasing civic responsibility, and contributing to community needs. The Association of American Colleges and Universities recognizes community-engaged learning and active learning practices, such as collaborative assignments and participation in learning communities, as high-impact educational practices (Kuh, 2008). Community-engaged and active learning practices overlap in some ways—such as drawing from the direct experience of students—but community-engaged learning extends active learning experience beyond the classroom to consider potential benefits to the community both through students' coursework and by fostering active and engaged citizens (Bringle, Clayton, & Hatcher, 2013). Distributing these and other high-impact practices throughout the curriculum is intended to increase student engagement, learning, and retention.

More recently, community-engaged learning also emphasizes student learning. Unlike community service work, which often involves "volunteering in the community with no direct relationship or application to course curricula, learning goals, structured reflections, and acquisition of skills" (Delano-Oriaran, 2015, p. xxxvii), community-engaged learning deliberately links community service with educational objectives (Bringle & Hatcher, 1999). Effective community-engaged learning projects must include student learning and achievement of educational goals; they must also provide something meaningful to the community (Jacoby, 1996). As such, a properly designed and implemented community-engaged active learning project benefits everyone directly involved, and, in some cases, benefits can extend to people indirectly involved. This chapter describes case studies seeking to do just that. Each of the examples involved a course in which one of the coauthors was involved or for which colleagues generously shared their experiences. These illustrative cases, both short-term and year-long projects, show the benefits to student learning and to communities that can bring together active and community-engaged approaches to learning.

Case Studies

One-Time Projects

We begin our analysis of active and community-engaged approaches to learning with several case studies that include one or more visits from students to locations, groups, or actors beyond the classroom. One-time projects are effective for taking active learning beyond the classroom without needing a longer-term commitment from community partners. The following case studies can be highly effective for increasing student exposure to diversity and multiculturalism and thus enabling students to rethink commonly held stereotypes and providing opportunities for students to link class content to life on the ground.

Seeing Sustainability in Action. This first case study describes a short-term engagement beyond the classroom and demonstrates how student engagement and understanding of topics relate to environmental citizenship. The course students attended is a new addition to UNC Charlotte's General Education Program. Many departments across the university offer the course on different topics but with similar goals of teaching critical thinking and communication. The course, available to sophomores, juniors, and seniors, is designed to offer a bridge of continuity between freshmen and the experience with first-year writing. Ideally, the course uses active and integrative learning to sharpen critical thinking and communication skills.

This case study focuses on a class taught by one of this article's coauthors. Student learning objectives include understanding citizenship as evolving to accommodate (or not) environmental rights and duties. A previous active learning project for the class was to take on an environmental challenge for an average of three weeks. A few examples of challenges included changing one's diet to vegetarianism or veganism, recycling all waste, and lowering one's carbon footprint with alternative modes of transportation. The assignment's learning objective was for students to learn through personal experience how difficult it is for the average person to make sustainable everyday life choices. This type of experiential learning would help students be equipped to identify the necessary system changes that need to be made for more sustainable living. Every semester, a handful of students in each class took the project seriously and were able to produce a meaningful narration of their experiences and to identify the necessary infrastructural and institutional changes needed for a person to have access to sustainable choices. For the rest of the class, personal narrations of experiences were largely flat, canned, and/or outright fabrications.

To address those deficiencies, the environmental challenge project was replaced with a fieldwork assignment in which students were required to visit a site or event that claims to promote sustainability. They could go alone or in groups, and they were expected to have a conversation with someone at the site or at the event. Using an ethnographic approach, the students then wrote about their observations, including critiquing how well the site or event was meeting sustainability goals. This assignment was well received and more effective for several reasons. First, it was not as daunting as a three-week life change, and thus students followed through with the assignment. Second, students were able to see sustainability/environmentalism on the ground within communities of people that, overall, are very much like themselves, their family members, and/or friends. What may have seemed exotic and foreign to them was normalized. The verbal engagement, whether a casual conversation, an informal Q & A, or a formal interview with fellow community members, can deepen this normalization of sustainability/environmentalism. Finally, students, especially when they visit with a friend or a group of classmates, do not experience the isolation of taking on an environmental challenge on their own. In this case, having students witness sustainability within their own communities as it is practiced beyond the classroom is more accessible, effective, and enjoyable than engaging in an individual act or simply discussing environmentalism in class. The following are two examples of fieldwork options in this class:

Charlotte Mecklenburg Recycling Facility. In a general education course focused on sustainability, students learned hands-on about recycling through a tour to the local recycling facility. The tours were led by the facility director who emphasized the three R's (reduce, reuse, recycle) throughout the tour that included seeing recycled benches used on site, a short video and discussion about the recycling process generally and in the county, a Q & A, and finally a short tour of the recycling floor. Students, dressed in safety vests and helmets, were able to see the trucks dump recyclables and trash, the workers sort through the materials, and the final bales of paper and plastic resources sold to other businesses. Students asked many questions during this leg of the tour that were answered with a good dose of southern humor by a person working on the floor.

Following the tour, students wrote about their fieldwork experience, and many made meaningful connections to class content and texts. Participants were able to see the process of recycling on the ground and were also able to learn things absent from the text, such as the biggest problem the recycling facility faces: people throwing things in their bins that cannot be recycled at that facility. It was illuminating for the students to hear firsthand from recycling staff, "Oh, everything can be recycled . . . just not here," along with references to plastic and paper as resources rather than trash. Furthermore, at one visit, students were able to meet a fellow community member there as a volunteer and hear her talk about the importance of helping to keep the city sustainable. Finally, by observing the actual process and getting to talk with facility staff and volunteers, students were encouraged to think critically about how well the facility was meeting its goals. Indeed, many students were quick to point out that the facility would do a better job with a better-educated public.

The fieldwork experience enhanced student learning objectives in several ways. First, students were able to think more critically about the recycling process because they were able to move beyond a theoretical description in a textbook. Second, students were able to identify ways that county sustainability efforts intersect with private businesses, highlighting the need for a wide range of community partnerships. Finally, students identified access to education and information as key for increasing productivity within sustainability efforts.

Earlier visits to the recycling facility fostered a working relationship between the course instructor and the facility director. Through this relationship, plans are underway for students to further engage with hands-on community issues through assisting the facility director with her tours for school-aged children. A select number of undergraduate students will work on devising an age-appropriate recycling art project and will enhance the tours with implementation of the craft project. The small group of select students will serve as a pilot program that will help us determine the viability of expanding the scope of involved students. Expanding the project will allow students to meet additional learning outcomes, including identifying children as active citizen participants and community stakeholders that should be included in sustainability efforts and recognizing the value of art as an effective tool for fostering community involvement.

Veg Fest. In another example, students were engaged in actively learning about sustainability through interactions with community groups at Veg Fest. Veg Fest, which was first organized and hosted by the Humane League, is an annual vegan expo event held in the fall in Charlotte. In 2018, Veg Fest was attended by more than 6,000 people of diverse socioeconomic and racial/ethnic backgrounds. Equally diverse vendors, ranging from local restaurant representatives, local and artisan food purveyors, botanical soap and oil makers, and animal and human health and hunger advocacy groups were present. The venue offered a rich cross-section of the multiple passions, concerns, and reasons behind the vegan movement.

For this event, students attended Veg Fest and had at least three separate conversations with representatives at any of the vendor tables about their goals and commitments to veganism. Students then wrote the observations and reflections in fieldwork assignments. Notable surprising observations, as recorded in their fieldwork write-ups, included that the hunger advocacy group, Food Not Bombs, prepared vegan meals for the homeless every Sunday, that many African Americans were into veganism, and that vegan food, especially from the food trucks, could taste so good. Students also observed how environmental groups are linked to more than animal welfare; many of the vendors advocated for human well-being and the mitigation of climate change by opting for a dietary change—ideas that linked to class content on environmental change. Students were also asked to consider how well the event met the goals of sustainability. This supported critical thinking as students reflected on how much consumerism was present at Veg Fest, admired efforts toward promoting animal well-being, and recommended ways vendors could broaden their sustainability goals by reducing their food and product packaging and eliminating plastic bags. Finally, this event also normalized veganism, which is often stereotyped as some sort of exotic fad movement. Building on these experiences, representatives from the local Humane League were invited to class to talk about animal welfare, human health, and the environmental impact of livestock.

Exploring a "Good Life" Through Community Visits and Interviews

This case study provides another example of taking active learning outside the classroom for an undergraduate general education course fostering critical thinking and communication. This course topic was "A Good Life" and was taught through a religious studies department. It examined definitions and ideas of a "good life" throughout western history in ethics, philosophy, religious studies, and psychology. A key learning objective was for students to use critical thinking to assemble evidence for generating their own valid and defensible definition of "the good life." Building on readings, writings, visitations, and interviews, students produced a final, polished ePortfolio. The class was fully flipped through consistently and seamlessly integrating short lectures, weekly quizzes, and team-based active learning projects. Active learning was further extended with community-engaged integrative learning.

Similar to the case study above, community engagement arises through active learning projects that immerse students in nearby communities to gain an understanding of the multiculturalism and diversity where they live. Community engagement was accomplished through two assignments: an interview with someone from a different generation and a visitation to a community center that promotes happiness and well-being.

Assignment 1: The Interview. Students interviewed a person from another generation using these guiding questions:

- **What is a good life?**
- **How does one go about living it?**
- **How is happiness defined and understood?**
- **What are the problems we humans must address?**

Students were assessed by a write-up of the interview where they were required to make connections between course content and the interview. A specific student learning outcome was the application of theoretical models of happiness to the interviewee's responses. Careful analysis of the interview allowed students to think critically about the strengths and limitations of theoretical models. These firsthand accounts of adversity and happiness also deepened the students' appreciation and understanding of the power of storytelling through interpersonal engagement.

Assignment 2: The Visitation. The visitation assignment required students to visit an *unfamiliar* religious or civic organization and submit a fieldwork write-up. Like the interview assignment, students were assessed by how well they were able to connect ideas and theories about happiness to their actual encounters with individuals and experiences at the community site. An additional key student learning outcome was reflection on how answers to "What is a good life?" were often dependent on cultural context.

Semester-Long Projects

Community-engaged learning courses that span a full semester enable collaboration between students and nonprofit organizations, city agencies, and other stakeholders on more in-depth projects. They also require more hands-on engagement from instructors and community partners and thus can be more of a commitment than the lower-stakes cases discussed above. This section provides two case studies to demonstrate how students can engage hands-on with course content through such collaborative research projects.

Public Computing Centers. The first project involved a small group of students in a geographic information systems (GIS) course. The GIS course, enrolling upper-level undergraduate and graduate geography and urban studies students, provided training on basic GIS skills. Learning outcomes focused on theoretical and practical uses of GIS, including representation of geographic information, creating GIS databases, and performing spatial analysis. It included lectures and working lab sections. In addition to lab assignments and a midterm exam, graduate students completed a community-engaged active learning project using GIS skills learned in class that produced not only a project for graduate students but also a report for the city agency working on the same topic.

To connect classroom content with hands-on learning in the community, students mapped locations of public computing centers (PCCs) for a municipal agency tasked with establishing new locations throughout the city. This project took place in an industrialized northeast U.S. city where, at the time of the project, nearly 40% of the residents did not have Internet access at home. To address this issue, the municipal government created centers with public computers and staff members in places such as libraries and community centers. These spaces provided access to computers and technology training as well as a community gathering space that helped to foster a low-stakes environment for residents to become familiar with the technology.

In collaboration with city staff, the students and instructor identified these research questions: Which PCC sites serve the most clients? Are those sites located in areas of low Internet adoption? What other accessibility factors impact utilization rates? The students then analyzed data routinely collected in existing PCCs, such as number of users, tasks, locations, etc. Specific skills learned in class and applied to the research included geocoding (or mapping geographic coordinates of specific sites), attaching data to those sites, spatial analysis comparing locations to demographic data (i.e., identifying sites serving clients located within 1,000 feet of block groups with low Internet adoption), and representing the data through maps. Students presented their report to city staff at the end of the semester. This engagement with a city research question enhanced student learning through hands-on engagement with real-life data. In a class already embedded in active learning pedagogy (through lab assignments), this project went one step further by asking students to identify a research question and then to apply a combination of learned skills to answer the question. It also enabled the students to learn about issues affecting the local region (such as a digital divide), thus increasing their civic consciousness.

Designing Qualitative Research. Another semester-long, community-engaged project provided active learning opportunities for graduate students enrolled in a qualitative methods class. This class involved graduate students in hands-on development of research instruments to support a local organization seeking to better assess its impact. Student learning objectives for the class focused on designing and implementing qualitative research methods including defining research questions, identifying the best methods to answer the questions (interviews, focus groups, surveys, etc.), and designing a related research protocol. The course instructor built on an existing community partnership to provide students a hands-on opportunity to apply those skills beyond the classroom. The local organization constructs aquaponics systems and implements STEM curricula in K–12 schools. The organization's leadership expressed a need to better understand the impact of its programming on students and teachers to improve its work. These goals could be matched with the student learning objectives to foster an active learning approach to community-engaged learning.

The project began with forming an agreement between the course instructor and the organization's leadership regarding the expectations of each partner, the process for the project, and the expected outcomes. This step is important for ensuring that all partners recognize the goals of both student learning and achieving organizational goals. Throughout the semester, the organizational leadership provided graduate students with detailed information about its research questions, mission, and operations. This knowledge-sharing occurred through the organization's staff visits to the graduate class, class visits to program sites, and graduate student interviews of relevant stakeholders (staff, students, teachers, and school decision makers). In addition to acquiring information to build research tools, students used each of these steps to practice different research methods, such as interviewing and participant observation.

In the classroom, graduate students worked together to define the research questions to be answered. Then as each method was discussed in class—interviews, focus groups, surveys, participatory action research, etc.—students considered the effectiveness of that method to answer the research questions. Once the top three methods were identified, students worked in groups to design research protocols for implementing that method. The protocols detailed how the research will be completed: questions that will be asked, identification of research participants, and how to embed the research into existing programming. Throughout protocol development, students and organizational staff developed tools best suited to the organization's needs. Students presented their final research instruments to the organization's leadership at the end of the course. The final product was a set of research protocols ready to be implemented by the partner organization.

This project enhanced student learning of qualitative research methods through hands-on experience designing research tools. Students also practiced implementing qualitative research through gathering and analyzing information needed to design the research. Finally, students learned more about the local context where they study and how to use skills learned in the classroom to impact that context. The community-engaged nature of this active learning project also produced a set of tools to support the mission of a local organization.

Year-Long Projects

Finally, we present a year-long case study that involves a longer-term commitment by both the instructor and students. While often requiring additional resources, such higher stakes projects can also yield higher impact on meeting student learning objectives. In 2001, UNC Charlotte established a learning community program that today offers 17 different residential and nonresidential opportunities for first year and new transfer students. Options are either discipline-specific or values- and skills-specific. Discipline-specific learning communities include business, communications studies, community psychology, computing and informatics, criminal justice, education, engineering, English, health, history, psychology, and sociology. Programs centered on developing values and skills include gender excellence, global village, leadership, passport leaders, SUCCESS, transfer students, and transition opportunities. Each program requires a two-semester commitment on the part of the student and the successful coordination of teaching faculty, staff, and peer mentors. The objectives of the program include helping students transition to campus life academically and socially and increasing student success in academics and community engagement. These goals are achieved in these learning communities through common courses, innovative curricula, and cocurricular activities (https://lc.uncc.edu/overview). The programs are designed with integrative learning that fosters critical thinking and collaborative problem-solving.

Whereas the common goal is to promote campus community engagement, many of the programs extend this engagement to the greater Charlotte community through community-engaged activities. The Health Connection program—the focus of this case study—is a residential learning community made up of first-year kinesiology, nursing, public health, and social work students that was established in 2004 by the College of Health and Human Services. Today, active learning is coupled with community engagement through a project performed at The Pines at Davidson, a retirement community of nearly 350 residents located in Davidson, North Carolina. The retirement community includes the Schramm Health Center that accommodates residents with assisted living needs, full-time care needs, or residents with dementia.

Students in the two-semester–long program are expected to commit 12 hours of community-engaged learning per semester at the Schramm Health Center. Students also enroll in a Prospect for Success course in the first semester and a liberal studies course titled Issues of Health and Quality of Life in their final semester. They also complete a capstone project by the end of the program. The community-engaged learning hours largely revolve around social interaction with the residents, such as playing games, taking walks, or simply sitting in conversation. These experiences provide students with opportunities not only to assist the residents but also to prepare for the design of their final project that will be a hosted event revolving around resident interests. Past events have included a Jenga game event, a Kentucky Derby party, a high tea, a baseball-themed event, and craft projects, such as making birdhouses, painted plant pots, and dining room centerpieces. The community-engaged learning hours provide students with enough interaction and socialization to plan for and create a multigenerational experience that culminates in a memorable social event.

Throughout the program, students are expected to apply course content to their community-engaged work and to the design and implementation of their final projects. For example, key course content includes the International Council of Active Aging (ICAA) Model that posits seven dimensions of wellness, nine principles of active aging, and a continuum of physical function. While performing their service hours, students can help seniors fulfill many of the ICAA Model's recommendations for well-managed active aging such as positive social interaction, emotional support, cognitive and intellectual exercise, and physical activity. A key component for student preparedness includes exercises employed by the instructor to simulate the experience of common physical limitations that come with aging. Students practice physical activities while using devices that impair their sensory and ambulatory abilities. For example, special goggles to limit vision and noise-canceling headphones to inhibit hearing allow students to virtually experience sensory deficits. Students wear thick gloves while tying their shoe laces to experience dexterity limitations, climb stairs while breathing through a straw to simulate the impacts of chronic obstructive pulmonary disease (COPD), and use walkers and canes to experience ambulatory challenges.

As with any community-engaged learning activity, there is a risk of posing a burden on the hosting community when students show up unprepared or disinterested. The course instructor mitigates this risk by preparing students for the lived realities of the residents, by requiring student commitment to the project in the form of a signed contract, and by personally intervening by conferencing with any problematic students. The commitment, energy, and resources (including assignments, but also meaningful working relationships with community partners) of the instructor are key to this project's success. The commitment of these resources, time, and energy also provides dividends in student learning. Students are exposed to the health care field with a group of people with whom they may not regularly interact. The projects benefit both the students and the seniors residing at the center. Students learn health profession skills and benefit emotionally through seeing positive results of their interaction with seniors; the community partners benefit from student resources for creating happier, more comfortable, and healthier spaces for residents. The success of this project opens up opportunities for similar partnerships with other health service centers in the region.

Case Study Possibilities and Pitfalls

There are several themes evident across the case studies in this chapter. This final section pulls together these themes through discussing possibilities and pitfalls that can inform future work seeking to integrate active and community-engaged learning pedagogies. We focus especially on how to prepare and the benefits of starting small; the importance of journals, debriefing, and otherwise engaging with student experiences back in the classroom; and balancing the expectations of students and community partners.

Starting Small. Low-stakes, one-day projects are, for many, the best way to start implementing community-engaged active learning. Planning is manageable, and committed relationships with community partners are not always necessary. At the very least, such projects offer more impactful active learning opportunities than those available in the classroom, but assignment directions must be clearly detailed and explicit with stated learning objectives. Using prompts in connection to writing assignments can assist students with clear articulation of how their community experiences have deepened understandings of in-class instruction. They can also expose students to different community landscapes and demographics and deepen their understanding of shared spaces. Last, such projects can offer instructors a sandbox experience: a place to begin with a student exercise that can be expanded into a more meaningful and immersive community project, a place where challenges and mistakes are better managed, and a place where instructors gain the necessary experience and community contacts to plan with precision a more ambitious project.

In-Class Reflection. Occasionally, students resist taking active learning pedagogy outside the classroom when they do not recognize the contributions to learning objectives. In the case studies discussed, a key aspect for fostering success is reflecting on out-of-classroom experiences back inside the classroom. Reflection journals and in-class debriefs are particularly helpful tools for enabling students to assess what they learned throughout the project. Students can take field notes on their experiences, complete in-class reflection journals, and/or engage in conversations regarding learning outcomes. In the Seeing Sustainability in Action case study, students were equipped with directions on how to prepare for the visit, how to take notes on site, and how to best synthesize all gathered content into an ethnography. In the Qualitative Methods case study, students wrote reflection journals at the beginning, middle, and end of the semester. These journals questioned students about baseline learning objectives asking: What are qualitative methods and what types of knowledge can be acquired with that methodology? The journals also asked students about the context within which they worked by posing questions such as: What have you learned about our social and ecological context, and how has your perception of the city changed throughout the semester? Encouraging students to reflect on these questions and then discussing them with classmates can help students recognize learning achieved during community-engaged active learning classes.

Balancing the Expectations of Students and Community Partners. Finally, in community-engaged active learning projects, objectives of multiple partners are pursued. From the academic perspective, achieving student learning objectives are critical. At the same time, it is necessary to contribute to community partner objectives to produce tangible impacts and continue favorable partnerships. All too often, classes or student research create products that are not relevant to community partners and/or are relegated to dusty shelves. To better contribute to community outcomes, projects must be designed in collaboration with community partners. To that end, for longer-term projects, a memorandum of understanding (MOU) can be developed between course instructors and community partners before a course begins. Such written communication clearly explains the roles and responsibilities of each partner (including the students), objectives, and deliverables. Developing projects in collaboration with community organizations ensures a more solid partnership that can maximize both student learning and community objectives (Blouin & Perry, 2009).

All parties must also be mindful of what can be accomplished based on the time available, student abilities, and constraints of learning objectives. In the Qualitative Methods example above, students were not asked to evaluate the community partner's program. Because students in that class were only learning how to design research, there was not sufficient time or student ability to also carry out such research within the confines of a single semester. To achieve learning outcomes relating to designing multiple methods of research, the students also spent class time discussing methods that were not likely to be implemented by the community partner for logistical reasons. To ensure that students had hands-on experience with designing a variety of types of research, students spent time on work that was not always directly relevant to the community partner. It is important to be clear at the outset about everyone's expectations for the collaborative work and to find ways to complement the course learning objectives with each community partner's objectives.

Conclusion

In this chapter, we argue that attending to both active and community-engaged learning pedagogies is effective for improving student learning outcomes and civic consciousness. Through several case studies, we presented a continuum of engagement from low-stakes, one-time visits to community events to higher-stakes, full-year projects of student cohorts collaborating with community partners. The examples provided were effective in a myriad of classes from lower-level undergraduate general education to graduate courses. These case studies all present ways to bring active learning pedagogy (learning through doing) outside the classroom to give students more meaningful and sustained opportunities to practice skills and concepts learned inside the classroom. We also highlight the importance of making clear connections between learning in and out of the classroom through field note assignments, debriefing, and journaling. To be effective, these projects require proactive planning and true collaboration with community partners that identify the objectives and capabilities of each stakeholder in the project early. We invite those just starting to implement active learning practice and seasoned practitioners to consider the promises afforded students from engaging community partners in their work. When accomplished successfully, such active learning projects open possibilities for greater learning and engagement with the environments we study.

References

Bell, B. S., & Kozlowski, S. W. J. (2008). Active learning: Effects of core training design elements on self-regulatory processes, learning, and adaptability. *Journal of Applied Psychology, 93*(2), 296. https://doi.org:10.1037/0021-9010.93.2.296

Blouin, D. D., & Perry, E. M. (2009). Whom does service learning really serve? Community-based organizations' perspectives on service learning. *Teaching Sociology, 37*(2), 120–135. https://doi.org:10.1177/0092055X0903700201

Bransford, J., Brown, A. L., & Cocking, R. R. (1999). *How people learn: Brain, mind, experience, and school.* Washington, DC: National Academy Press.

Bringle, R. G., Clayton, P. H., & Hatcher, J. A. (2013). Research on service learning: An introduction. In R. G. Bringle, P. H. Clayton, & J. A. Hatcher (Eds.), *Research on service learning: Conceptual frameworks and assessments* (pp. 3–25). Sterling, VA: Stylus Publishing.

Bringle, R. G., & Hatcher, J. A. (1999). Reflection in service learning: Making meaning of experience. *Educational Horizons, 77*(4), 179–185. Retrieved from http://www.jstor.org/stable/42926911

Delano-Oriaran, O. (2015). Introduction. In O. Delano-Oriaran, M. W. Penick-Parks, & S. Fondrie (Eds.), *The SAGE sourcebook of service-learning and civic engagement* (pp. xxxvii–xliv). Los Angeles, CA: SAGE Reference.

Gilboy, M. B., Heinerichs, S., & Pazzaglia, G. (2015). Enhancing student engagement using the flipped classroom. *Journal of Nutrition Education and Behavior, 47*(1), 109–114. https://doi.org:10.1016/j.jneb.2014.08.008

Jacoby, B. (1996). Service learning in today's higher education. In B. A. Jacoby (Ed.), *Service learning in higher education: Concepts and practices* (pp. 3–25). San Francisco, CA: Jossey-Bass Publishers.

Kuh, G. D. (2008). *High-impact educational practices: What they are, who has access to them, and why they matter.* Washington, DC: Association of American Colleges and Universities.

CHAPTER 10

Design Patterns for Active Learning

MARY LOU MAHER, NASRIN DEHBOZORGI, MOHSEN DORODCHI,
AND STEPHEN MACNEIL

Flipped classrooms, active learning, and peer learning are innovations in education receiving the attention of educational researchers and instructors. Our previous papers describe several strategies for adopting the concept of flipped classrooms in various courses within a computer science education context (Maher, Latulipe, Lipford, & Rorrer, 2015; Latulipe, Long, & Seminario, 2015). As part of our experience with flipped classrooms, we introduced the concept and practice of lightweight teams. The integration of lightweight teams in both introductory computing courses and data structures creates a social learning environment that has led to improvements in academic performance (Latulipe et al., 2015; Latulipe, MacNeil, & Thompson, 2018). In this chapter, we present a more comprehensive view of active learning as pedagogical design patterns, patterns that have emerged from our own practice of active learning.

Active learning has two primary benefits: First, in-class activities create a more engaging learning experience for students, and second, active learning allows for misconceptions to be corrected before assessment (Prince, 2004). Student engagement and collaboration are features of active learning that are often contrasted with a traditional lecture setting where students typically listen to and receive information from the instructor (Prince, 2004). It can be challenging for students to maintain their attention and motivation for the entire lecture period, and many students lose their focus after the halfway point (Köppe & Portier, 2014). Active learning requires students to engage in meaningful learning activities and think about what they are doing (Bonwell & Eison, 1991). These class activities are done either individually or in teams to solve a given problem. This suggests that active learning can be considered as a continuum along which varying amounts of activity can be included throughout a class period.

Although there is some variation in how active learning is defined and discussed, there are some generally accepted definitions that help to distinguish it from nonactive learning (Prince, 2004). Many different types of pedagogy could be classified as active learning, such as team-based learning (TBL) (Smith et al., 2009), cooperative learning (Millis & Cottell, 1997; Feden & Vogel, 2003), collaborative learning, problem-based learning (Prince, 2004), or studio-based learning (Narayanan, Hundhausen, Hendrix, & Crosby, 2012). Although there are instances where students may work on activities alone, active learning usually emphasizes collaboration and learning from peers. Team-based learning (TBL) has the potential to enhance student learning outcomes (LeJeune, 2003) and has been applied across many domains, such as computer science (CS) education (Biggers, Yilmaz, & Sweat, 2009). In many institutions, the classic lecture-style format of teaching is gradually shifting to a practice-based model in which students work in teams while actively and collaboratively developing their understanding of the concepts (Lasserre, 2009). Research in TBL has identified several critical issues related to the successful implementation of teams, including team formation principles, assigning grades to teams, and improving the quality of the experience of working in teams (Michaelsen & Sweet, 2008; Mennecke & Bradley, 1998; Johnson, Johnson, & Smith, 1991). Decisions made by instructors about team formation and grading have an impact on group cohesion and effectiveness. These decisions should not be made solely based on the instructor's intuition but should also consider this research.

Incorporating activities into scheduled class time is a unique opportunity for students to work together under the supervision of an instructor without scheduling conflicts. This type of active learning centers around the social construction of knowledge. Design decisions about team formation, grading, and even the physical structure of the classroom can facilitate or disrupt this social construction of knowledge. In a lecture classroom, desks are often placed in rows to increase seat accessibility and maximize the number of seats that can fit facing forward. In active learning, the physical structure of the classroom can facilitate social interactions, such as placing tables and chairs together so that students can see each other and talk. Given these many design decisions and their effects on learning, best practices and research should be considered by instructors.

Successful implementations of active learning require goal-oriented pedagogical practices based on empirical evidence and research. We present an approach to formalize successful practices in active learning using pedagogical design patterns. Pedagogical design patterns define successful ways to solve recurring problems using a language of problems and solutions, similar to the concept of design patterns in software engineering (Dehbozorgi, 2017). They provide a formalism for capturing emerging successful pedagogical techniques (Dehbozorgi, 2017). Instructors can use pedagogical design patterns as a tool to formulate their teaching practices in a lecture or active learning setting. Many of the existing design patterns in the literature focus on teacher-centered pedagogy and lecturing methods (Dehbozorgi, Maher, MacNeil, & Dorodchi, 2018). Our design patterns serve to fill this gap by focusing on student-centered pedagogy and active learning.

Design patterns help educators share their design ideas in a structured style and also provide a framework for thinking about and comparing design decisions (Preiss, 1999). Design patterns and pattern languages originated in the writings of Alexander et al. on architecture and town planning (Alexander et al., 1977). Alexander et al.'s intention was to democratize architecture and town planning by offering a set of conceptual resources that ordinary people could use in (re)shaping their environment. Their work provides a principled, structured, but flexible resource for vernacular design. In Alexander et al.'s own words, a pattern "describes a problem which occurs over and over again in our environment, and then describes the core of the solution to that problem, in such a way that you can use this solution a million times over, without ever doing it the same way twice."

Design patterns in education provide a set of design ideas in a structured format that combines problems with solutions and also offers a rationale that connects research-based evidence with experiential knowledge. Identifying and using design patterns helps instructors encode and apply the knowledge and experience of best practices in education in an iterative and fluid process of designing course materials and activities (Goodyear, 2004).

Identifying a relevant design pattern is the first step in the process of applying that pattern to the practice of teaching. As the number of patterns increases, it becomes harder to find relevant patterns that address a specific problem. In this case, having an object model with multiple attributes may help in indexing the patterns. We have developed an object-based design pattern model that makes explicit the principles of active learning. The core structure of our model is derived from Alexander et al.'s model (Alexander et al., 1977), however, it has been extended to include components and attributes that capture features of active learning and collaboration. The modular structure and defined attributes keep the problem and solution concise. This allows patterns to be easily indexed and allows for the use of concept map representations to show the relationships among patterns. The object-based model representation makes pattern components and their attributes more obvious and cues designers to think about these aspects as they design their course.

We present our object-based design patterns in active learning that describe problems that occur over and over again. We associate those problems with active learning solutions. Our intent is similar to Alexander et al.'s: the solutions are described as patterns that can be used differently every time to adapt to each classroom's unique context. This provides instructors with the freedom to create their own learning activities and environment. The use of patterns is a way of bridging theory, empirical evidence, experience, and the practical problems of design (Goodyear, 2004). In our case, we are focused on designing course materials and learning activities.

Flipped Classrooms and Active Learning

Flipped classrooms and active learning promote the use of in-class activities for students as an alternative to long lectures and have been successfully implemented in introductory science, technology, engineering, and mathematics (STEM) courses (Hakimzadeh, Adaikkalavan, & Batzinger, 2011; Heines, 2015; Dorodchi et al., 2018). In active learning, the class time shifts from passive learning to active learning. Students are presented with new problems and apply concepts that were introduced prior to coming to class. Class time serves to test student understanding of concepts, address gaps in that understanding, and apply newly learned concepts to increasingly complex problems (Lasserre, 2009). Motivations for creating an active learning classroom are to provide a rich interactive environment, to foster better student engagement, to involve students in collaborative and cooperative problem-solving, and to promote com-

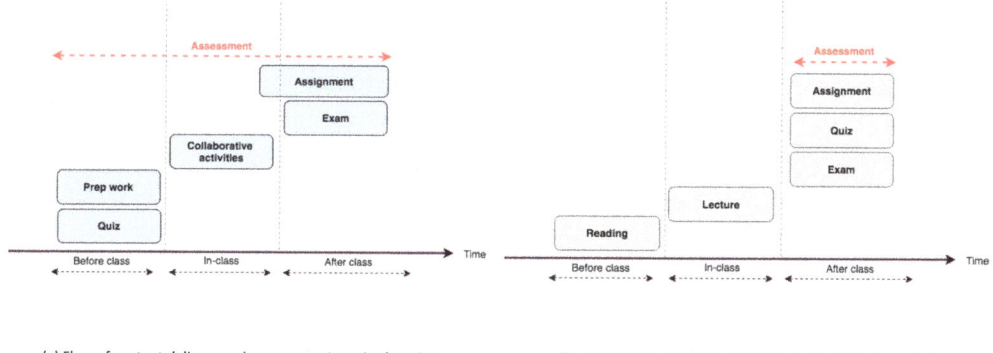

(a) Flow of content delivery and assessment in active learning   (b) Flow of content delivery and assessment in lecture-style

Figure 10.1. Active learning and lecture-based flow of content delivery and assessment.

putational thinking (Hakimzadeh et al., 2011) while socializing and having fun (Dorodchi & Dehbozorgi, 2017). In an active learning classroom, assessment is integrated into all stages of the learning process. This differs from the traditional lecture classroom in which assessment occurs periodically after the lecture and reading, as illustrated in Figure 10.1.

Students typically work in teams in an active learning class to recognize that peer discussion encourages students to come prepared and engages students in explaining while learning. TBL is valuable to student success, even when peers initially did not understand the concepts (Lasserre, 2009). Accountability (positive independence; Johnson et al., 1991) and immediate feedback are two key ingredients of TBL. Accountability can be ensured by evaluating individuals first and teams second. Competition between teams is also used to initialize interest and accountability. Immediate feedback is provided through various means, ranging from traditional materials (cards, scratch tests, color pins, small boards) to technological materials (spreadsheets, in-class scanner, clickers). Students are also encouraged to deepen their understanding by challenging the instructors' questions if they discover errors or ambiguities (Lasserre, 2009).

Teams in Education

We review the literature on teams in education to inform the development of our design patterns for active learning because our approach to active learning has a focus on student engagement and learning from peers. Forming teams that work well together is a hallmark of effective team-based learning. Michaelsen and Sweet's seminal work posits that cultivating cohesion within the team is essential to the success of those teams (Michaelsen & Sweet, 2008). But success in the context of TBL has many definitions. One common way to measure success in teams is to evaluate the quality of the artifact generated by those teams, such as in a capstone course. Examples of these artifacts are group presentations, documentation, and project demonstrations. These artifacts are one important aspect of the TBL experience because in industry these artifacts are highly valued by the company. Teams are formed to maximize the performance of the team in the context of both TBL and professional software engineering. There are a number of guidelines for team formation and composition with this performance goal. Students can be grouped together randomly, by each individual student's preference, or by the instructor when initially forming teams. Randomly formed teams are often preferred because they reduce coalitions (Michaelsen & Sweet, 2008) and homophily (McPherson, Smith-Lovin, & Cook, 2001). A compromise between randomly selected and instructor-selected teams means that teams are chosen algorithmically. For example, CATME attempts to integrate instructor-specified criteria while avoiding scheduling conflicts within teams (Layton, Loughry, Ohland, & Ricco, 2010). The decision about how to form teams is dependent on the purpose of the teams. In active learning, there is a broader set of purposes for teamwork that go beyond the use of teams for project-based learning.

The artifact represents a significant portion of each team member's grade in teams that collaborate on one final artifact. Therefore, teams should be chosen as fairly as possible. This can be challenging because IRATs (individual readiness assessment tests) and other individual performance metrics (such as grade point average [GPA]) only represent one aspect of team performance (Michaelsen & Sweet, 2008). Positive interdependence and individual accountability, which are not accounted for in GPA, are also essential components of collaborative learning (Johnson et al., 1991). Finally, because teams can only deliver one final artifact, they must be able to come to a consensus. For this reason, conflict resolution styles (Forrester & Tashchian, 2013), personality (Peslak, 2006), and leadership styles (Shen, Prior, White, & Karamanoglu, 2007) are sometimes considered when forming software engineering teams.

A broader view of success in the context of TBL might also consider that students construct their professional identities socially within a team. Similarly, students can share metacognitive learning skills, such as techniques for organizing information, test-taking strategies, or problem-solving policies within their teams. Beyond these intended TBL experiences, students who enjoy working together might continue to collaborate after the project or course ends and form informal learning communities.

Different factors should be considered when forming teams to achieve social and collaborative benefits from the team experience. For example, there is a significant negative correlation between teams in which some members have preexisting friendships and performance on a group project (Maldonado, Klemmer, & Pea, 2009). This is one of the reasons that self-selected teams should be avoided; however, these teams can also provide opportunities for students to develop their friendships so that they are more connected to other students in their major (Barker, McDowell, & Kalahar, 2009). Persistence in an academic program has been correlated with a student's sense of social support (DeBerard, Spielmans, & Julka, 2004). So, although some of the factors in forming teams may not lead to high performing teams, they may lead to TBL experiences.

Choosing an appropriate size for teams is task dependent, and recommendations for optimal sizes vary widely in the literature (Adams, 2003). Dyads are a popular choice for CS courses in the form of pair programming. There are two other common recommendations for team size: three to five and five to seven. Three to five is typically recommended for activities that require less structure (Adams, 2003). Larger teams can be considered for more structured interaction. LeJeune recommends five to seven to ensure that the team has enough breadth of skills to complete the task while minimizing social loafing and promoting positive interdependence (LeJeune, 2003). We refer to these two functional sizes as small and medium, respectively. Large can be considered a catchall for other sizes; however, it is generally associated with class-wide activities, such as discussions.

Roles are one way to ensure positive interdependence (Johnson et al., 1991). Assigning roles to students ensures that they work collaboratively and rely on each other. The use of roles has been shown to improve cohesion in programming teams (Mennecke & Bradley, 1998). We identify two types of roles: task-specific and team-specific. Examples of task-specific roles are driver and navigator for pair programming, programmer and documenter in a traditional programming team, and tester. Team-specific roles are designed to keep the team on track. Examples of team-specific roles are timekeeper, encourager, and devil's advocate (Adams, 2003). Roles can be assigned by preference, personality tests, or randomly. Cruz, da Silva, Monteiro, Santos, and Rossilei provide a review of personality tests in software engineering education. The study names Myers–Briggs, Kersey Temperament Sorter, and Neo Five Factor Model as the three most common tests for forming teams (Cruz, da Silva, Monteiro, Santos, & Rossilei, 2011).

It is difficult to assess and grade teams because each individual, and the team as a whole, need to be considered. Grading schemes for assessing individual students often have students share one grade that was assigned to the team, have their individual contributions evaluated, take quizzes to assess individual competencies, or have a cross-validating approach that combines more than one of these schemes (Dehbozorgi, MacNeil, Maher, & Dorodchi, 2018). In Michaelsen and Sweet's original teams, they suggested using individual readiness assurance tests as a way to ensure each student was developing individual competency and cross-validating the individual's contribution to the team (Michaelsen & Sweet, 2008). Peer and self-evaluation are very common methods of assessment because teams may work outside of class time, and the instructor may not be aware of the team dynamics to ensure fair and successful team experiences. Surveys are employed for this kind of assessment, and these surveys can include Likert scales, partner ranking, descriptive word matching, short answers about peers, and journaling about their effort and experiences (Hayes, Lethbridge, & Port 2003). Finally, the weight of the grade is either provided by the instructor in the form of a standard rubric, or the weight of each component is negotiated between the instructor and the students (Michaelsen & Sweet, 2008).

In the next section, we draw on our review of teams in educational settings to describe our model for active learning design patterns that includes TBL.

An Object-Based Model for Pedagogical Design Patterns

Design patterns represent known problems and solutions in a standardized way to enable the sharing of emerging best practices. Design patterns allow designers to research a problem they are currently facing and use practiced solutions rooted in learning theories or empirical rationale. A wide range of pedagogical practices in CS education originates from instructors' expertise. Mapping these pedagogical practices to existing learning theories can be challenging and time consuming for new instructors. Instructors often rely on their intuition or on pedagogies that they have observed in their time as students.

Researchers have adapted different formats for their design patterns. Most pedagogical design patterns in the literature consist of specific parts, such as the "problem" and the "solution" to address that problem. Each set of design patterns has a specific format and language. Our observation of the related research showed that most scholars apply the general structure of patterns proposed by Alexander et al. (1977) regardless of design pattern category. Depending on the context, some researchers used an adapted version of Alexander et al.'s format and added more attributes to the patterns. Most published pedagogical design patterns (Bergin, 2006; Goodyear, 2004; Köppe & Portier, 2013; Köppe & Schalken-Pinkster, 2015; Köppe, 2011) adapt Alexander et al.'s pattern format (Alexander et al., 1977). The beginning section of each pattern is a short summary of the context that explains in what circumstances the solution should be applied, and this is followed by three diamonds. The second part of the pattern includes the problem (in bold) and the forces that shape and refine the problem. These forces that are intended for deeper understanding of the nature of the problem are followed by three diamonds. The next parts of the pattern consist of the solution (in bold), solution details, positive and negative consequences, and a discussion of the possible implementations. Finally, there is the example of pattern implementation that is explained in italics.

Format 1: [Context, <u>Problem</u> {forces}, <u>Solution</u> {solution details}, Positive/negative consequences, Pattern implementation, Examples, Related patterns]

We have developed an object-based design pattern model derived from Alexander et al.'s format (Alexander et al., 1977). This model facilitates selection and adaptation to a new context. Our object-based model emphasizes solutions that include teams to engage students in peer learning. Our model uses dimensions to build on research in TBL (Mennecke & Bradley, 1998; MacNeil, Dorodchi, & Dehbozorgi, 2017; Dehbozorgi, 2017; Dehbozorgi, MacNeil, Maher, & Dorodchi, 2018). Figure 10.2 illustrates this model, its components, attributes, and related values. This model has three main components:

- Pattern name: Describes the general characteristics of the pattern.
- Metadata: Provides high-level information about the pattern. It provides information about the high-level category of the problem this pattern addresses and its goal (e.g., content delivery, assessment or getting students' feedback, individual vs. teamwork, etc.; Smith et al., 2009).
- Pattern core: This component has four main attributes: problem, solution, rationale, and pitfall. The solution includes second-level attributes that are "teamwork" (Smith et

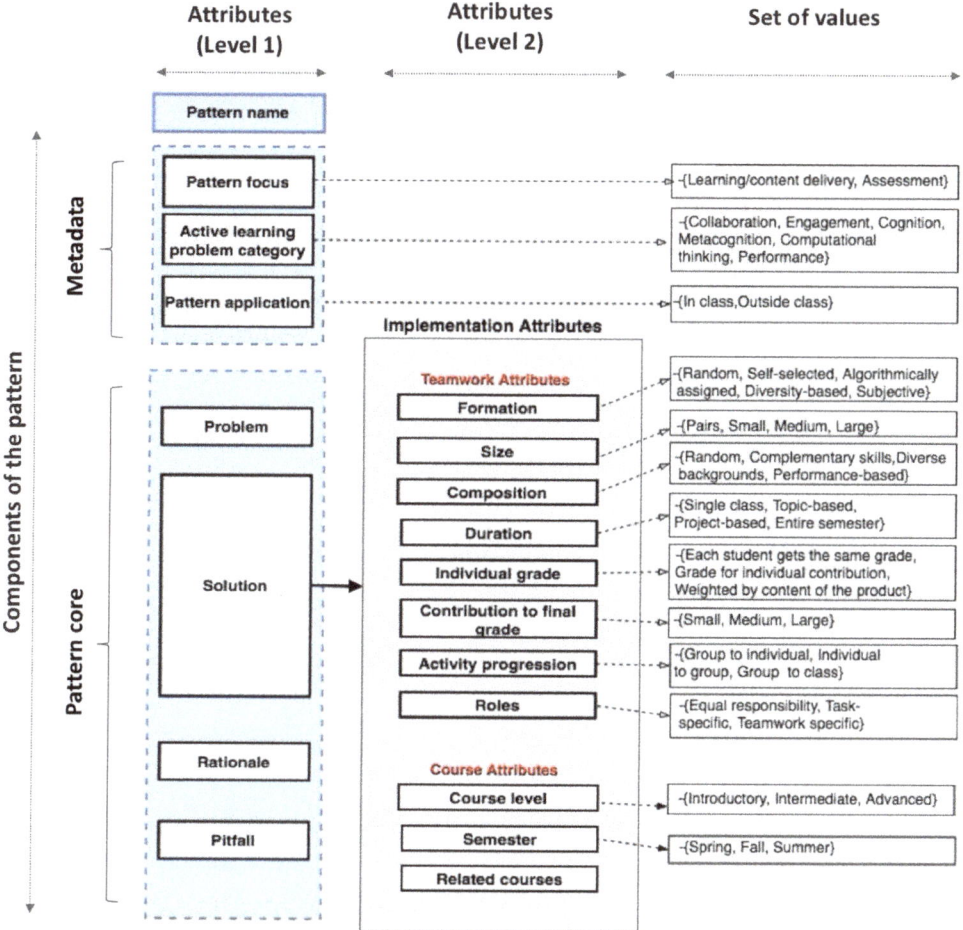

Figure 10.2. Object-based pedagogic design pattern model.

al., 2009) and "course" attributes. The teamwork attributes are: team formation, team size, duration of teamwork, individual grade in teams, teamwork product contribution to final grades, activity progression, and roles in teams. The course attributes provide insights about application of the pattern in a course- or context-specific domain. The course attributes are: course level, semester, and related courses. Depending on how the solution is going to be applied, different values can be assigned to the second level attributes.

Different variations of the teamwork attributes can be practiced in applying the solution. Therefore, several examples of the solution can be provided by setting different values for the teamwork and course attributes. The third attribute of the "pattern core" is the "rationale." "Rationale" connects research-based evidence with experiential knowledge to justify why the solution is appropriate for the corresponding problem. Design patterns can have unintended

PATTERN NAME: Low-stakes (lightweight) teams in class	
METADATA	
Pattern focus	Learning/Content delivery
Active learning problem category	Collaboration/Engagement
Pattern application	In class
PATTERN CORE	
Problem	Students' performance in teams is negatively affected by the importance of the grade.

Solution	Create teams for activities that do not have a significant contribution to final grades and encourage students to learn from each other.
	
	 Suggested teamwork attributes (optional*):
	 `{formation, size, composition, duration, individual` `grade, contribution to the final grade, activity` `progression, roles}`
	 Suggested course attributes (optional*):
	 `{course level, semester, related CS courses}`

Rationale	Reduces students' stress to perform well to get a good grade and encourages social learning.
Pitfalls	Students may still worry about unequal contribution to teamwork. Students may get discouraged by low grade contribution.

Figure 10.3. Abstract "low-stakes teams in class" pattern class.

or undesirable side effects. This aspect is captured in the fourth attribute as "pitfall" that warns about how the pattern's solution may lead to a different problem that may be addressed by another pattern.

According to the literature, patterns should be "simple and elegant solutions . . . [which] capture solutions that have developed and evolved over time" (Köppe & Schalken-Pinkster, 2013). The intention of the components and attributes in our model is to highlight the pattern details and features. In simpler terms, there is no need for the pattern designer/user to narrate/look for all the details in a verbose pattern description. Instead, this abstract representation is concise and flexible, allowing the practitioners to adopt different variations of attributes while implementing the pattern. Any pattern can have multiple examples of implementation (objects) by setting different combinations of values to teamwork and course attributes. We demonstrate how this model can be used to generate meaningful design patterns for active learning with an example pattern shown in Figure 10.3 and Figure 10.4. The "low-stakes team" pattern has been selected as the abstract representation of the pattern, and two objects are derived from this pattern by setting different values to teamwork attributes. This pattern addresses the problem that students need applied practice with course concepts to go beyond a theoretical understanding they develop during lecture or during prep work. In this example, the only attribute that has the same value in both objects is the "contribution to final grade" that is the basic characteristic of the concept of the low-stakes team.

Lightweight teams Object No. 1:
Teamwork attributes
Formation: random
Size: medium (2-3)
Composition: complementary skills
Duration: Entire semester
Individual grade: grade for individual contribution
Contribution to final grade: small
Activity progression: group to individual
Roles: equal
Course attributes
Course level: introductory, intermediate
Semester: any
Related CS courses: any

Lightweight teams Object No. 2:
Teamwork attributes
Formation: self-selected
Size: medium (3-4)
Composition: diverse background
Duration: Entire class
Individual grade: weighted by team product
Contribution to final grade: small
Activity progression: individual to group
Roles: task specific
Course attributes
Course level: introductory
Semester: Fall
Related CS courses: programming

Figure 10.4. Example of two objects derived from the "learning activity in class" abstract pattern.

As shown in Figure 10.3, the concise model clearly addresses students' collaboration and engagement issues. The attributes of "metadata" components provide higher-level information about the pattern. Since this pattern addresses the collaboration issue between students (as read in metadata), the teamwork attributes relate to this solution. By setting different values for teamwork attributes, multiple examples can be generated from a single pattern. Figure 10.4 shows two sample implementations of the "low-stakes teams in class" pattern by assigning values to teamwork attributes in the form of two derived objects from the abstract pattern.

Active Learning Design Patterns

Based on the object model, we have developed 15 patterns focusing on general problems of active learning. These patterns address the problems in four main categories: (a) Prep work patterns, (b) In-class activity patterns, (c) Teamwork patterns, and (d) Reflection and feedback patterns. Below we describe the abstract patterns in each of these four categories using our object-based model.

Prep Work Patterns. The students need to be prepared before coming to active learning classes. The following set of tables shows different patterns and methods of preparation.

In-Class Activity Patterns. Designing meaningful activities in active learning classes can be a challenge for instructors. The following set of patterns give some insights into in-class activities.

Teamwork Patterns. Teamwork is one of the important aspects of active learning environments. Forming teams, balancing time, and assigning grades to students can be a challenge. The following patterns include some guidelines about teamwork in active learning.

Reflection and Feedback Patterns. Frequent feedback and formative assessment is an important aspect of active learning. The feedback can be both about students' experiences during

Table 10.1 Prep Work Pattern: Short Lectures Before Class

Short lectures before class

Metadata	
Pattern focus	Learning/Content delivery
Active learning problem category	Engagement/Cognition
Implementation	Outside class
Pattern core	
Problem	Long lectures encourage passive learners, and many students fall asleep in long lectures during class.
Solution	Create short video lectures and make them available online for students to watch before attending a scheduled class activity.
Rationale	Reduce passive learning during class time. Students have more time to ask their questions and get guidance from the instructor during the class.
Pitfalls	Breaking course content into chunks and the process of making a video may be a challenge for the instructor. Students may choose not to watch the video before class. Students may feel that watching videos online and alone is too passive. Watching videos is a form of passive learning that needs a follow-up learning experience.

Table 10.2 Prep Work Pattern: Prep Work Forcing Function

Prep work forcing function

Metadata	
Pattern focus	Learning/Assessment
Active learning problem category	Cognition
Implementation	Outside class
Pattern core	
Problem	Students might skip doing the prep work before attending the class.
Solution	Do not allow the students to access the in-class material until they have indicated that they have completed the prep work.
Rationale	Students take more responsibility in doing prep work.
Pitfalls	Students might acknowledge that they did the prep material while they have not completely finished the prep work.

Table 10.3 Prep Work Pattern: Short Quiz Before Class

Short quiz before class	
Metadata	
Pattern focus	Learning/Assessment
Active learning problem category	Engagement/Cognition
Implementation	Outside class
Pattern core	
Problem	Students might not pay enough attention to the prep material or skip doing it. Instructors need to know the students' preparedness level before proceeding with the class activities.
Solution	Have students answer a short quiz after completing the prep work.
Rationale	This quiz can act as a forcing function to complete the prep material. The quiz provides an opportunity for students to learn from their mistakes. Based on the quiz grades, instructors can monitor how many have done the prep work and also assess their level of knowledge after finishing the prep work.
Pitfalls	Because of the low grade contribution of prep quizzes, some students might skip doing them. Some students might need additional instruction to learn the content and do well in the quiz even if they have done the prep work. Designing the prequiz with the right challenge level needs to be well thought-out.

Table 10.4 Prep Work Pattern: Collaborative Online Activities Before Class

Collaborative online activities before class	
Metadata	
Pattern focus	Learning/Content delivery
Active learning problem category	Collaboration/Engagement
Implementation	Outside class
Pattern core	
Problem	Students lack motivation to learn the material and be prepared before the class.
Solution	Design some activities related to the lecture video that students watch before coming to class and have them work collaboratively. Every badge that any individual earns by solving the problems can be rewarded to the whole group.
Rationale	Students are motivated by peer pressure and reward.
Pitfall	Some students might rely on their teammates and not put much effort in solving the problems. Some students may feel that the reward does not have enough direct impact on their grade.

Table 10.5 Prep Work Pattern: Collaborative Online Videos Before Class

Collaborative online videos before class

Metadata	
Pattern focus	Learning/Content delivery
Active learning problem category	Collaboration/Engagement
Implementation	Outside class
Pattern core	
Problem	Watching videos alone is passive, and students may get distracted easily.
Solution	Use anchored collaboration techniques to embed forums into video watching sessions. Require that student groups submit a consensus on the most important points of the video lecture before class to get credit for preparation work.
Rationale	Students can interact with their peers and engage more actively as they consume content online.
Pitfall	Determining a student's participation can be a challenge for the instructor.

Table 10.6 In-Class Activity Pattern: Interactive Real-Time Quiz Questions Activity in Class

Interactive real-time quiz questions activity in class

Metadata	
Pattern focus	Assessment
Active learning problem category	Collaboration/Engagement/Performance
Implementation	In class
Pattern core	
Problem	Students are not always motivated to study preparation materials for the class.
Solution	Develop interactive real-time quizzes that students take during the class. Engage students to answer either individually or with the team. The use of interactive quizzes makes the results visible anonymously to everyone and allows students to see their own and others' mistakes instantly.
Rationale	Engages students in the material with feedback available to them instantly. Helps in learning with low stress. Interactive quizzes are the basis for peer learning while the students are not dependent on their teammates to answer.
Pitfall	Designing quizzes requires time and effort for the instructor. If a student did not do the preparation study, the learning benefit is diminished. Students may not have learned some of the concepts in the preparation study and need more instruction. Most real-time interactive quizzes are multiple-choice questions, and these kinds of questions only address recall, potentially missing application and synthesis learning.

Table 10.7 In-Class Activity Pattern: Applied Learning Activity in Class

Applied learning activity in class	
Metadata	
Pattern focus	Learning/Content delivery
Active learning problem category	Collaboration/Engagement/Cognition
Implementation	In class
Pattern core	
Problem	Students need to use the concepts from the lecture to learn in more depth and resolve their misunderstandings.
Solution	Expose students to in-class activities performed in small groups that require the knowledge in the preparation work to complete the activity.
Rationale	Students go beyond memorizing generalizations and apply what they are learning. Students figure out if they really understand the material being presented. Students get motivated to do the prep work before coming to class because of the social pressure of working in teams.
Pitfall	Designing class activities and maintaining consistency in the preparation activities with class activities can be a challenge for the instructor. Determining the contribution of the class activities to final grades can also be a challenge for the instructor. Students may not know how to solve problems and will need more time to complete the activity.

Table 10.8 In-Class Activity Pattern: Short Lectures on Demand in Class

Short lectures on demand in class	
Metadata	
Pattern focus	Learning/Content delivery
Active learning problem category	Cognition
Implementation	In class
Pattern core	
Problem	Students are not able to connect the content of preparation work to a class activity.
Solution	Provide short (5–10 min) lectures during in-class activities that address emerging student misconceptions.
Rationale	Students learn more from minilectures since they are in demand of information and guidance.
Pitfall	Instructors should be careful that the minilectures do not exceed a certain time frame.

Table 10.9 In-Class Activity Pattern: Active Listening Activity in Class

Active listening activity in class	
Metadata	
Pattern focus	Learning/Content delivery
Active learning problem category	Collaboration/Engagement
Implementation	In class
Pattern core	
Problem	Students need to practice and learn how to listen to other students.
Solution	Ask students in a team to respond to a prompt (Why did you choose this major? How did you answer the quiz question?). Have each student provide a response while the others listen. The listening students are not allowed to interrupt or speak. The student providing the response is given a fixed amount of time to answer. If the student speaking does not need the entire time allocated, then there is silence.
Rationale	Students will learn to listen if they are told not to ask questions or interrupt the student who is speaking.
Pitfall	Identifying the prompt and the amount of time for each student to speak may be difficult.

Table 10.10 Teamwork Pattern: Think-Pair-Share in Class

Think-pair-share in class	
Metadata	
Pattern focus	Learning/Content delivery
Active learning problem category	Collaboration/Engagement/Cognition
Implementation	In class
Pattern core	
Problem	Group activity can reduce time for individual reflection.
Solution	Structure group activity so that there is time for individual reflection before the group discusses and submits a solution.
Rationale	By providing time for individual reflection and teamwork, different learning styles are accommodated.
Pitfall	Keeping teams on the same schedule is a challenge because students need different amounts of time for reflection.

Table 10.11 Teamwork Pattern: High-Stakes Teams in Class

High-stakes teams in class	
Metadata	
Pattern focus	Learning/Content delivery
Active learning problem category	Collaboration/Engagement/Cognition
Implementation	In class
Pattern core	
Problem	Students do not demonstrate enough collaborative and social skills to perform well in teams outside the class.
Solution	Assign students to teams during the class and have them work on activities together in senior-level classes.
Rationale	Students learn many concepts from their peers. Class time is more dynamic, and students learn how to work in teams to prepare for being computing professionals.
Pitfall	Students need some time to reflect on concepts individually and not fully rely on teammates to solve problems. Teamwork can impose some grade stress on students (especially high achievers). Fair task distribution in teams and assessing individuals can be a challenge.

Table 10.12 Teamwork Pattern: Low-Stakes (Lightweight) Teams in Class

Low-stakes (lightweight) teams in class	
Metadata	
Pattern focus	Learning/Content delivery
Active learning problem category	Collaboration/Engagement/Cognition
Implementation	In class
Pattern core	
Problem	Students' performance in teams is negatively affected by the importance of the grade.
Solution	Create teams for in-class activities that do not have significant contribution to final grades and encourage students to learn from each other in introductory-level classes.
Rationale	Reduces students' stress to perform well to get a good grade and encourages social learning.
Pitfall	Students may still worry about unequal contribution to teamwork. Students may get discouraged by low grade contribution.

Table 10.13 Teamwork Pattern: Low-Stakes Team Grade Assignment

Low-stakes team grade assignment	
Metadata	
Pattern focus	Assessment
Active learning problem category	Collaboration/Engagement/Performance
Implementation	In class
Pattern core	
Problem	Lightweight teams (Table 10.1) with the grade assigned based on team results disadvantages well-prepared and high-achieving students.
Solution	Assign grade for team activity as the average or the higher of the individual and group grade. This works best with clicker quizzes when you can repoll each question.
Rationale	Encouraging students to come to class prepared.
Pitfall	Low performing students will continue to come unprepared.

Table 10.14 Reflection and Feedback Pattern: Reflection on Teamwork

Reflection on teamwork	
Metadata	
Pattern focus	Assessment
Active learning problem category	Collaboration/Engagement
Implementation	Inside/Outside class
Pattern core	
Problem	Students' reflection on their participation and interaction in teams does not happen unless it is requested.
Solution	Ask students to fill out a short survey (request for reflection) about their teamwork experience after each teamwork activity.
Rationale	Encouraging students to talk about collaborative/cooperative experience encourages learning through self-assessment. This is in contrast to the assessment made by the instructor.
Pitfall	Low-performing students in groups may not provide the necessary details. Students may not appreciate the benefit of reflection and may need to see how it relates to their grade before they take it seriously.

Table 10.15 Reflection and Feedback Pattern: Reflection on Learning

Reflection on learning	
Metadata	
Pattern focus	Assessment
Active learning problem category	Cognition/Metacognition
Implementation	Inside
Pattern core	
Problem	Students do not have many opportunities to reflect on learning in teams, and it does not happen unless it is requested. Instructors are unaware of student challenges in course content; teamwork submission may not reveal each individual's gap in understanding the class material.
Solution	Have students fill out a two-question survey before leaving the class: "What did you learn in this class?" and "What was the most challenging concept for you in this class?"
Rationale	Develops metacognitive skills because it encourages students to think about their learning. Improves learning through self-assessment in contrast to the assessment made by the instructor. The student responses to these two questions can also help the instructor understand what the students found challenging. Reflection is super short so students are more likely to do it.
Pitfall	Asking students directly about their learning may not always reveal valuable information. Some students may not answer the forms thoughtfully.

the active learning class and working with teams or about their learning process (metacognition) and concepts they learned or did not learn in class. Depending on the course level, the required assessment can be different. For example, in capstone courses, teamwork has a higher contribution to students' final grades than in introductory courses. The following patterns are examples of reflection and assessment practice in active learning.

Relating Patterns Using Concept Maps (Pattern Language)

Evaluating individual design patterns can be challenging because each pattern addresses an instructional problem encountered in the classroom. However, concept mapping is a novel approach when considering how patterns interact and may be used to locate potential pitfalls that could occur while following instructional designs. According to Alexander et al. (1977), combining patterns provides a more valuable outcome to overall instruction technique; it further develops pattern language, a method of describing instructional design practices. In education, developing good instructional pattern language is crucial to addressing various student, instructor, and classroom needs. Existing patterns are largely based on Alexander et al.'s approach: design space encoded in narrative. In our study, we utilize and build on similar concept mapping to visualize relationships between object-based pedagogical structures.

In Figure 10.5, we show an object-based representation of the relationships between several patterns. Each pitfall leads to an existing or corrective pattern; the corrective pattern then addresses that pitfall as a problem. For example, a short lecture before class contains two pitfalls: students may not have learned some concepts during preparation for class, and students may not have watched the lectures or other information given prior to class. These two pitfalls then lead to possible corrective patterns: in-class lectures on demand and in-class, interactive, real-time quiz activities. However, these corrective patterns also contain their own associated pitfalls.

In our concept map, we address pitfalls associated with both collaborative and noncollaborative learning. Note that Figure 10.5 only simplifies a larger body of instructional patterns while providing an overview of how multiple patterns may or may not fit together. These overviews can lead to a more holistic understanding of the decisions made when designing classroom experiences. Likewise, links between patterns are not prescribed or absolute; they serve as suggested pathways through the design space.

In object-based patterns, all relationships are directional and are described in pitfall sections; this supports the idea that potential complications are important components of instructional design patterns. Conversely, in narrative formats, relationships between patterns are defined by upper case KEY_WORDS that are integrated into the narration; the reader is then left to identify relationships between patterns by reading the pattern narrative.

In the Student **Minors** pattern (Köppe & Schalken-Pinkster, 2013), a similar narrative format, relationships between patterns are largely implied. The names of related patterns within the structure are not always descriptive, making the relational interpretation even more challenging. In our study, we attempt to identify the types of relationships mentioned in the solution of the Student Minors pattern.

According to our research, there are four types of patterns in the Student **Minors** model: originating patterns, similar patterns, course-specific patterns, and related patterns. Throughout the model, we found that relationship diversity tends to make pattern language less consistent and interpretable in this model.

In the object-based model, we introduce the idea of specific attributes, which eliminates the needs for similar patterns or course-specific patterns in the pattern language. We include solutions to various classroom problems by developing examples of abstract patterns, which have different values assigned to the pattern core and avoid redundancy. In the resulting object-based pattern language, we have a hierarchy of problem–solution pairs, including those associated with active and collaborative learning, that generate pitfalls directed to other patterns as possible solutions.

Active learning and collaboration are often coupled with flipped classrooms. Flipped class-

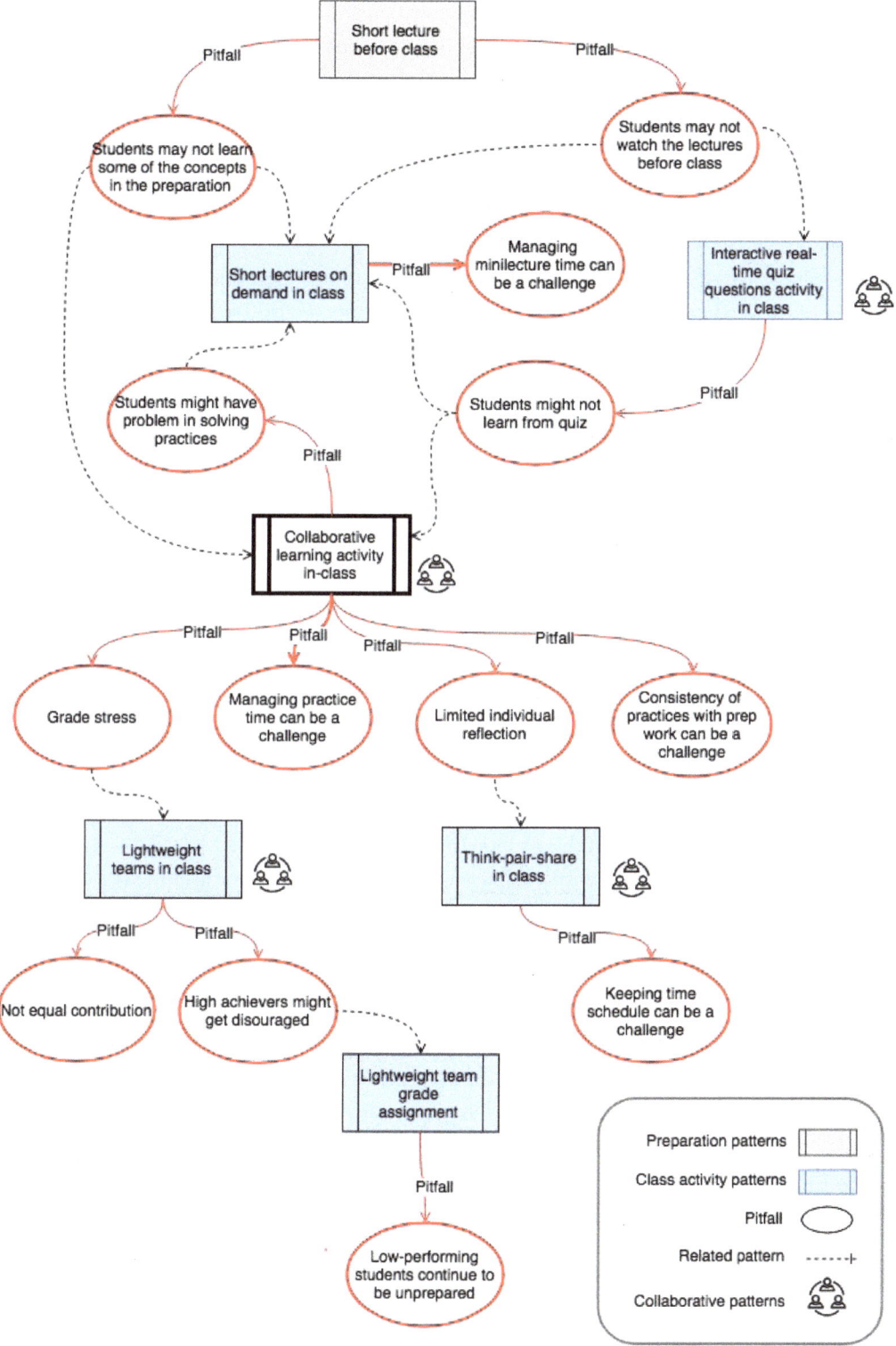

Figure 10.5. An object-based representation of the relationships between several patterns.

rooms provide students with an opportunity to become familiar with the materials at home, get practice with it in class, and then extend their understanding through after-class assignments. This complexity means that implementing one single pattern would not likely be sufficient to create a successful collaborative learning environment. Instead, multiple patterns should be combined to consider the many problems faced by instructors and to account for potential challenges that are an unavoidable part of any pedagogical technique. This aspect highlights the importance of a usable and comprehensive pattern language that can be applied by various designers.

Our object-based pattern language with concept map representation describes how a sequence of patterns can be combined and applied together. Narrative lecture-based patterns, however, suggest several patterns are related, but they can be verbose and difficult to interpret. As the number of patterns grows, the narrative format can become overwhelming. Ultimately, an object-based approach makes it easier to find the pattern that you need and apply it with confidence, knowing that pitfalls can be mapped to other patterns.

Evaluation of Design Patterns

Our design patterns were evaluated in two ways: (a) by measuring the frequency that patterns were applied, and (b) by evaluating how the application of these designs impact CS faculty. To collect the data necessary to evaluate these two aspects, we held a series of active learning design pattern workshops.

In May 2016, we held a summer institute for active learning at our college with 15 participating faculty. The purpose of this institute was to share the design patterns that we were developing. During the institute, we presented several of our emerging design patterns and our object-based model for structuring active learning design patterns. The following semester, those faculty members adopted the patterns in their classes.

This workshop provided us with feedback about what was happening in the classroom and helped us adapt our patterns to the many problems and solutions that were emerging in our instructors' classrooms. To get a better sense for the existing active learning pedagogies that are being practiced at our college, we conducted a second summer institute in May 2017; 19 faculty members attended. We asked instructors to self-report which active learning design patterns they used in their classes during the previous academic year.

The "Learning Activity in Class" and the "Lightweight Teams in Class" patterns were the two most commonly used patterns. The "Teamwork in Class" pattern was not developed at the time of this summer institute. This explains why data were not provided for this pattern application at that time. The list of patterns with resulting application frequency data is presented in Figure 10.6.

To evaluate how the application of these patterns impacted the teaching practices of faculty, we distributed a survey to the participants. We also conducted a focus group discussion in May 2018. The research question that we wanted to answer for this evaluation was "How does the application of design patterns impact the practice of active learning?" To answer this research

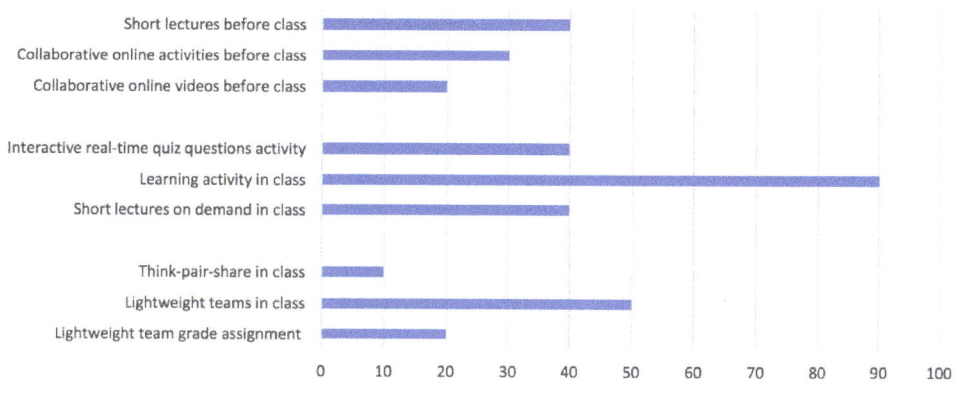

Percentage of instructors who applied the patterns

Figure 10.6. Application frequency of active learning design patterns during 2016.

question, we reached out to faculty in our college. Our college has approximately 30 CS faculty members that engage in active learning. We introduced our design patterns and the concept maps to these faculty members though digital handbooks. We shared updates to these patterns continually from 2016 to 2018. In this study, 21 of the 30 faculty members responded to a survey. The survey includes two sections, consisting of four five-point Likert scale responses and two open-ended questions. The four response statements probed the faculty members' experiences when they applied the design patterns in their classes. We asked about their agreement with the following statements:

- I found the use of design patterns helpful in my active learning classes.
- Applying design patterns has improved my active learning teaching experience (i.e., for providing material, managing class time, etc.).
- These design patterns have helped me develop a more structured approach to active learning (i.e., raising awareness of team formation, problems and solutions, pitfalls, etc.).
- One or more design patterns has provided new insights and ideas for my teaching.

The following open-ended questions were developed to capture faculty interest in applying or not applying our research patterns in the future. We also encouraged the faculty to provide examples of how design patterns improved active learning practices in their classrooms.

- Question 5: Which pattern(s) are you planning to use during fall 2018? (mark all that apply).
- Question 6: Provide some examples on how design patterns can improve active learning (AL) practices.

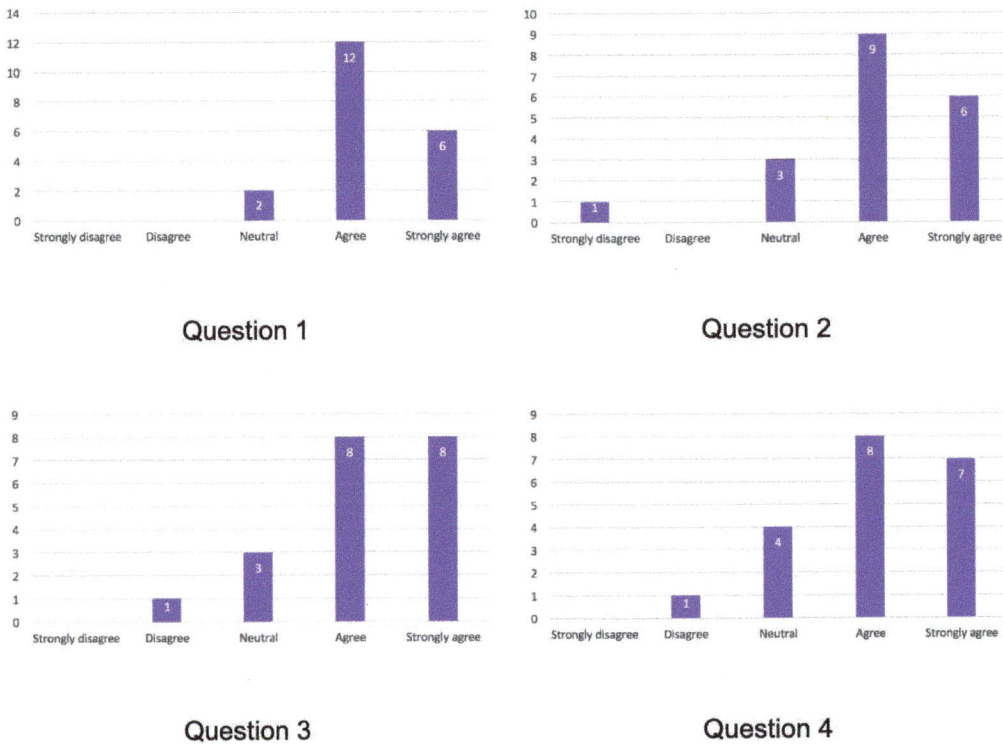

Figure 10.7. Distribution of answers about the impact of design pattern on active learning practices.

Faculty responded to the four statements using a five-point Likert scale (*Strongly disagree* = 1, *Strongly agree* = 5). The distribution of answers is presented in Figure 10.7. These results show that most (76%) of the faculty members who responded to the survey support the benefits of design patterns in their practices of active learning (Figure 10.8).

Figure 10.8 presents the result of Question 5, which shows that the top two patterns selected by faculty were "Learning Activity in Class" (90%) and "Teamwork in Class" (90%). The result is somewhat consistent with pattern application frequency analysis that we performed one year before in 2017. In the 2017 summer institute, the teamwork pattern was not developed; the only pattern that denoted teamwork in class was "Lightweight Teams." This pattern was also one of the top two most frequently used patterns that year. The second one was "Learning Activity in Class," which again ranked highest in the 2018 study. These popular patterns are related to incorporating opportunities for collaboration into the classroom.

We conducted a thematic analysis of the answers to Question 6. Figure 10.9 shows the identified themes and patterns in Question 6 answers. Four of the seven themes related to providing more structure for classroom activities and for novice instructors. Having design patterns can help new instructors get up and running with the current best practices in our college. This can save them time, but it also prevents them from reverting to their familiar and comfortable

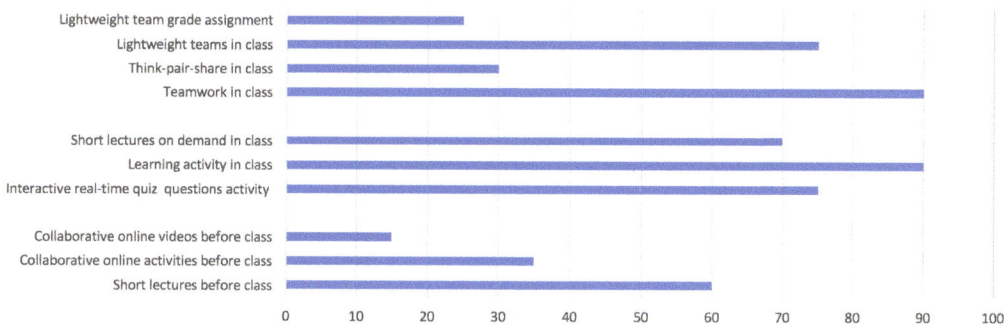

Figure 10.8. Distribution of answers about application of the patterns.

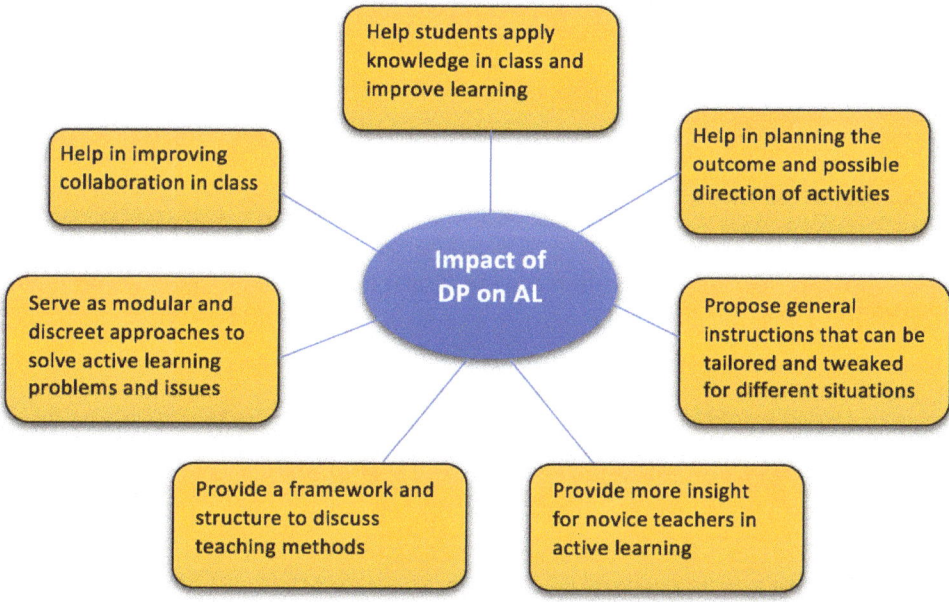

Figure 10.9. The result of thematic analysis on "Impact of Design Pattern (DP) on Active Learning (AL)" dataset.

lecture-based teaching practices. Helping to improve collaboration was also a theme here that reiterates the responses received for our 2018 rankings of which design patterns were most adopted, with the top two being related to collaboration.

We also conducted a focus group with eight CS faculty members who applied design patterns in their active learning practices. The goal of the focus group was to discuss their concerns, satisfaction, practices, and understanding of active learning and the role that design patterns play in their practice of active learning. One part of this focus group was dedicated to

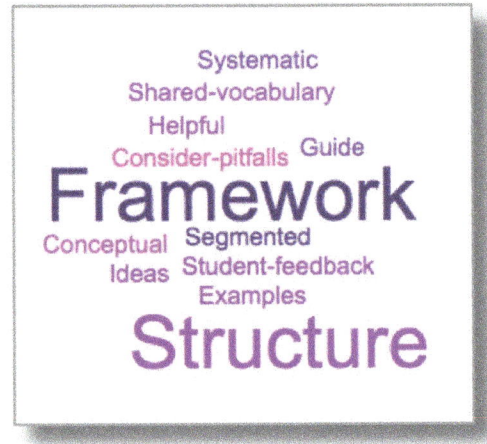

Figure 10.10. Focus group active learning and design pattern word cloud.

an activity in which we asked participants to write their perceptions about active learning. We also asked them to explain design patterns in single words separately on sticky notes and stick them on the wall. After all of the participants had done so, we asked the participants to talk about what they wrote and share their insights with others.

Keywords collected from the participants are illustrated in the form of a word cloud in Figure 10.10. In this presentation, the most frequently used keywords are larger in size. The result shows that the faculty members associated active learning keywords such as *Engagement*, *Collaborative*, *Effective*, and *Learning* more frequently; they related the concept of design patterns with keywords such as *Framework* and *Structure*. Our analysis of this activity shows that the design patterns serve the purpose of providing a framework and a structure for their active learning practice. Results from the focus group indicate that design patterns are achieving their goal of communicating the successful practice of active learning in a structured way that can be applied by faculty.

Conclusion

In this chapter, we present active learning design patterns that have emerged from our practice of active learning in CS education. We developed an object-based design pattern model that captures the attributes of active learning combined with team-based learning. As part of our research, we applied our object-based design patterns in various classrooms with diverse numbers of students and various course topics. Understanding that design patterns can facilitate developing an active learning practice, it was important for us to provide a holistic solution to classroom pedagogy, one that considers inherent limitations and potential complications that any one pedagogical technique may face.

Throughout our study, we were able to identify design patterns for active learning techniques that focus on peer learning. We developed an object-based model in contrast to the narrative format to avoid the difficulty in identifying the links between problems, solutions, and pitfalls in related patterns. We claim that explicit dimensions that capture pitfalls can assist in avoiding potential complications.

Our object-based design patterns simplify problems and solutions by making patterns more readable. They highlight dimensions that are important for team-based active learning, such as team formation, size, roles, and grade weight. They also highlight the importance of readability, flexibility, and functionality in diverse classroom environments. We are confident that instructors can more easily apply pedagogical patterns for active learning with this model leading to more successful student learning.

Acknowledgments

This work is supported by the National Science Foundation Award 1519160: IUSE/PFE: RED: The Connected Learner: Design Patterns for Transforming Computing and Informatics Education.

References

Adams, S. G. (2003). Building successful student teams in the engineering classroom. *Journal of STEM Education Innovations and Research, 4*, 1–6.

Alexander, C., Ishikawa, S., Silverstein, M., Jacobson, M., Fiksdahl-King, I., & Angel, S. (1977). *A pattern language: Towns, buildings, construction*. Oxford, England: Oxford University Press.

Barker, L. J., McDowell, C., & Kalahar, K. (2009). Exploring factors that influence computer science introductory course students to persist in the major. *Proceedings of the 40th ACM Technical Symposium on Computer Science Education (SIGCSE '09)* (pp. 153–157). New York, NY: Association for Computing Machinery (ACM).

Bergin, J. (2006). Active learning and feedback patterns: Version 4. *Proceedings of the 2006 Conference on Pattern Languages of Programs (PLoP '06)* (article 6). New York, NY: Association for Computing Machinery (ACM).

Biggers, M., Yilmaz, T., & Sweat, M. (2009, March). Using collaborative, modified peer-led team learning to improve student success and retention in intro CS. *ACM SIGCSE Bulletin, 41*(1), 9–13.

Bonwell, C. C., & Eison, J. A. (1991). *Active learning: Creating excitement in the classroom* (ASHE-ERIC Higher Education Report No. 1). Washington, DC: The George Washington University, School of Education and Human Development.

Cruz, S. S., da Silva, F. Q., Monteiro, C. V., Santos, P., & Rossilei, I. (2011). Personality in software engineering: Preliminary findings from a systematic literature review. *Evaluation & Assessment in Software Engineering (EASE 2011), 15th Annual Conference* (pp. 1–10). IET.

DeBerard, M. S., Spielmans, G. I., & Julka, D. L. (2004). Predictors of academic achievement and retention among college freshmen: A longitudinal study. *College Student Journal, 38*(1), 66.

Dehbozorgi, N. (2017). Active learning design patterns for CS education. *Proceedings of the 2017 ACM Conference on International Computing Education Research* (pp. 291–292). New York, NY: Association for Computing Machinery (ACM).

Dehbozorgi, N., Maher M. L., MacNeil, S., & Dorodchi, M. (2020). An object-based pedagogical design pattern model for collaborative active learning. (manuscript to be submitted).

Dehbozorgi, N., MacNeil, S., Maher, M. L., & Dorodchi, M. (2018, October). A comparison of lecture-based and active learning design patterns in CS education. *2018 IEEE Frontiers in Education Conference (FIE)* (pp. 1–8). IEEE. doi:10.1109/FIE.2018.8659339

Dorodchi, M., & Dehbozorgi, N. (2017, June). Addressing the Paradox of Fun and Rigor in Learning Programming. In Proceedings of the 2017 ACM Conference on Innovation and Technology in Computer Science Education (pp. 370-370). doi:10.1145/3059009.3073004

Dorodchi, M., Benedict, A., Desai, D., Mahzoon, M. J., MacNeil, S., & Dehbozorgi, N. (2018, October). Design and Implementation of an Activity-Based Introductory Computer Science Course (CS1) with Periodic Reflections Validated by Learning Analytics. In 2018 IEEE Frontiers in Education Conference (FIE) (pp. 1-8). IEEE.

doi:0.1109/FIE.2018.8659196

Feden, P. D., & Vogel, R. M. (2003). Methods of teaching: Applying cognitive science to promote student learning. New York, NY: McGraw-Hill Humanities, Social Sciences & World Languages.

Forrester, W. R., & Tashchian, A. (2013). Effects of personality on conflict resolution in student teams: A structural equation modeling approach. *Journal of College Teaching & Learning* (Online), *10*(1), 39.

Goodyear, P. (2004). Patterns, pattern languages and educational design. In R. Atkinson, C. McBeath, D. Jonas-Dwyer, & R. Phillips (Eds), *Beyond the comfort zone: Proceedings of the 21st ASCILITE Conference* (pp. 339–347). Retrieved from http://www.ascilite.org.au/conferences/perth04/procs/goodyear.html

Hakimzadeh, H., Adaikkalavan, R., & Batzinger, R. (2011, November). Successful implementation of an active learning laboratory in computer science. In Proceedings of the 39th annual ACM SIGU CCS conference on User services (pp. 83-86). doi:10.1145/2070364.2070386

Hayes, J. H., Lethbridge, T. C., & Port, D. (2003, May). Evaluating individual contribution toward group software engineering projects. In 25th International Conference on Software Engineering, 2003. Proceedings. (pp. 622-627). IEEE. doi:10.1109/ICSE.2003.1201246

Heines, J. M., Popyack, J. L., Morrison, B., Lockwood, K., & Baldwin, D. (2015, February). Panel on flipped classrooms. In Proceedings of the 46th ACM Technical Symposium on Computer Science Education (pp. 174-175). doi:10.1145/2676723.2677328

Johnson, D. W., Johnson, R. T., & Smith, K. A. (1991). *Active learning: Cooperation in the college classroom.* Edina, MN: Interaction Book Company.

Köppe, C. (2011). Continuous activity: A pedagogical pattern for active learning. *Proceedings of the 16th European Conference on Pattern Languages of Programs (EuroPLoP '11)* (article 3). New York, NY: Association for Computing Machinery (ACM).

Köppe, C., & Portier, M. (2014). Lecture design patterns: Improving the beginning of a lecture. *Proceedings of the 19th European Conference on Pattern Languages of Programs* (p. 16). New York, NY: Association for Computing Machinery (ACM).

Köppe, C., & Schalken-Pinkster, J. (2013, October). Lecture design patterns: improving interactivity. In *Proceedings of the 20th Conference on Pattern Languages of Programs* (pp. 1-15). doi:10.5555/2725669.2725697

Köppe, C., & Schalken-Pinkster, J. (2015). Lecture design patterns: Laying the foundation. *Proceedings of the 18th European Conference on Pattern Languages of Program (EuroPLoP '13)* (article 4). New York, NY: Association for Computing Machinery (ACM).

Lasserre, P. (2009, May). Introduction to team-based learning. In *Proceedings of the 14th Western Canadian Conference on Computing Education* (pp. 77-78). doi:10.1145/1536274.1536296

Latulipe, C., Long, N. B., & Seminario, C. E. (2015, February). Structuring flipped classes with light-weight teams and gamification. In *Proceedings of the 46th ACM Technical Symposium on Computer Science Education* (pp. 392-397). doi:10.1145/2676723.2677240

Latulipe, C., MacNeil, S., & Thompson, B. (2018, October). Evolving a Data Structures Class Toward Inclusive Success. In *2018 IEEE Frontiers in Education Conference (FIE)* (pp. 1-9). IEEE. doi:10.1109/FIE.2018.8659334

Layton, R. A., Loughry, M. L., Ohland, M. W., & Ricco, G. D. (2010). Design and validation of a web-based system for assigning members to teams using instructor-specified criteria. *Advances in Engineering Education, 2*(1), 1–28.

LeJeune, N. (2003). Critical components for successful collaborative learning in CS1. *Journal of Computing Sciences in Colleges, 19*, 275–285.

MacNeil, S., Dorodchi, M., & Dehbozorgi, N. (2017, October). Using spectrums and dependency graphs to model progressions from introductory to capstone courses. In 2017 IEEE Frontiers in Education Conference (FIE) (pp. 1-5). IEEE. doi:10.1109/FIE.2017.8190599

Maher, M. L., Latulipe, C., Lipford, H., & Rorrer, A. (2015). Flipped classroom strategies for CS education. *Proceedings of the 46th ACM Technical Symposium on Computer Science Education,* 218–223.

Maldonado, H., Klemmer, S., & Pea, R. D. (2009). When is collaborating with friends a good idea? Insights from design education. *Proceedings of the 9th International Conference on Computer Supported Collaborative Learning (CSCL '09), International Society of the Learning Sciences, 1*, 227–231.

McPherson, M., Smith-Lovin, L., & Cook, J. M. (2001). Birds of a feather: Homophily in social networks. *Annual Review of Sociology,* 415–444.

Mennecke, B., & Bradley, J. (1998). Making project groups work: The impact of structuring group roles on the performance and perception of information systems project teams. *Journal of Computer Information Systems, 39*(1), 30–36.

Michaelsen, L. K., & Sweet, M. (2008). The essential elements of team-based learning. *New Directions for Teaching and Learning, 116*, 7–27.

Millis, B. J., & Cottell Jr., P. G. (1997). *Cooperative learning for higher education faculty* (Series on Higher Education). Phoenix, AZ: Oryx Press.

Narayanan, N. H., Hundhausen, C., Hendrix, D., & Crosby, M. (2012). Transforming the CS classroom with studio-based learning. In *Proceedings of the 43rd ACM Technical Symposium on Computer Science Education* (pp. 165–166). New York, NY: Association for Computing Machinery (ACM).

Peslak, A. R. (2006). The impact of personality on information technology team projects. In *Proceedings of the 2006 ACM SIGMIS CPR Conference on Computer Personnel Research: Forty-Four Years of Computer Personnel Research: Achievements, Challenges and the Future* (pp. 273–279). New York, NY: Association for Computing Machinery (ACM).

Preiss, B. R. (1999). Design patterns for the data structures and algorithms course. *SIGCSE '99: The Proceedings of the Thirtieth SIGCSE Technical Symposium on Computer Science,* 95–99.

Prince, M. (2004). Does active learning work? A review of the research. *Journal of Engineering Education, 93*(3), 223–231.

Shen, S. T., Prior, S. D., White, A. S., & Karamanoglu, M. (2007). Using personality type differences to form engineering design teams. *Engineering Education, 2*(2), 54–66.

Smith, M. K., Wood, W. B., Adams, W. K., Wieman, C., Knight, J. K., Guild, N., & Su, T. T. (2009). Why peer discussion improves student performance on in-class concept questions. *Science, 323*(5910), 122–124.

Vlissides, J., Helm, R., Johnson, R., & Gamma, E. (1995). Design patterns: Elements of reusable object-oriented software. *Reading: Addison-Wesley, 49*(120), 11.

Wilkins, D. E., & Lawhead, P. B. (2000). Evaluating individuals in team projects. In S. Haller (Ed.), *Proceedings of the Thirty-First SIGCSE Technical Symposium on Computer Science Education (SIGCSE '00)* (pp. 172–175). New York, NY: Association for Computing Machinery (ACM).

CPSIA information can be obtained
at www.ICGtesting.com
Printed in the USA
LVHW071159200821
695727LV00026B/1273